WHERE TO DRINK WINE

The essential guide to the
world's must-visit wineries

CHRIS LOSH

quadrille

CONTENTS

INTRODUCTION

If there's one thing that sets wine apart from other drinks, it's the fact that it can taste different depending on where it comes from. Sure, winemakers have an influence – of course they do. But you can take grapes from two different vineyards, treat them exactly the same way and each will have its own distinctive character – sometimes even if the vineyards are only a few metres apart. The French, as you might expect, have a word for it: terroir – the untranslatable term that takes in everything from climate and vineyard orientation to soil and the general habitat.

And that, frankly, is what this book is all about. Because drinking a wine at home is one thing, drinking it in the place where it's grown quite another. Being able to take in the terroir as you sip is the difference between colour TV and high-definition 3D – it all just seems more, well... real.

Slither your way up the slatey slopes of the Mosel, or crunch across the alluvial soils of the Médoc, and the cool, stony punch at the heart of the wines starts to make sense. Taste the light-footed lift of an English white wine or the tang of a manzanilla sherry, and you'll remember the chalky breeze on your face in the Hampshire vineyard, the whisper of sea-salt and anchovies of an Andalucian lunchtime. And going there doesn't just connect you to the land, but to the past as well.

As you kick up dust-trails in the heat of the Douro's terraced vineyards it's easy to imagine square-sailed *barcos* carrying their casks of port to the waiting cellars, warehouses and merchant ships of Porto hundreds of years ago. Visit the original house of Dr Christopher Penfold outside Adelaide or the old cellars of Ksara in Lebanon and you are in the places that gave birth to an entire country's wine industry. It's a pilgrimage as much as a visit. Taste in situ, in other words, and flavours, history, terroir – they all start to make sense.

Clearly, given there are tens of thousands of wineries in the world, it's not possible to cover everything. But in this book I've tried to cover as many countries and regions as I can, so wherever you happen to be or are thinking of going, there should be great visits within striking distance.

We go from some of the highest vineyards in the world to ones practically dipping their toes in the sea. From vineyards on the edge of cities to ones that are perfect for seekers of solitude. From wineries steeped in tradition to new arrivals intent on ripping up the rule book.

There are visits with games for kids, swimming pools, zip-wires and boules, and others that are little more than a shack with passionate staff; places where you can ride horses and bikes through the vineyard, and ones with slick visitor experiences. All manner of life is here.

So whether you're a seasoned visitor or a first-timer, a retiree or a student, a young couple or a young family, I hope you will feel inspired to visit. Partly because there are bound to be dozens of wineries out there that are perfect for you. But mostly because, in wine, what you taste and where you taste are the same thing, and making that connection is the most thrilling thing of all.

FRANCE

If you were to force an oenophile, sommelier, drinks writer or wine trader to choose wines from just one country to drink for the rest of their life, most would probably pick those of France. Charles de Gaulle's 'land of 246 types of cheese' also makes wines in a staggering array of styles, many of them reference points for the world.

CHAMPAGNE

I wonder if there's ever been a greater dislocation between a place and its product? After all, champagne the drink is glamour, celebration and bling; flappers, Art Deco and the Roaring Twenties; Oscars and anniversaries. Yet the countryside of Champagne the region is as forgettable as a party-bore's joke.

The drive from Calais could be fairly renamed '300km of nothing' – just pale wheat field after pale wheat field – offering horizons more Oklahoma than Orléans. And anyone who's been looking for a place to kill a couple of hours on their way back to the Eurostar will know that, bar the odd First World War battle site, non-wine-related tourism options in this north-eastern corner of France could politely be described as limited.

But from this landscape, Reims rises like an oasis: a buzzy, food-centred town chock-full of history, restaurants and, of course, champagne. It's the drink's unofficial capital, and names that you'll recognise from wine lists and retailers' shelves around the world are everywhere.

Southwards from the city lie a cornucopia of vineyards, wineries and ancient cellars. Annoyingly, many of the most famous houses aren't open to tourists at all – not even by ringing ahead – but there's still a decent selection of bigger players, small growers and a sprinkling of co-operatives that will open their doors (and cellars) to you.

Unless you're a serious champagne anorak, I doubt you'd choose Reims for a two-week holiday, but it's a good place to visit for a long weekend, en route to Alsace and Germany or even as part of a 24-hour whistle-stop visit from Paris, which is commutably close to the west.

One piece of advice: don't visit in the darker months. The coldest I've ever been was in a wine cellar in Champagne, and this particular part of northern France can be bleakly, damply, unforgivingly bone-chilling in winter. A day trudging numbly round the cold muddy vineyards in January can only make you wonder at the fortitude of the soldiers who spent month after month in the trenches that ran through the heart of this region 100 years ago.

As you reach for a second jumper, however, you can comfort yourself with the knowledge that this chilliness is very much part of the secret of Champagne.

These are France's most northerly vineyards, and they shouldn't be able to produce ripe grapes at all. Indeed, if they were planted on the flat, marly plains, they simply wouldn't. But just south of the city lie the curved slopes of the Montagne de Reims and, south of that, of the Côte des Blancs. Vines here use the slopes like a sun-lounger, banking up to absorb the rays, shielded from the westerly winds, and luxuriating in the chalky soils that drain well and also retain heat. This allows the grapes to get to the perfect level of 'almost ripeness' that you want for champagne – of apple and citrus flavours and that thrilling crispness that's so key to all top fizz.

Champagne is a story of three grape varieties. There's Pinot Noir, which you'll find scattered around the eastern and southern slopes of the Montagne de Reims. Its cheerful, less intellectual relative, Pinot Meunier, plays along the banks of the Marne river, while the Côte des Blancs, just south of Épernay, is the spiritual home of the zesty and elegant Chardonnay grape.

In such a marginal climate, different areas and different grapes tend to perform very differently from one year to the next, which is where Champagne's great USP comes in: blending. Of course, you can get vintage champagne (made from one year), single-varietal champagne (made from one grape variety) and single-vineyard champagne (made from one site). But the region's success has been built on mixing everything together in the name of consistency: different grape varieties, different areas and – in the case of non-vintage champagne, which makes up the vast majority of the region's production – different years.

Use any trip to the region to get a handle on this diversity: visit a couple of small growers who specialise in certain areas to see what makes their village special, as well as a co-operative or larger producer that takes fruit from across the region to understand blending.

And, of course, leave plenty of room in your car boot or suitcase to fit in some further research for back home.

REIMS

CHAMPAGNE POMMERY

Champagne has a long history of wine businesses that have been taken over and made bigger and better by strong women widowed at a young age. Pommery is one of them. When Mr P shuffled off this mortal coil in 1858, his widow – still not yet 40 – took over the reins and grew the company for the next 30 years. Clearly a confident, forward-thinking woman, she also set up a pension fund for her employees and founded the orphanage in Reims. On her death, her daughter Louise (by then happily married to a suitably aristocratic partner) took over and the winery's top wine, Cuvée Louise, is named after her.

There are two elements that set Pommery apart. One is its interest in modern art – there are often installations in both the grounds and cellar, from giant sculptures to video screens, to check out. The other is the grounds themselves. It's hard to imagine enough zeroes to calculate the worth of an estate as large and impressive as this so close to the centre of Reims – Domaine Pommery is only ten minutes from the main station. But the 'Elizabethan-style' vision begun by Madame Pommery in 1868 is incredibly photogenic, both above ground (with its architecture and gardens) and below, where its 18km of interconnected tunnels provide an elegant resting place for the wines.

Visits are understandably popular and phoning or emailing ahead to reserve a place is recommended, particularly at weekends.

CHAMPAGNE TAITTINGER

Taittinger – or 'Taitt', as it's affectionately known – is one of the few globally recognised Champagne marques still to be independently owned and run by the family. Over the years *la famille* have accumulated a number of vineyards – getting on for 300 hectares' worth – which, given the stratospheric land prices in Champagne, is no small commitment. It's also a significant amount for a house that, despite its fame, is only really a medium-sized player, and means half of its wine comes from its own vineyards.

The house's signature is Chardonnay – the variety traditionally takes up a greater proportion of its bottles than those produced elsewhere in the region – and it makes for wines of elegance, aroma and finesse rather than power and mouthfeel. Whether or not you love them depends if you like fine-boned, skippy top-notes or more muscular purpose in your glass – but that's part of the fun of exploring a region.

Taittinger's visitor centre is at the Place Saint Nicaise – only a couple of minutes from Pommery's wondrous fairy princess-style estate. In Roman times this was the site of a large chalk pit, adapted 900 years later by monks to form the underground cellars of the Saint Nicaise Abbey. Now, in among the monks' arches and buttresses sit thousands of bottles of Taittinger.

The tour isn't free, but does include a glass to sample – and you can 'customise' your tasting at the end according to whether you'd like to try rosé, off-dry, vintage or a wine from the grand cru vineyards.

MONTAGNE DE REIMS

CHAMPAGNE MAILLY

There are disadvantages to being a luxury product like champagne. When times are good everyone wants to be your friend, but when the world is counting its pennies or just generally miserable, you're the flash relative no one wants to know.

The depression that swept across the world in the 1930s caused major problems in Champagne, with many growers struggling to keep going. But it was also the seed from which Champagne Mailly was born. A group of growers united to form the co-operative; cultivating grapes and making wine together, then marketing it under one name. For 30 years, members of the co-op even took turns during the winter to dig the 1km of tunnels for cellaring the wines. Now that's commitment!

There is no shortage of co-ops in France (or, indeed Europe), but Champagne Mailly is unusual. It makes wine only from grapes grown in the village of Mailly – one of only 17 Champagne villages classified at the top level of grand cru. In other words, forget any preconceptions you might have about co-ops being low-rent; these guys are farming right at the top of the quality pyramid.

Not only that, but since Mailly, on the north-eastern slopes of the Montagne de Reims, is famous for its Pinot Noir, they have a very distinctive Pinot-centric house style that makes an interesting contrast to other champagnes.

There's no tour, but the tasting is well worth the visit, and if you go at the weekend, some of the 80-odd growers are usually around to take you through their wines.

MARNE VALLEY

CHAMPAGNE GEOFFROY, AY

There are any number of reasons to visit Champagne Geoffroy in Ay – not least the fact that its family story is representative of much of the Champagne narrative over the centuries.

Like those of so many others in the region, the Geoffroys' roots here run deep. Their ancestors have been growing grapes in Cumières (just to the west of Ay) for over 400 years, handing their vineyards down from generation to generation and, in that very French way, getting to know every wrinkle of the vineyards and vagary of the weather. Then, 60 years ago, the family decided to stop selling their grapes to other people and start making their own wines. It was a big decision, requiring a lot of confidence and commitment, but it's paid off in spades. Nine years ago, they relocated their business to a rather lovely house in the neighbouring grand cru village of Ay.

It's still a family-run affair, with Jean-Baptiste and his wife Karine running you through the cellars, barrels and bottle-stores with a line-up of wines to finish.

As well as a brut nature and a non-vintage, they have a white made mostly from red grapes (Pinot Noir and Pinot Meunier) and one made mostly from Chardonnay, offering a fascinating comparison of how the same winemaker can treat the different varieties. As well as vintage wines, there's a chance to taste a rosé de saignée – a relative rarity in Champagne, made by taking the first juice off the Pinot Noir grapes before it takes on too much colour.

CHAMPAGNE COLLET, AY

Want to know what the oldest co-operative in Champagne is? Well, this is it. Collet is the brand of the General Co-operative of Winemakers (COGEVI), which was founded back in 1921 as a display of unity by growers worried about the prevalence of counterfeit champagne.

In fact, the co-op itself is located on the site of a building that the furious growers burned in protest – an act that eventually led to the creation of the Champagne appellation. Visiting this site genuinely connects you to a key moment in the drink's history.

Not that it's all anger and rebellion. Collet-COGEVI's Cité du Champagne (City of Champagne) is a fantastic experience that gives you everything from the usual cellar and wine shop visits to a museum explaining the birth of the Champagne appellation and the story of the co-op itself.

There's also a collection of old, traditional wine growing and wine-making tools, from ancient ploughs and tiny wheezing tractors, to the first corking machines, while a floor-to-ceiling glass window gives you an inspiring panorama out over the vineyards of Ay.

Since I'm a sucker for all things Art Deco, my personal must-visit is the second and third floors of the Cité's Villa Collet, which is dedicated to the Roaring Twenties. The books, posters, bottles and clothes capture the post-war hedonism of the Jazz Age beautifully. From anger to excess and modern success, it's the story of Champagne in a nutshell.

Cellar vie

Chalk is a big part of champagne. Its vineyards are full of the stuff – particularly on the Côtes des Blancs – and a visit to a cool dark cellar, hewn out of the thick chalk seams, should be on everyone's to-do list.

Most of these cellars were initially excavated by the Romans, who mined the rock in the first century AD. Many of them were taken over in the Middle Ages by monks and, after them, by champagne houses.

The appeal of these cellars is that they are consistently cold and dark all year round – a great environment for wine to age in. But the shock of stepping from a summer's afternoon to a 10–15°C cellar 20m below ground can be significant. If you're going to do cellar tours, which often take around an hour, make sure you tak a jumper or coat with you.

CHAMPAGNE
LEGRAND-LATOUR,
FLEURY-LA-RIVIÈRE

Soil is important in wine production, and the Champenois are rightly proud of their chalky land. Chunks of it lie around in the vineyards, and it forms a cool white backdrop to every cellar tour. But small grower Legrand-Latour in Fleury-la-Rivière has taken this love of the white stuff to a whole new level of engagement.

Its Cave aux Coquillages – the cellar of shells – is home to an impressive array of fossils dating back 45 million years when the region was a shallow sea and playground to the kind of snails (40cm long) you wouldn't want to meet at night on your patio. While kids can have a go at sifting through chalk and learning how to prepare fossils, parents can get stuck into a tasting to see if they can spot the influence of the defunct gastropods in the wine.

The winery has three well-priced *chambres d'hôtes*, too, if you're on a budget.

CHAMPAGNE
COLLARD-PICARD,
VILLERS-SOUS-CHÂTILLON

The big-name houses of the Champagne region might be known throughout the world, but it's arguably the small growers that make up the soul of the area. They're the people in touch with their vines on a daily basis, and the fact that more and more of them are choosing to make their own wines rather than sell their fruit to bigger players, is a definite plus for the region.

Champagne Collard-Picard is the result of the coming together by marriage of two separate growing families from different parts of the region: Olivier Collard, whose family have mostly red-grape vineyards in the Marne Valley, and Caroline Picard, whose heritage is from the white grape heartland of the Côte des Blancs, south of Épernay. Under their unified banner, the couple now have a wine shop in the latter (15, Avenue de Champagne) and a cellar over in Villers-sous-Châtillon.

Collard-Picard only owns 15 hectares, and farm it with as little intervention as possible, using old-style techniques such as ploughing and cover crops rather than dousing the vineyards in fertilisers. Phone ahead to make an appointment with Olivier at the cellar and he'll tell you all about it.

CHAMPAGNE PANNIER, CHÂTEAU-THIERRY

Champagne Pannier's home, the village of Château-Thierry, lies just off the main A4 motorway linking Paris and Reims. Its location means that Pannier offers an impressive Champagne visitor experience not that far from the French capital, so if you're looking for a day trip by car from the City of Light, this could be the one to go for.

Pannier is a fairly traditional champagne house, in that while it's based in the Marne Valley, it takes grapes from all over the region to make its blends. It has a wide range of wines, from super-dry 'zéro dosage' offerings through blanc de blancs, blanc de noirs, rosés and sweeter demi-secs.

The 2km of medieval cellars, initially excavated in the 12th century, are beautiful, and you can see an ancient carving of an archer etched into the rock by some budding artists hundreds of years ago. The symbol has been adapted into the winery's logo.

There's a one-hour tour, complete with films teaching you how the wine is made, a visit to where it's aged and a tutored tasting afterwards. There's also the chance (on request) to compare and contrast three different cuvées or to try a bit of champagne and food matching. It's slick, accessible and a recommended experience for first-timers.

CHAMPAGNE BARON ALBERT, CHARLY-SUR-MARNE

Sisters are doing it for themselves at this winery. Set up by Albert Baron in 1947 and passed down through a couple of generations since, this house is now entirely run – from vineyard to winemaking to sales – by Monsieur B's grandchildren, Claire, Lise and Aline, aka the Baron Sisters, which makes them sound vaguely like a Motown tribute act.

The winery is on the western edge of Champagne, about halfway between Reims and Paris. Not too far off the main A4, it's a handy stop between the two cities, and offers you the chance to tour the old cellars and taste two or three cuvées of wine completely free of charge.

ÉPERNAY

MOËT & CHANDON

With over 1,100 hectares of vineyard and contracts with squillions of growers, Moët & Chandon is the biggest champagne producer by a country mile, and there's a case for saying that if you are only going to visit one house while you're in the region, this should be it.

If the size of the operation is slightly daunting, the timescale is even more so. Jean-Rémy Moët, grandson of the founder, is credited with being the figure who really took sparkling wine out from being a local drink into the rest of France and the world. One of his most loyal customers, apparently, was Napoleon, which, in case you were wondering, is where the 'imperial' in Moët & Chandon's Brut Imperial comes from.

Another fan, the Marquise de Pompadour – the 18th-century It Girl/Insta Influencer of her day – is credited with the neat-sounding, but somewhat questionable quote that 'champagne is the only wine a woman can drink without becoming ugly.' Mind you, she was the mistress of Louis XV, so she could probably say what she wanted...

With over 250 years of history, there's no shortage of such historical nuggets on offer at the Moët cellars in Épernay. An hour and a half from Paris (by car or train) and just five minutes from the main station, this is a visit that you could feasibly work into a day trip from the capital.

You can, of course, visit the Moët shop any time you like, but the tour is nicely put together, with a short film and a range of cellar visits. They're all around 90 minutes, and cover the history of Moët and how its champagnes are made, but vary in price depending on which wines you sample afterwards.

CÔTE DES BLANCS

CHAMPAGNE JACQUES SELOSSE, AVIZE

Jacques Selosse set up his winery in the 1950s and for the last 30 years it's been run by his son, Anselme. He studied winemaking in Beaune, and the Burgundian influence makes itself felt in his champagnes. He's one of the most interesting and forward-thinking winemakers in the region, using lots of oak barrels and even starting to experiment with terracotta amphorae for ageing the wine. He's also a big proponent of biodynamics.

Selosse is a small producer – barely 60,000 bottles a year, from 37 hectares of vineyard – and doesn't have a vast range of wines. Nor does he have a glitzy visitor experience. But if you're a serious wine lover who wants their horizons expanded, you should pay him a visit.

You'll need to call ahead (ideally well in advance) and hope that the great man is free. But perhaps if you stay/eat at the rather good hotel and restaurant that he and his wife set up a few years ago – Hôtel Restaurant Les Avisés – it might work in your favour. Even then, there's no guarantee you'll actually be able to take home any wine. Selosse's bottles are sold strictly on allocation all over the world, so it depends on whether he thinks he has any left once he's fulfilled those commitments. Yes. He's that good...

CHAMPAGNE DOYARD, VERTUS

Doyard, at the southern end of the Côte des Blancs, has been a fixture in Vertus for a long time. Twelve generations of the Doyard family have been growing grapes in the area, dating back to the 17th century, and they've been making wine for four generations. With just ten hectares of vines (mostly in the Côte des Blancs), they are genuinely bijou producers, but interesting ones, and key members of the 'artisans du champagne' group of small growers.

They use oak to add breadth and texture, and recently launched La Libertine – the result of ten years of research to try to recreate the style of champagnes drunk in the 18th century. The wine is a 100 per cent Chardonnay that's a fair bit sweeter than the majority of champagnes, has been aged for 12 years, and comes in a bottle wound round with hemp cord. It's definitely one of the more unusual creations out there.

Visits include a tasting of two wines with the price depending on what you sample. You need to contact them in advance, though, either by phone (recommended) or email. Your best bet might be to stay at their Le Clos Margot, which comprises five *chambres d'hôtes* that adjoin the actual cellars. A visit to the vineyards and winery can be included as part of the accommodation.

SOUTH

CHAMPAGNE
DEVAUX

It's tempting to think that Champagne ends at the foot of the Côte des Blancs. Tempting but wrong. If you're heading south/south-west towards Burgundy, it's worth making sure you go through Bar-sur-Seine.

The Côte des Bars is 100km or so south of Reims, and feels less coolly maritime and a bit more bucolic and, well, Burgundian. The warmer temperatures and south-facing slopes are great for Pinot Noir, and the place is justly famous for its work with the red grape and for its rosés.

Champagne Devaux has been going since the 1840s and it's another of those champagne houses where women widowed at an early age took the reins and drove the business forward. In this case not once, not twice, but three times, creating a remarkable legacy of 'champagne widow' owners.

Devaux's Manoir building, 1.5km or so outside Bar-sur-Seine, on the road towards Dijon, is across the way from the winery, so while there's some interesting 'introduction to champagne' stuff, there's no tour of the cellars.

Still, it's a lovely atmosphere in which to stop off and taste wines and see how the offerings from Champagne's southern edge compare stylistically with those further north – they're quite distinct. You should try its non-sparkling and rare Rosé des Riceys, too.

BURGUNDY

If you want a region that captures the essence of France, it has to be Burgundy. At first sight, there's nothing particularly extraordinary about the place – the scenery is gently attractive rather than spectacular, and so what if there are vineyards everywhere? That's true of much of the country.

But Burgundy is about detail. Those defiantly homespun restaurants? They're often great. Those simple local dishes? They'll give you a gastronomic experience you'll remember for years. And those unassuming, beaten-up vans buzzing around? Well, the men in blue overalls inside are tending arguably the most sought-after vineyard plots on the planet.

Essentially, Burgundy is very simple. While there are bits of Sauvignon Blanc (around St Bris) and Aligoté in the region (plus Gamay in Beaujolais), this is a story of just two grape varieties: Chardonnay and Pinot Noir.

But the same grape grown in different villages will taste markedly different. Try the metallic, bloody punch of a Pommard next to the lifted perfume of a Chambolle-Musigny and you'd almost swear they were different varieties. But it gets more complicated. A great grower in a B-list site might well make better wine than a lazy or poor grower with a five-star village name on his bottle. There is, it must be said, an awful lot of indifferent Puligny-Montrachet out there...

Burgundy is a place where it pays not just to know your vintages and your villages, but your growers, too.

All of which makes the region fascinating, if frustrating. It's the kind of place where you can lose yourself happily for days at a time exploring what's on offer and (just to be rigorous, you understand) testing it with the food.

Beaune makes a great base. It's a beautiful town, stuffed with fabulous places to eat and drink and smack in the heart of the Côte-d'Or. Just about all the best vineyards are west of the main road that runs north-south through the region, so it's easy to navigate, and you can taste/visit pretty much the whole way down from Dijon to Lyon. Autumn is a particularly wonderful time to visit. The vines turn golden (which is what gives the Côte-d'Or its name), smoke from vineyard fires fills the air, and the earthy tang of the season finds a perfect reflection in the region's wines.

BEAUNE

JOSEPH DROUHIN

There are few better locations for a winery visit than this. The Drouhin Oenothèque is at 1 Cour du Parlement – smack in the old centre of Beaune, between the famous Hospices de Beaune and the Notre Dame Collegiate Church. In other words, at the beating, historical heart of probably the most famous and sought-after wine region in the world.

While there are some useful maps and interesting objects scattered around the Oenothèque (including a 500-year-old wine press and several near-2,000-year-old Roman artefacts), the real highlight is the chance to visit and taste in the old cellars where the wines age and the bottles rest.

Built on the remains of an old Roman fort, this 13th-century cellar belonged to the Dukes of Burgundy, who used to pass legislation in the great hall above. Such nobility has a price, however, and the tours are certainly not the most economical around – though they do include a tasting of six wines.

If there's anything you like, the shop has pretty much everything from the winery's huge production across Burgundy (including Chablis and Beaujolais), plus back vintages and wines from the Drouhins' collaboration in Oregon (p201).

DOMAINE LYCÉE VITICOLE DE BEAUNE

Just to the west of Beaune town on the Auxerre road lies a highly unusual operation. Owned by the local school, La Viti de Beaune (as it's called locally) is a kind of 'learn on the job' winery, where students can gain first-hand knowledge of all aspects of grape growing and winemaking. It receives no funding from the state, but pays for itself entirely by making and selling its wine.

The winery owns 23 hectares of vineyard scattered between Chorey-les-Beaune in the north to Puligny-Montrachet in the south, which must make it one of the most asset-rich schools in France. Recently the pupils had the bright idea of introducing a guided tour round six of their vineyard sites near the winery. Up and down the slopes of the Côte de Beaune, it's a three-hour, 10km walk, so you'll need to be reasonably fit, though the gradients are gentle rather than vertiginous. As a way of seeing the different slopes, soils and terroirs of Burgundy close-up, it could hardly be bettered, and the experience makes the wines taste all the better afterwards.

By the way, while the winery itself is on the Avenue Charles Jaffelin, 1km or so further on, the road becomes the magnificently named Route de Bouze…

NUITON-BEAUNOY

The address – Route de Pommard – tells you much of what you need to know about the location of this co-op. It's located on the south-western edge of Beaune and if you're heading out into the famous villages to the south of town (Volnay, Meursault, Puligny-Montrachet...), you're almost certain to go past it.

With members scattered (mostly) across the vineyards of the Côte de Beaune, it has a solid selection of wines on offer, from AC Bourgogne rouge and blanc up to premier and grand cru bottles, including some from vineyards in Volnay, Savigny and Meursault, and up into Nuits-St-Georges in the Côte de Nuits.

By Burgundy standards, prices are reasonable, plus there's loads of parking, animals are welcome and it even has a children's play area – not exactly common. All of which makes it a handy one-off visit for a family in a hurry.

PATRIARCHE

There are some impressive numbers associated with this Burgundy house in the northern half of town. Not only did Jean-Baptiste Patriarche first begin making and selling wine back in 1780, meaning it's been around for some 250 years, but it also has the biggest cellars in Beaune: 5km of labyrinthine arches, cool stone and wine barrels. Interestingly, it acquired its impressive network of galleries by buying properties around town, keeping the cellars, and selling off the houses above.

It's an attractive place that's well set up for visitors. Audio guides in nine languages mean you can wander on a self-guided tour around the cellars to your heart's content, learning about everything from production methods to the impact of the French Revolution.

When you arrive, you are given a tastevin (a shallow silver tasting cup) as part of your entry fee, and can use this to sample some of the dozen or so wines that are left out in a room in the cellar as part of the tour. Slip any bottles you want to buy into a bottle-carrier and pay for them on the way out. And if you can manage two visits in quick succession, Chanson is on the same street.

On your bike

Beaune's excellent local tourism website (www.beaune-tourism.com) is a great place to start planning a visit to the region. It's a mine of information on everything from spas to tasting visits and guided tours round the town itself. But if you only want to do one thing, I'd suggest hiring a bike for a day. A leisurely cycle ride is perhaps the best way to take in Burgundy's quiet country roads, plethora of well-known villages and the gently changing aspect of its vineyards. There are companies that organise guided tours and drop bikes at your hotel, and there's no shortage of regular bike hire places, either. Working up an appetite sufficient to justify that second bottle of Montrachet with your dinner couldn't be easier.

CÔTE DE NUITS

DOMAINE ARMELLE ET BERNARD RION

The Côte de Nuits is Pinot Noir country, so if you're a fan of what many wine lovers consider the best red grape in the world, it's the place to come. And this small domaine, passed down through the generations since 1896, has plenty to recommend it.

Not least, of course, the wines. Like most Burgundy growers, it has multiple (small) vineyards, in this case all in the Côte de Nuits – Vosne-Romanée, Chambolle-Musigny, Nuits-St-Georges and Vougeot. You can do a basic 'turn up and taste' for nothing, but it's better to book in advance and pay to get higher-standard wines and more engagement from the family. The tours vary from the regular VIP option (with some food) to the blow-out Immersion in Burgundy – perhaps disappointingly, this doesn't involve a Cleopatra-style bath in grand cru wines, but you will learn about everything from food matching to pruning.

The family are massively big on truffles (and have started importing and breeding some rather cute poodle-lookalike dogs from Italy to sniff them out), and their two-hour Burgundy Truffle Secrets tour gives you a chance to hunt some and taste them with the wines.

But for me the Art of Wine lesson – essentially a two-hour masterclass with the winemaker for four to eight people – is an unrivalled opportunity to get right under the skin of a fascinating region. And you still get to try the wines with some truffles afterwards.

CÔTE DE BEAUNE

OLIVIER LEFLAIVE, PULIGNY-MONTRACHET

There have been Leflaives growing grapes in Burgundy for 17 generations, but Olivier initially got waylaid by a career in TV and radio (much to his father's chagrin), before eventually setting about making beautiful music in the vineyard in the mid-'80s.

The winery has a hotel in the Place du Monument, in the heart of Puligny-Montrachet. Pricey, but nicely done, it gets consistently high scores on travel recommendation websites and has the advantage of being within staggering distance of any number of wineries and several decent restaurants.

From here you can arrange a 90-minute vineyard visit or a cellar tour – the latter is free if you're eating at the hotel. The restaurant offers a couple of three-course tasting menus with six or nine wines, which is an interesting way of finding out how different crus of Burgundy work with food.

HENRI DE VILLAMONT, SAVIGNY-LÈS-BEAUNE

You won't regret a stop at the village of Savigny-lès-Beaune, just north-west of Beaune. For starters, it's pretty, and it also has a château full of motorbikes, racing cars and fighter planes (!) if you have fractious kids to cheer up – not to mention some pleasant walks through woods and, of course, vineyards.

Henri de Villamont is a 130-year-old-plus wine estate housed in a distinctive 19th-century building built by the flamboyant Léonce Bocquet. Designed by the leading architect of the day, the place took an extraordinary eight years to build. Its cellars are large, unusually high-ceilinged (up to 6m in places) and, at 2.5km², pretty sizable too.

The tours run most days and take in everything from vineyard to cellars and winery, and include a tasting of three to five wines – though it can also accommodate more bespoke tastings on request.

CHÂTEAU DE MEURSAULT

While there are châteaux everywhere you look in Bordeaux, there are hardly any in Burgundy, so if you've had enough of 'small and homespun' and fancy a bit of camera-friendly glamour, Château de Meursault and Château de Santenay (below) are worth a look.

What began as a fairly humble manor house 1,000 years ago has been expanded over the years to the rather grand edifice you see today. Apparently, the higher the tower of a building's dovecote, the grander it is – and this is certainly a biggie!

Château de Meursault offers tours and tastings all year round, and if you're not a fan of white Burgundy, don't worry – despite the name, it makes wines from across the Côte de Beaune, from Puligny-Montrachet (and Meursault, *bien sûr*) to the red wine crus of Corton, Volnay and Pommard.

CHÂTEAU DE SANTENAY

One of the biggest vineyard owners in Burgundy (98 hectares, which is huge for this region), Château de Santenay is a U-shaped building with a typically colourful Burgundian glazed tile roof and a suitably aristocratic history. It was once the home of Philip the Bold, who, as Duke of Burgundy, was the biggest *fromage* in 14th-century France, and, in wine terms, is famous for banning the (red) Gamay grape and forcing growers to concentrate on Pinot Noir. Wine lovers, in other words, owe him a lot.

At the southern end of the Côte de Beaune, it's a recommended final stop if you're on your way towards Mâcon, Beaujolais and Lyon. Tours are reasonably priced, and include a visit to the ninth-century cellars and a tasting.

Jura cell

Head east out of Burgundy through the chicken town of Bresse towards Switzerland and you'll come across the Jura wine region. Its bottles don't make it on to many international wine lists (and even fewer on to retailers' shelves), not because they're no good but because a) it doesn't produce very many, and b) they're all a bit left-field.

Jura producers use grapes that you probably don't know. Yes, OK, some Pinot Noir and Chardonnay, but also Savagnin, Poulsard and Trousseau. And they do weird things with them. The region is best known for its vin jaune wines, which are nutty and tangy and taste rather like dry (white) sherry, but they also have straw wines (where the grapes are dried on straw mats to make a sweet wine), and Macvin du Jura, which is made by taking late-picked (sweet) grapes and fortifying them with marc (pomace brandy).

The 80km wine route is probably one of the less-well-travelled in France, but also – for adventurous wine lovers, at least – one of the most interesting, with dozens of quirky small producers all the way along.

CHABLIS

In wine terms, Chablis is part of the Burgundy appellation – but since it sits 100km or so north-west of the rest of the region, it seemed logical to give it a section of its own. In truth, Chablis and Burgundy are more half-sisters than 100 per cent blood relatives. They share some DNA – in this case the Chardonnay grape – but they're quite different. While there's a self-confident, almost jolly warmth to Burgundy, Chablis has the chilly tang of the ascetic about it.

This is not a criticism. If you ask sommeliers to describe Chablis in one word, they'll probably settle on 'mineral'. It's a term that sounds like wine-nerd nonsense. But taste a cool vintage Chablis next to the generosity of a Meursault or a more obviously fruity New World Chardonnay, and it starts to make sense. There's a pale, steely core to these wines that isn't quite fruit and isn't quite acidity – as if you'd taken a mouthful of wine, then popped in a cold pebble from a mountain stream as well. And that cool, crunchy, almost saline flavour profile lies at the heart of what Chablis is all about. It makes it a superb food-matching wine, and explains why it's both one of the first names on wine lists across the world and shorthand for 'dry white wine' for so many people. In other words, it might be Chardonnay, but labelling it by grape variety only tells part of the story. Like all good wine, chablis is a product of where it's grown: of the cold northern winters and late, damp springs; of gentle summer sunshine and limestone slopes.

The best (grand cru) vineyards are just to the north of the town on land tilted towards the south-west. The combination of good soil and great exposure means more ripeness (and expression) in the wines. A couple of years ago, these were extremely good value for money. A series of short vintages, plus an upward gravitational pull from soaraway Burgundy, means they're no longer the bargains they once were, but compared to their high maintenance half-sister to the south, the best ones very much over-deliver.

For visitors, Chablis has the big advantage of being a small region with a definite centre. You can stay in the town, and easily visit three or four wineries in a day with a typically French lunch and dinner thrown in. It's also halfway between Paris and Dijon, so you can stop off en route to Burgundy.

JEAN-MARC BROCARD

When Jean-Marc Brocard was young, he was told by an experienced winemaker, Louis Petit, to keep his eyes and ears open, his mouth shut and to learn from the land and those around him. The youth spent hours at his mentor's side, absorbing the rhythms of the earth and vines, and learning how to translate the interaction between plant and soil into the wine.

When Jean-Marc planted his first vines in the early 1970s, the old man's wisdom came back to him, and today, the name of Jean-Marc Brocard is one of the most respected in Chablis. His winery – now run by his son, Julien - makes an impressive range of wines from across the appellation, with standard chablis, four premier crus and four grand cru wines. His description of Chablis as about 'precision, strength and freshness' is about as good a definition as you'll get.

The estate is one of the most committed to eco-friendly farming methods in the region – 60 of its hectares are organic and 40 of those are farmed biodynamically. On top of a hill 5km to the south-west of the town (near a rather lovely 15th-century church), the domaine has impressive views over a wide swathe of Chablis vineyards, making it a great place to get a feel for the region.

Brocard also owns an impressive array of gîtes. These cover everything from the whopping Maison de Louis a couple of kilometres from the winery, which sleeps up to 18 people, through a pair of apartments and an attractive townhouse in the centre of Chablis, to two farmhouse cottages in the Morvan Regional Natural Park, within striking distance of Burgundy's Côte de Nuits.

LA CHABLISIENNE

The economic reality of the 1920s blew through Chablis like the region's famously chilly winds and to withstand the buffeting, a group of growers decided to pool their wines as a group.

Initially, the ensuing company, La Chablisienne, used to mix these wines together into varying blends, then sell them. But by the 1950s the company's ethos had subtly changed. Growers no longer delivered finished wine, but must – the unfermented grape juice – allowing the co-operative to take control of the entire winemaking process and create its own style.

Nowadays, with 300 members, La Chablisienne is a powerful force in the region. It owns two wine shops, one in the centre of Chablis, and the other in Vézelay, a small village about a third of the way to Burgundy. With its impressive Benedictine Abbey, it makes a good stop-off.

The beauty of La Chablisienne for the visitor is the sheer range of wines on offer. Responsible for a quarter of all chablis production, it makes 30 different wines from every corner of the appellation, including 13 premier crus, seven grand crus and (very unusual for Chablis) a single-estate wine from the magnificently named Château Grenouilles.

DOMAINE LAROCHE

The investor Warren Buffett based much of his success on the dictum of 'be fearful when others are greedy. Be greedy when others are fearful.' The young Michel Laroche followed much the same strategy to great effect in Chablis. In the 1960s the region was struggling with low prices and a string of frost-affected vintages. Growers were going broke, giving up and selling their vineyards, and Laroche made the most of it, accumulating an impressive range of some of Chablis' best sites.

Laroche was somewhat ahead of his time in everything he did, from his embrace of modern packaging and screw-caps (to avoid cork-taint issues), to the idea of building a brand name. That forward-thinking is also evident in the kind of activities he offers visitors to the region.

Of course, there's the chance for a tour and tasting at the Obédiencerie – the 1,000-year-old former monastery in the heart of Chablis that now houses the domaine's winery and offices. But there are also vineyard picnics (complete with electric bikes), a terroir tour in a Citroën 2CV, and various health- and food-driven packages at Laroche's boutique Vieux Moulin hotel.

DOMAINE LONG-DEPAQUIT

If you like attractive manor houses, beautiful gardens and high-quality wines, you'll love Long-Depaquit. It's in the heart of Chablis town, so easily walkable from the likes of Laroche's hotel/winery and the La Chablisienne shop.

The Bichot family who own it have been in Burgundy for the small matter of 800 years, and still have the same coat of arms – which features a *biche* (or doe). Tasting-wise, at the Orangerie, there are five grand crus, six premier crus and the curious La Moutonne to choose from. The latter is produced from a single vineyard, owned entirely by the family, which spreads across two separate grand cru sites: Vaudésir and Les Preuses. It's in a kind of south-facing bowl, meaning that it probably gets the best sun exposure of anywhere in Chablis. In warm years, this may not be a good thing, but in cooler ones it gives a wine of rare intensity and balance.

Free visits are available without reservation and give you a guided tasting of a chablis, a premier cru and a grand cru and the chance to ask questions. Winery and cellar visits are also available for larger groups (over ten).

BEAUJOLAIS

Beaujolais sits at the bottom end of the Mâconnais, the southernmost outpost of Burgundy. Officially, it's part of the wider Burgundy appellation, but it's a rather odd fit. While Burgundy inspires visions of aristocratic grape varieties and drooling collectors, Beaujolais is all cheap and cheerful Gamay and 'quaff-me-quick' Beaujolais Nouveau in zinc-countered bistros.

The plus side of this is that while Burgundy has stratospheric price tickets and soaring land values, Beaujolais remains one of the world's great wine bargains, and its growers are more likely to be driving Peugeots than Mercedes. All of which, frankly, makes it an excellent place to visit.

Its ten villages – Fleurie, Brouilly, Moulin-à-Vent et al – are familiar to most wine lovers, and, in a north-south line just off the A6, are easy to get to. Tasting a line-up of wines from these different villages next to each other is one of the best ways of understanding just how land can influence a wine's character.

Plus, of course, Beaujolais can be really, really good. The region might be best-known for its super-young wine, Beaujolais Nouveau, which makes it to market barely eight weeks after vintage and prompted all manner of faintly embarrassing shenanigans on Beaujolais Nouveau Day, the third Thursday of every November, in the 1980s. But its wines from the 'cru' villages have a lot more about them.

Grown on a range of rolling granite hills, Gamay attains a zip and poise that it lacks in more humble terroir, and gives wines with character, and in the case of some, such as Morgon or Moulin-à-Vent, serious ageability. These are the kind of wines that sommeliers drink when they're not at work and, therefore, paying with their own money: charming, refreshing and criminally undervalued.

For the tourist, Beaujolais is an interesting base. It's not far from Lyon – France's undisputed gastronomic capital – and the slopes make for beautiful (if energetic) cycling and walking. It pays to linger a bit, but if you're en route elsewhere and in a rush, you can still get a flavour of the area in a couple of days.

GEORGES DUBOEUF, MOULIN-À-VENT

Duboeuf is the biggest producer in Beaujolais, a tireless advocate for the region and a proud local whose ancestors have been making wines in this part of southern Burgundy for hundreds of years. He famously used to strap bottles of the family's wine to his bike to take samples to top chefs in Lyon, and after years of pedalling (and later driving) the back lanes west of the motorway, his knowledge of the region is second to none.

His Hameau Duboeuf (Duboeuf Hamlet) is billed as the first wine and vine park and it's a fabulously ambitious attempt to create a mini vinous Disneyland, with everything from a cinema and crazy golf to bike rides and (faintly terrifying) automated puppets. Plus, of course, museum, cellar and winery visits. If you have a young family and want to do one winery visit in France, this should probably be it.

CHÂTEAU DU MOULIN-À-VENT

The Moulin-à-Vent appellation gets its name from the old windmill that sits on top of the Thorins hill. For many observers, it's the classiest of all the Beaujolais crus, blending the region's perky fruit with structure and ageability.

Records show that this estate has been making wine since the 1730s (it used to be called Château des Thorins, after the hill, but changed its name when the appellation was created in the 1930s). It owns a number of amazing vineyards, containing some seriously old vines – the average age is 40 years.

There are no tourist 'extras' here, but if you want to get to know one of the region's best producers in one of the best areas, this is where to come. It's a small, family operation, though, so ring ahead to book first.

DOMAINE DE LA MADONE, FLEURIE

A couple of kilometres from the village of Fleurie lies the slope of La Madone. One of the best grape growing sites in the appellation, it's also home to the estate of the same name, which nestles below the chapel on the summit.

As well as making 'typical' Fleurie – subtle, perfumed and elegant – it also produces a string of less usual versions from a variety of sites and plays with oak-ageing to create wines of more ambition, power and ageability. Going through its various Grille Midi, Oak Cask and Domaine du Niagara wines provides a fascinating education in how different aspects of an estate can be used to create very different expressions.

The domaine is well set up for visits, and even has a modern gîte (which sleeps six to seven) in the heart of the vineyards if you want to use it as a base.

CHÂTEAU DE JAVERNAND, CHIROUBLES

Sometimes, the wines of an area mirror the place itself and that's the way it is with Chiroubles. It's one of the prettiest parts of Beaujolais, yet unpretentious and honest. And, stylistically, its wines tend to be equally fun, charming and accessible.

In this, Château de Javernand, which celebrated its 100th anniversary in 2017, is right on message. Despite its decent history, it's neither stuffy nor grand and is pretty rather than showy, affording beautiful views out over the hills down to the flat lands of the east.

The winery is thoroughly welcoming to tourists – it prefers if people book in advance, but it's also happy for you to turn up unannounced on the chance that someone won't be far away. The usual tours and tastings, including the opportunity to simply wander around, are all free and if you're in a larger group, it can also provide food.

A couple of times a year the domaine has open-door weekends, when you can picnic out on the lawn, take a scenic walk through the vines and play *pétanque* and croquet.

JEAN-PAUL THÉVENET, MORGON

If you're a fan of natural wines, you may well already know about Monsieur Thévenet: he was one of the Beaujolais 'gang of four' who ushered natural wine production into the region. He's in the cru of Morgon, which tends to give some of the fullest-flavoured and structured versions of Gamay around here. Indeed, there are plenty who feel that these wines don't just benefit from a bit of age on them, but demand it.

Thévenet uses no artificial nasties in the vineyard, as well as non-synthetic yeasts, and after a bit of time in oak, bottles his wines without filtration. Truly, what you see is what you get.

JULIEN MERLE, LÉGNY

At the other end of the scale from Duboeuf is Julien Merle, a young winemaker making a range of good, very well-priced, unpretentious wines in as natural a style as possible. He's down in Légny, at the southern edges of Beaujolais, a long way from the region's more prestigious slopes. There are no daily cellar or vineyard tours, but Julien is passionate, interesting and, for want of a better word, real. Ring if you're in the area and try to set up a visit.

BORDEAUX

It's hard to think of any other decently sized city in the world so associated with one product. Bordeaux might be a big, bustling, modern metropolis, but first and foremost it's all about wine.

Along with Burgundy and Champagne, this is one of the most-recognised wine regions in the world – and unlike Burgundy, at least, it also knocks out a lot of bottles, which is handy if you're coming to south-west France for a visit. Handy, but daunting... Everywhere you look there are vines and vineyards. Until fairly recently, Bordeaux produced more wine than Chile.

Bordeaux is most famous for its red wines, though its whites – usually Sauvignon Blanc with a splash of Sémillon to add depth – are shockingly under-appreciated, and capable of superlative quality, particularly those originating from the gravelly soils of Pessac-Léognan, where there's a smoky crunch and elegant lift that ages beautifully.

Further down the River Garonne, the vineyards of Sauternes and Barsac benefit from fog rolling up off the water to create some of the most elegant dessert wines in the world. If you're a fan of 'stickies', a visit here should be on your bucket list.

That said, if you don't like red wine, this probably isn't the ideal region for you: 80 per cent of all the plantings are rouge. Cabernet Sauvignon, Merlot and Cabernet Franc are the 'big three' with the likes of Petit Verdot and Malbec adding delicate dashes of seasoning from time to time.

Growers in Tuscany, Napa and Margaret River might disagree, but for most wine lovers, the 'Left Bank' vineyards to the west of the Garonne are Cabernet's spiritual home. Here, the gravelly soils – washed down from the Pyrenees a bajillion years ago – do two things the grape likes: they drain well, and they absorb the sun's rays and reflect heat back up on to the bunches.

This is important. Cabernet takes its time to get fully ripe – essential for softening its notoriously tough tannins. In less than ideal years, the wines can be a little tough on the gums. And even in good years, there's a faint savoury undertone to these Cab-dominant Left Bank creations: a cigar-box/pencil-lead element that doesn't really occur anywhere else in the world and gives the wines a distinctive personality. These are wines that have a tweed-waistcoated formality to them.

The Médoc is not, frankly, the most beautiful wine-growing region in the world – it's low-lying and bereft of striking features. But it's a place of subtlety rather than picture-postcard beauty – instead of looking up, you're probably best off looking at what's beneath your feet.

The gravels are at their most intense at the southern end of the Médoc, petering out slowly as the spit of land heads towards the coast. This shifting balance of gravel and clay in the famous villages is a large part of what gives the likes of St-Julien, Margaux, Pauillac and St-Estèphe their character.

You could spend years exploring this part of Bordeaux alone, but the wine tourist can get a good flavour of it in just a few days. It's worth the effort.

The other big region of Bordeaux for wine tourism is the Right Bank. Spreading out from the town of Libourne on the other side of the Dordogne river, down towards (and past) St-Émilion, it's quite different in feel to the Médoc. The countryside is more rolling, the towns less dour and wind-blown, and the wines, too, are friendlier. On these cooler clay and limestone soils, the haughty Cabernet Sauvignon struggles to get ripe, and its more approachable counterpart Merlot takes over, usually with a good splash of winsomely aromatic Cabernet Franc to add charm to its plumpness.

St-Émilion itself is a lovely place to make your base, with a strong Roman and monastic past. A walking tour of the town is recommended, as is renting bikes to potter round the vineyards that carpet the region.

With almost 10,000 growers in Bordeaux, there's no shortage of potential visits. But for most of them, you'll need to book in advance, and for goodness' sake make sure you arrive on time.

Also bear in mind that many of the big names vet their visitors carefully. If you're in the trade or a regular customer, you'll get in. If you're just a wine-curious tourist, however much you plead, you're just not going to get that tour and tasting at Le Pin. Sorry.

So plan ahead and use the expertise of the various regional tourist offices.

THE LEFT BANK – THE MÉDOC

CHÂTEAU KIRWAN, MARGAUX

Head to the Médoc from Bordeaux and Margaux is the first great wine commune you come to. It's got the thinnest, most gravelly soils in the Left Bank, which is what gives the region's wines their beautiful perfumed elegance in good years. In bad years, they can be a bit bony.

Château Kirwan has been in the hands of the same family for eight generations and, impressively for a Third Growth château, it has embraced the idea of opening for tourists. With eight nicely pitched visits to choose from, there should be something for everyone. For beginners, the basic tour is a 45-minute whizz through the vineyards and the winery, plus a tasting of two wines. The more committed will prefer the longer tours/tastings with three wines and a ham/cheese accompaniment. And if it's your birthday, go for the full guided tour, which gives you the opportunity to taste decanted wines from your birth year. Obviously, you need to book the latter experience well in advance – and it's worth first checking to see whether or not your birth year was a good one for Bordeaux. If it was, it could be an unmissable opportunity.

CHÂTEAU LANGOA BARTON/CHÂTEAU LÉOVILLE BARTON, ST-JULIEN

The Barton family have been involved in the wine trade in Bordeaux since Thomas 'French Tom' Barton arrived in Bordeaux in 1725. From an Irish merchant family, they originally bought and exported wine, but, having navigated the turbulent waters of the French Revolution, Hugh Barton managed to buy a small wine estate – Château Langoa – and, in 1826, added a small vineyard from the large Léoville estate next door, naming it Léoville Barton.

During the famous Bordeaux Classification of 1855, Langoa was awarded Third Growth status, while Léoville Barton went one better, and is one of only 14 Second Growths. It remains among the most reliable wine estates in St-Julien – and is also frequently one of the most reasonably priced, even in stellar vintages.

Léoville Barton, which is just a vineyard, uses the Langoa cellars to make and age the wine. Visitors have access to the cellars, as well as the beautiful Bordeaux château, which is justly renowned for its fabulous gardens, particularly its roses. Visits are conducted in French and English four-and-a-half days a week and include the chance to taste the latest vintage. Be sure to book in advance, though.

CHÂTEAU PICHON LONGUEVILLE, PAUILLAC

Pauillac is probably the starriest of all the Médoc communes. Three of the five First Growths are here: Mouton Rothschild, Lafite and Latour. Getting in is, to say the least, difficult. But if you're a wine lover, you can't come to this part of the world and not sample some top-class wine. There's a sleek, high-toned glossiness to good Pauillac that has the balance of power and elegance of a top racehorse, and you owe it to yourself to check out a couple of thoroughbreds while you're here.

Pichon Longueville is, at Second Growth status, only just below the top level, but its wines are very, very good. Even better, it's possible to get a visit, provided you contact them well in advance. The vineyards were bought by a local bigwig wine merchant back in the 17th century, and became part of his daughter's dowry when she married Baron Pichon de Longueville. The charming château – like something out of a Disney movie – was built in 1851, four years before the estate acquired its Second Growth status.

Note: don't confuse Château Pichon Longueville (aka Pichon Baron) with the neighbouring Château Pichon Longueville Comtesse de Lalande. The latter doesn't accept visits from the public.

CHÂTEAU PHÉLAN SÉGUR, ST-ESTÈPHE

St-Estèphe is the most northerly of the great wine communes of the Médoc, and the great gravel banks are starting to disappear. You'll see stones in the vineyards here, and more sand and clay.

If you visit Phélan Ségur during the week, you'll get a chance to see this in the company of the estate's chef de culture. To be taken on a tour of the vines of a Third Growth with the man in charge of managing them is quite an opportunity. With its pebbly vineyards sloping down towards the Gironde, it gives you a real sense of what Left Bank Bordeaux is all about. What's more, the tasting includes a vertical of wines from three different vintages – an absolute bonus.

The estate was another of those bought by Irish wine shippers in the 18th century, though it now belongs to a French family, the Gardiniers, who own some of France's top restaurants. You can also book a meal at the château prepared by the estate's chef de cuisine.

CHÂTEAU CASTERA, MÉDOC

The northern end of the Médoc contains the final stretch of vineyards before the Atlantic, and it's liberally dotted with estates – though few are as welcoming as this one.

Like many Bordeaux estates, Château Castera has seen plenty of ups and downs since it started growing vines in the Middle Ages. But it's on a definite upswing now. The owners have spent a lot of money creating a friendly, open winery. It's well set up for families, with a beautiful garden and park – a handy place for little ones to run off steam – and an emphasis on child-friendly winery tours.

The most wine engaged should try the Premium Tour, which includes the kind of activities normally reserved for industry professionals: tasting wine direct from the barrel with the cellar master and a vertical tasting. It's a great way of seeing how the same estate's wine, made in the same way each year, can differ from vintage to vintage.

PESSAC-LÉOGNAN/GRAVES

CHÂTEAU LA LOUVIÈRE

This château belongs to the André Lurton stable, one of the best-known names in Bordeaux. When it was established in the 14th century, the area was all-but uninhabited and its wildness is thought to explain the name of the château – La Louvière means 'den of wolves'.

It's easy to reach from town, and the listed château is beautiful. The shop, where you can try and buy wines from all seven of the Lurton wineries has limited opening hours, but three bookable tours. The basic Art of Wine visit gives you information about the company and the Pessac-Léognan region, plus a tasting of five wines. Splash out on the top Wine Club Buffet tour and you get an extra hour, nine wines and various cheeses and charcuterie. But you're probably better off saving the money and spending it on a few bottles of the estate whites. If your only experience of Sauvignon Blanc is from the Loire or Marlborough, these can be real eye-openers. The famous gravelly soils of the Graves give the wine an elegant mineral crunch that becomes more textured and honeyed with time.

CHÂTEAU PAPE CLÉMENT

Archbishop of Bordeaux Bertrand de Goth was one of the first owners of this estate, which was given to him when he was appointed to the position, and he was heavily engaged with growing the grapes and making the wine. But when he was appointed pope in 1305 (taking the name Clement V), the small matter of becoming God's emissary on earth made it hard for him to devote as much time to tending the vineyards and he was eventually forced to hand them over to his successor in Bordeaux. The estate, however, has been named in his honour ever since.

Located inside the Bordeaux ring-road, the château is one of the closest to the city centre (though First Growth Haut-Brion, just a few kilometres down the road, is even closer). Cabernet Sauvignon can be particularly attractive off its gravelly, sandy, shell-filled soils, and in good years it's capable of really singing.

There is a wide range of possible tours. Though a more intriguing option is the chance to play winemaker and blend your own Bordeaux.

CHÂTEAU SMITH HAUT LAFITTE

Near the southern edges of the Pessac-Léognan appellation, Château Smith Haut Lafitte is not like most wine estates. Wander over during springtime and you won't see anyone frantically spraying with pesticides to keep away beasties. No, you'll see them manually turning over the soil with a plough. Pulled by a horse.

Yet, while committedly eco-friendly, this winery is also a gleaming shrine to modernity and uses drones to assess the ripeness of the grapes. The vineyards are run organically, which means biodiversity and no chemicals. Rainwater and waste water are recycled, solar panels provide energy, and vine cuttings are either turned into compost or used for heating.

There are a whole raft of other tours and workshops, too. The chance to experience the daily life of a vineyard manager in a Bordeaux château looks like a great present for the wine lover in your life.

If you're visiting Smith Haut Lafitte, it makes sense to check out Les Sources de Caudalie. There is a superb hotel and cottages, a restaurant, bar and award-winning spa that focuses on vinotherapy. If you've ever felt the urge for a crushed Cabernet scrub, you now know where to go...

SAUTERNES/BARSAC

CHÂTEAU DUDON, BARSAC

If you like sweet wine, you have to come to Sauternes and Barsac. That's the rule, sorry.

The Dudon estate is in Barsac, which is a bit less glitzy than Sauternes, but still has some wonderfully famous names such as Châteaux Doisy-Daëne, Climens and Coutet. It's a stone's throw from this trio, and that relative rarity for this part of the world: an organic producer. Moreover, the wines are fabulous: opulent but balanced. There's an undeniably aristocratic feel to each one, which is darkly fitting given one of its previous owners was guillotined in front of Barsac's church during the French Revolution for supporting the king.

It has a small wine museum and a model of the château made out of 30,000 matchsticks(!). But the tasting aside, best of all is the chance to stay in a gîte next to the lovely old château, with views out over the vineyards.

CHÂTEAU SUDUIRAUT, SAUTERNES

True disciples of Sauternes may wish to shell out the cash to worship at the altar of the sublime Château d'Yquem. But if that's a bit rich for your tastes, and you just want to taste some top-class sweet wine from some of the region's best vineyards, Château Suduiraut offers better value.

After all, it has plenty of history – the estate was founded in 1580 – and plenty of pedigree, too: it was classified as a First Growth in 1855. The sandy, gravelly soils of the vineyard warm up and radiate heat back on to the grapes, giving them a particularly ripe style and a natural opulence: pineapple, mango, apricot, beeswax and honey are all typical.

Trying to discern all those in a glass can be somewhat overwhelming, though, which is why Suduiraut's Aroma Gallery is such a brilliant idea. Here, you get to taste two wines alongside nine aroma jars containing some of their key flavours. It really helps get your head round the various scents wafting up your nasal cavity.

THE RIGHT BANK

CHÂTEAU SIAURAC, LALANDE DE POMEROL

One of the particularities of Pomerol is that, for all the stellar wines, it's pretty short on five-star architecture. While the Left Bank seems to have an indecent number of imposing buildings, this bit of the Right Bank seems more shed than château. Which is why Château Siaurac might come as a relief to anyone feeling starved of photo opportunities since crossing the two rivers. Built in the late 1800s in an 18th-century style, it appears to have been carved out of vanilla ice cream. It also has one a fine 'English-style' garden – though since 15 hectares of vineyard were pulled up to create it, you might feel ambivalent about that.

The cheaper tour takes in the vineyard and cellars with a tasting of the first and second wines. But the Grands Vins tasting is a better bet. The tour is the same, but you get to try a Pomerol, a St-Émilion and Siaurac's Lalande de Pomerol – a ripe chance to compare the differences between the three most recognisable Right Bank appellations.

CHÂTEAU FAUGÈRES

Château Faugères is towards the eastern edges of St-Émilion, on the south-east facing slopes of a limestone plateau. Admittedly, this is hardly Mosel levels of steepness, but it's more photogenic than many parts of Bordeaux and its modern (and modernist) 'cathedral of wine', designed by Swiss architect Mario Botta, has become a justly famous landmark in the region. Moreover, the winery and vineyards – run on organic principles – are clearly on the up under new owner Silvio Denz, owner of Lalique perfume: the estate was upgraded to Grand Cru Classé status in 2012.

The attraction is not just the chance to look around the vineyards and try the rapidly improving wines, but also to do a tasting in the airy space at the top of the cathedral's tower. From here, soaking up the views out over the vineyards of St-Émilion, glass in hand, is an unforgettable experience.

CHÂTEAU DE PRESSAC

Located on a *tertre* or small hill, Château de Pressac offers some of the best views of St-Émilion, with its terraced vineyards and white-stone walls

As you'd expect from a limestone and clay terroir, almost all of its 40-hectare estate is planted with Merlot and Cabernet Franc. The combination leads to wines that are approachable at a younger age than those produced by your average Left Bank château.

This is a laudably comprehensive visit. You might not get to go inside the château itself, but you get a tour of the exterior (complete with history from the Middle Ages onwards), an explanation of the terroir and the full winemaking and blending process. Plus, of course, the chance to put your new knowledge to the test with a tasting of several Château Pressac vintages.

CHÂTEAU MAUVINON

On the flatter lands south of St-Émilion, heading towards the Dordogne, Château Mauvinon is almost entirely given over to Merlot and Cabernet Franc. It used to be owned by a *grand fromage* in the St-Émilion co-op, and the wine was blended with the fruit of many other estates as a result. But since 1990 it's been run by Philippe and Brigitte Tribaudeau, who bottle it under their own label. The soil is lighter and sandier here, and the wines tend to be softer – albeit less age-worthy – than those from the limestone hills to the north.

The joy of this visit is that not only do you get the chance to taste how Merlot performs on lighter soils, but also to look round every bit of a simple, unpretentious wine estate in the company of the people who own and run it. At just 6.5 hectares, it's a boutique operation, and a visit to the vineyards and small winery will give you a real flavour of what you might call the real world of wine.

CHÂTEAU NODOT

This estate, about 20 minutes off the main A10 motorway north of Bordeaux, could be a handy (and quirky) stop on your way through the region. The vineyards are organically certified and there's a small wine museum with old bits of paraphernalia. The big attraction, though, is the themed dinners.

There aren't many wineries where you can take part in a full-on medieval day. Participants dress up in period costume, cut grapes by hand, tread them by foot, then tuck into an olde-style banquet accompanied by the kind of flavoured wines drunk at that time. If you just want the food without the theatre, at certain times of year you can tour the vineyards and winery and sample seven of the estate's wines before an alfresco dinner. This time with a full set of modern cutlery.

ENTRE DEUX MERS

CHÂTEAU BAUDUC

This middle area between the Garonne and the Dordogne is especially good for rosé and full of small, unpretentious wine estates making standard AC Bordeaux at a reasonable price. Some, however, are more worth a look than others, and Château Bauduc is definitely one to put on your list.

Gavin and Angela Quinney fell in love with this place in the late '90s and moved from London to start a new life as wine producers. They've done a great job. The family conducts tours of the vineyards and cellar with a tasting. There's also an old farmhouse with pool on the property that they rent out. Situated about half an hour from both St-Émilion and Bordeaux, it could be a homely base if you're planning a week's exploration of the area.

THE LOIRE

The Loire is France's longest river. But if you're harbouring dreams of tasting and visiting right the way along its 1,000km length, from its source in the Massif Central to the Atlantic, you'll need to reconsider. The first two-thirds of the river's journey from the mountains, as it first hurries, then trudges north, is all-but vine free. But once you get to Pouilly-sur-Loire and Sancerre – and this most indolent of waterways has slowed to a sluggish amble – the serious vineyards begin. And from Orléans to the coast at Nantes, you're looking at over 300km of almost continuous vine action.

The Loire is the dividing line between 'cool, temperamental, northern France' and 'warmer, sunnier southern France', and its spread of wine styles reflects this. It makes good sparkling wine that isn't quite as cool-hearted as champagne from the north, and Sauvignon Blanc that's tighter and less ostensibly fruity than Bordeaux to the south.

In good years its Cabernet Francs can be perfumed, joyous and as light-footed as springtime lambs; in bad years they have all the charm of a wronged teenager. There are succulent sweet whites and unambitious off-dry pinks, the bone-dry quayside blasts of young Muscadet and the haunting, autumnal flavours of old Vouvray. This is a place that makes a lot of interesting styles of wine – some world-famous, some half-remembered, others all-but anonymous – and for the wine-curious tourist, this is good news. In short, it's a real chance to broaden your wine education.

It helps, of course, that the Loire is a very easy region to like. This was the summer stomping ground of the French royal court – Paris is just over 100km away at its nearest point – and the aristocratic invasion has left the place with a string of fairy-tale châteaux stretching from Orléans to the coast. If you're looking to work in five days of wine visits with more mainstream touristy stuff, this is the perfect region.

The Loire's western edges round Nantes are the home of Muscadet. For rather too long, drinking its wares was like drinking the colour white – neutral, fresh wines that paired well with the local seafood or perked up your palate on a hot afternoon, but couldn't do much else. But the growth of the 'sur lie' process – where the wine is left in contact with its lees (the deposit left after fermentation) for a while before bottling – has generated wines with more texture and complexity. They're not showy, but they're good.

Lovers of Chenin Blanc should base themselves around Angers, where along one 30km stretch of river you'll find every style of which the grape is capable showcased – from rather good sweeter whites (Coteaux du Layon and Bonnezeaux) through the taut, dry, age-worthy beasts of Savennières to the sparklers of Saumur. The Chenin love-in picks up again as you pass Tours and enter Vouvray – but first you have to go through the Loire's best red-wine enclave round Chinon.

While Cabernet Franc is a key element in Bordeaux, there it's part of a blend. In the Loire it takes centre stage. In good years, the wines are medium-bodied, with an attractive leafy freshness behind the red fruit. They're the kind of bottles that you find yourself reaching for to cheer up a Tuesday night, or putting in ice buckets on summer days.

Having said all that, if you had to pick one grape variety that defines this region, it would be Sauvignon Blanc. The best and most famous versions are, perhaps somewhat counter-intuitively, produced far away from the cool sea breezes in Sancerre and Pouilly-Fumé. There, the limestone slopes (atypical for the Loire) help give the wines a smokiness and zing that takes them beyond Sauvignon Blanc's in-your-face fruit flavours.

The distances in the Loire might look intimidating, but there are motorways all the way from the coast at Nantes to near Sancerre, so getting around is relatively painless. And if you're heading from the north to the south via Bordeaux, it's likely to be en route, so it makes sense to at least work in a couple of days round Tours, Chinon or Saumur.

DOMAINE PIERRE LUNEAU-PAPIN, MUSCADET

Monks brought the Melon de Bourgogne grape to this part of France from Burgundy 500 years ago, and this winemaking family, now in their ninth generation, must have arrived not that long after. They produce pretty much every style that it's possible to do in the region, including the less-usual Gamay (red) and Folle Blanche (white), and have a wide range of expressions of them, from 'young and fresh' to 'aged and complex'.

They'll let you come and taste with an appointment – typically five or six wines – though visits to the winery are out. Alternatively, if you simply want to try a tonne of Muscadets rather than visit a domaine, you could pop into La Maison du Muscadet in Vallet. The store stocks over 80 wines from 27 local producers.

DOMAINE DE LA BERGERIE, ANJOU

In the Loire's occasionally erratic climate, you need guts to cast aside artificial treatments and go organic, so hats off to the Guégniard family for managing it. Their portfolio of wines is a great showcase for the diversity of this mid-western part of the Loire. While some areas of France might concentrate on a couple of styles, Domaine de la Bergerie, in the Coteaux du Layon, south of Angers, makes sparkling wine, sweet wine, dry reds, dry whites, medium-sweet whites and rosé, using combinations of Chenin Blanc, Chardonnay, Cabernet Sauvignon, Cabernet Franc and the local Grolleau grape.

The family's eldest daughter, Anne, worked for years as a sommelier and is married to a talented chef, so the winery has duly set up a restaurant of its own, La Table de la Bergerie, which has picked up a Michelin star. It's a superb place to see how myriad styles of wine from this part of the Loire can work with great food.

BOUVET LADUBAY, SAUMUR

If the western side of the Loire is about clay and dark schist soils, there's a very obvious shift around Saumur – one that you can see in the town itself. All the buildings are made out of limestone excavated from the surrounding land and the practical locals used the newly created tunnels to store their wines.

Like Chardonnay on the Côte des Blancs, Chenin Blanc likes the chalky white soil and the team at Bouvet Ladubay is making the most of it. For a crash course in the Loire's sparkling wine, this is the place to come, offering an enormous spread of styles, from quaffable and good value, to complex and ambitious.

The place is set up for all kinds of visitors, from those with restricted mobility to children – little ones even get their own tasting (of sparkling apple juice).

If you're able to book in advance (and don't have anyone under 14 in your party), the chance to do a one-hour tour of the ancient limestone cellars by vintage bicycle should not be missed.

COULY-DUTHEIL, CHINON

If you're feeling a bit 'whited out' by the preponderance of vins blancs in the Loire, this is somewhere you'll want to stop. In the appellations of Chinon, St-Nicolas-de-Bourgueil and Bourgueil, Cabernet Franc rules.

The vineyards are a mix of limestone on the slopes and sandy or gravelly soil on the flatter lands near the river, and they give quite different wines. Those from the former are dense, structured and ageable; the latter lighter and more perfumed.

Now approaching its 100-year anniversary, Couly-Dutheil is one of the region's best producers. The basic 90-minute tour – which takes in the vineyards, cellar, history and most of what you need to know about the region, plus a tasting of three reds – is incredible value.

HENRI BOURGEOIS, SANCERRE

Sauvignon Blanc is not, for the most part, a wine that commands big bucks. But Pouilly-Fumé and Sancerre are the exceptions. On these limestone slopes, in the right years, the wines can attain a poise and complexity that knocks your bog-standard Sauvignon Blanc into a cocked *chapeau*: a combination of fruit, leafy greenness, tropical perfume and (in certain places) an undeniable smoky whiff of gunflint.

The problem is they don't deliver these things every year. Get a wine from a bad vintage – or from a lazy producer who's chasing volume and trading on the Sancerre or Pouilly-Fumé name – and you end up with something little more than crisp, fresh and massively overpriced.

So Henri Bourgeois is worth a look. From one of the best villages in Sancerre, Chavignol, it makes no less than ten Sancerres, from a variety of sites and in a variety of styles. Tasting them is a fascinating exercise in how one variety from one area can give very different results in the hands of winemakers who properly understand its character.

MICHEL REDDE, POUILLY-FUMÉ

Ten kilometres from Sancerre lies Pouilly-Fumé, the other great Sauvignon Blanc appellation. The Redde family has records of one François Redde growing grapes in the village nearly 400 years ago, though the current branch of the name only started in the 1930s.

Redde is essentially a Pouilly-Fumé specialist, and has a portfolio of Sauvignon Blancs from a variety of soils – from flint through limestone to marl. Adding further to the complexity, some of the wines also spend time in varying sizes (and ages) of oak container. The result is a range of wines from freshly aromatic to rich and complex. A tasting here offers a rich exploration of what Sauvignon Blanc can do on different terroirs and with different treatments in the winery.

ALSACE

If Alsace were a restaurant dish, it would probably be described as 'fusion'. After all, most of the place names sound German, the half-timbered houses look German, the local food is what we think of as German, even the fluted wine bottles look German – but, of course, this is still France.

Germany butts up against Alsace's eastern edge and has annexed the place twice: in the Franco-Prussian War of 1870-71, then again in the 1940s. Which is perhaps why when I once idly remarked to a local winemaker that the place 'looked quite Germanic', his face turned the colour of a plate of *choucroute* (or should that be sauerkraut?).

Wine-wise, it's a real Franco-German mash-up. The superstar white grape might be Riesling, backed up by Gewürztraminer and Pinot Gris, but their expressions are quite different from the typical German ones. For starters, the Alsace versions are usually – though not always – dry, and often much bigger and richer than their German equivalents.

This is because Alsace is a suntrap. This far north (the region is about level with Champagne), you may not have the heat of the Mediterranean, but it's one of the driest places in France, getting about the same amount of rain as Perpignan in the south. Not only is it a long way from the sea, but the Vosges mountains, which line Alsace's western edge, act as an effective 1,400m-high barrier to all but the most persistent of rain clouds.

The region's vineyards stretch along the Vosges' eastern foothills in a long snaking band from north to south. The vineyards are not especially high – few sit above 350m – but they benefit from both the granite slopes, which drain better than the flat lands further east, and more exposure to the sun.

There's enough heat and sunlight to create good Pinot Noir in Alsace, though not necessarily every year. In any case, the locals often drink lush, smoky, vaguely red-fruited Pinot Gris with their darker meats – and it works. You should also check out the oily, powerful Gewürztraminers – especially with the local cheese or slightly spicier dishes.

But if there's one thing you must do in Alsace, it's get into the Rieslings. The grape is famous for its ability to taste very different depending on where it's grown, so checking out a range of them can be fascinating.

The best way to do this is to try the Rieslings from some of the 51 grand cru sites. They are all single vineyards, from across the appellation, and come from a wide variety of soil types, altitudes and exposures. In the difference between a floral, elegant Schlossberg Riesling and a more peppery, mineral Rosacker, just 5km to the north, you can appreciate so much about what makes wine fascinating.

For the wine tourist, Alsace is in the premier league. It's a relatively small appellation, it's easy to navigate and, running north/south, it's easy to work winery visits into a regular tourist itinerary without feeling like you're going miles out of your way.

Oh, and it's jaw-droppingly beautiful. The succession of medieval villages, with their walls, courtyards and overhanging gables, makes this perhaps the most consistently rewarding route des vins in the world. Riquewihr is the most picturesque (and busiest) of the wine villages, but you'd have to be exceptionally hard-to-please to feel disappointed by any of them.

Throughout the long summer and golden autumn days, camper vans trundle along the roads that run along the foothills of the Vosges as gastro-tourists go to stock up on wine, cured meats and joie de vivre. But cycling is a popular way of getting around, too. The villages are regularly spaced, not too far apart, and more easily accessible on two wheels than four. And after a couple of hours of negotiating the slopes, you can more easily justify that tarte flambée or whopping great ham hock at lunchtime.

The wine experience in Alsace is one of small family firms, and few offer much beyond a tasting and perhaps a cellar visit. But that's all part of the charm. Even small producers tend to have a disproportionately large number of wines to offer from different sites. And that, particularly with an expressive grape like Riesling, makes this a fabulous place to do comparative tastings.

JEAN-BAPTISTE ADAM, AMMERSCHWIHR

The Adam family have been making wine in Alsace for four centuries and they remain beautifully welcoming to tourists. Their tasting shop and cellar in Ammerschwihr is in the heart of some of the most prestigious vineyards in Alsace, so make sure you try their Kaefferkopf Riesling and Gewürztraminer from the nearby grand cru. You should also check out the organic and biodynamic wines, too.

The cellar is open seven days a week in high season and six days a week outside that, making it easy for a drop-in visit. The family's vines aren't directly outside the cellar, so you can't just wander in and take a look. But they might be amenable to taking you out for a view in a four-by-four provided you call ahead. And of course, it's always possible to visit the cave. Unlike in Burgundy, for instance, wood doesn't play a big part in the Alsatian wine production process – so you'll find a handful of stately oval *cuves* rather than rows of barrels.

ROLLY GASSMANN, RORSCHWIHR

When the Rolly and the Gassman families joined together through marriage in 1967, it marked the union of a combined 700 years of Alsace winemaking. And given the centuries of experience, it's no surprise they like doing things their own way.

Their wines are big and powerful: very ripe, with a hefty chunk of residual sugar, but plenty of acidity to balance. The style is about as fashionable as corduroy with most consumers, but these guys pull it off quite brilliantly. Not least because they hold on to the wines for several years before releasing them when they think they're starting to show well. Their cellar has getting on for five years' worth of sales in it (a million bottles if you don't feel like counting) and they're not a big producer by any means. It's quite a statement of intent, and one that, presumably, their accountant feels is more than justified by the quality of the wine.

The firm's little shop in the sleepy village of Rorschwihr is wonderfully unreconstructed – it feels a bit like tasting in somebody's garage, surrounded by bottles, cases and pallets – but the range of wines certainly makes an impression. You won't like all of them, but others you'll fall in love with. And they are fabulous with food, particularly full-flavoured or spicy dishes.

One final tip: if you stay in the pretty nearby village of Bergheim, you can reach the cellar via a pleasant half-hour walk through the vines.

HUGEL, RIQUEWIHR

With their gold and yellow labels, Hugel's bottles are among the most distinctive in the wine world. By Alsace standards, they're reasonably plentiful, too – around a million are produced each year – and since most are exported, for many wine drinkers, Hugel *is* Alsace.

One of the advantages of making a bit more wine is that there's a wide range of bottles to try. Beyond the usual Pinot Gris, Gewürztraminer, Riesling and Pinot Blanc, you also find Muscat, Sylvaner, Pinot Noir and dessert wines. The whole range is available for tasting at the shop, where the opened bottles are kept fresh under inert gas.

Tours of the cellars are limited to professionals and members of wine clubs, and even then only by appointment. But that doesn't matter. The staff in the shop are great, and the chance to taste in a medieval building smack in the centre of the utterly gorgeous village of Riquewihr, with vineyards encircling the town walls, is a real treat.

DOMAINE PAUL BLANCK, KIENTZHEIM

Based in Kientzheim, the Blanck family know their land. They've been here a long time and have a disproportionately high percentage of vineyards in excellent sites: 70 per cent of their vines are either in cru, grand cru or 'lieu-dit' (small, specific plot) areas.

Their cellar is open all year round, bar Sundays and holidays. The best bet is to move beyond the varietal wines to compare and contrast those from the myriad different crus and grands crus. As well as a straight wine tasting, they offer a food and wine matching, prepared by the winemaker, and the opportunity to try the Blanck wines with a picnic of your own.

Best of all, though, is the chance to have a tutored tasting in the vineyards surrounding the winery with Frédéric Isselen who is in charge of growing the grapes. On the prestigious slopes of the Kaysersberg, you'll get an expert explanation of which varieties perform best where, and how slope, aspect and soil impact on the flavour and structure of the wine.

The chance to taste these differences first hand in the vineyards where they were grown, in the presence of the man in charge of their cultivation, is a five-star opportunity to get to grips with the concept of terroir. A stimulating visit in some of the most beautiful scenery in Alsace.

THE RHÔNE

Over 800km long, the Rhône is one of Europe's great rivers. To follow its determined trudge to the Mediterranean is to observe the final shift from urban (and urbane) France, with its bustle, elegance and fine-dining, to the drowsy heat and light of Van Gogh's Provence.

This split is very much reflected in the region's wines, too. The bottles from the northern Rhône and the southern Rhône might share the river's name on their label and use some of the same grape varieties, but there are big differences – ones that, in a way, mirror their environments.

The northern Rhône is the third great red region of France, after Bordeaux and Burgundy. Until recently, even its best wines were eminently affordable, and although prices have risen sharply over the last decade, they remain good value for what are bottles of undoubted pedigree.

There are pockets of white grapes in Hermitage and, especially, Condrieu – which is home to the best expressions of Viognier on the planet. But, for the most part, Syrah is king here, grown on slopes that climb up from the mighty waterway below at gradients that vary from gentle to practically vertical.

The best sites all have one thing in common: granite soils, and it's these that give the wines their particular character – an inner minerality and tension that peeks out from under the Syrah fruit to add elements that can shapeshift from metallic through peppery to meaty. If you're planning to spend a few days in the region, exploring these differences is compelling.

Head out into the vineyards of Côte-Rôtie, St-Joseph and Hermitage – the latter's wines were once deemed on a par with the best from Bordeaux and Burgundy – and you'll also notice something else. Here the vines are not strung up on wires like in so much of France and the rest of the world, but instead are tied to huge stakes driven into the earth. This is a defence against the mistral, the northerly wind that howls down the valley for 120 days of the year with such ferocity that it's reckoned to drive men and horses mad. More prosaically, it also reduces wire-trained Syrah vines to tatters.

But the mistral does have its plus points. It blasts the vineyards free of diseases and damp, and is thus one reason why so many of the wineries here are increasingly interested in trying organic grape growing – because, simply, they can.

The white wine appellation of St-Péray marks the end of the northern Rhône, and then there's a 50km or so gap round the nougat town of Montélimar before the vines start up again. The heart of the southern Rhône is the town of Orange. Famous for its Roman architecture, it's a good base from which to explore the vineyards and the gorgeousness of Avignon. Though if you're visiting during the world-famous Chorégies opera festival, you'll need to book way in advance.

The villages of Gigondas, Vacqueyras and Rasteau are perfect places to go if you like gutsy, powerful reds. These Rhône blends – mostly Syrah, Grenache, Mourvèdre, Carignan and Cinsaut, though plenty of other grapes get the odd look-in – are both crowd-pleasing and good value, though not necessarily subtle.

But if it's unique terroir you're after, it's hard to beat Châteauneuf-du-Pape. Once the country bolt-hole of the Avignon popes, it's better known among wine lovers for the hefty 'galet' pebbles that litter its vineyards. Left behind when the Alpine glaciers melted, long before the Rhône Valley even existed, they absorb heat and radiate it back up on to the grapes. The result is boisterous wines with a heady, exotic, savoury/spicy character, often accompanied by head-spinning alcohol.

Cyclists looking for a healthier way of making the blood course through their veins might want to take on the might of Mont Ventoux. Situated 40km east of Orange and rising up 1,900m, 'The Beast of Provence' is a famous – and occasionally fatal – part of the Tour de France, and not for the faint-hearted. Those who like to take things a bit more leisurely, however, will no doubt prefer to be pointed in the direction of the growing number of excellent wineries on its slopes.

NORTH

GUIGAL, CÔTE-RÔTIE

Guigal is based in Ampuis, the village at the heart of arguably the Rhône's finest appellation, Côte-Rôtie. Though the estate was only established after the Second World War, the family have created a truly impressive reputation for themselves since then. While they also make wine from some of the big-name appellations of the southern Rhône, it's their Côte-Rôties that you should try (and buy) if you visit.

They do tours on weekdays (with the usual two-hour break for lunch from midday). These can be in English and are free – though they stipulate a minimum group of five people and a maximum of 20. The visit, which goes from the reception area for the grapes through to the barrel cellar and even the bottling line, takes about an hour and they say to allow a further hour for the tasting room.

Unsurprisingly, given their lack of cost and long duration – not to mention the prestige of the winery – the tours are enormously popular and priority is given to professionals and semi-professionals should demand exceed supply. For that reason, it's best to call ahead to see what's available, and probably wise to avoid peak 'entertaining the trade' times, such as vintage.

CHAPOUTIER, HERMITAGE

Chapoutier can lay a decent claim to being one of the most forward-thinking wineries in France. It got into organic and biodynamic grape growing early and has remained solidly committed to the practice; it has bought a string of wine estates across Australia (not exactly a common move for a French winery) and – a nice touch – it prints all of its labels in braille. The family's motto is *Fac et Spera* – do and hope – which sums up their combination of dynamism and humility rather well.

The Chapoutiers have been growing grapes here for just over 200 years, with the magnificently named Polydor Chapoutier the first to switch to making wine. The current scion is Michel Chapoutier, who might not share his moniker with a record label, but is obsessed with the differences of various vineyards and vintages. If you're looking for homogeneity or consistency, go elsewhere: this is a winery that's all about changes from one year and one site to the next. The family make wine from vineyards across the region, from Côte-Rôtie in the north to Luberon in the south, and to suit all pockets – from heady, expensive single-vineyard wines to well-priced intra-regional Côtes du Rhônes.

All visits begin with a tour of the vineyards, conducted by a sommelier, to help guests understand the terroir. Then you have a terrific variety of tasting lineups to decide between, including the Tour de France (a trip down the eastern side of the country from Beaujolais through the Rhône to Provence); a focus on different expressions of Rhône Syrah, and a kind of terroir special – not to mention the Fac et Spera option, which looks at wines from special vineyard sites.

If you're splashing out, though, the aptly named two-day Pack Prestige includes pick-up from the airport/station, visits to famous vineyards, dinner in a great restaurant, a top wine selection, accommodation in the winery's bijou Tour du Pavillon gîte and a tame sommelier at your beck and call.

If that seems a bit much, the wine school offers a series of superb *ateliers*, ranging from weekly wine discoveries and monthly workshops to fancier themed tastings of fine wines at competitive prices for committed enthusiasts.

Chapoutier's range of five gîtes across the northern appellations are also a wonderful opportunity. The aforementioned Tour du Pavillon, situated in an old watchtower in the heart of the Ermitage vineyard in St-Joseph, might not suit those who measure contentment in square metres of floor space, but it has character to burn.

BERNARD ANGE, CROZES-HERMITAGE

If Bilbo Baggins decided to hang up his precious and start a winery, this is probably what it would look like. Bernard Ange set up his cellar in 1998 with his wife Josiane, taking over an old hotel on the banks of the river between Tain l'Hermitage and Romans-sur-Isère. From the outside all looks normal. But head to the cellar and you're straight into *Lord of the Rings* territory: an arch with a doorway in it leads directly into the rocks behind.

The ancient stone quarry (Bernard Ange calls it his 'troglodyte cellar') makes for an interesting visit as well as a great, constantly cold place for the Anges' Crozes-Hermitage wines to age. And if you're a fan of northern Rhône Syrah, bottles from Crozes-Hermitage are significantly cheaper than those from the area's other appellations.

JEAN-LUC COLOMBO, CORNAS

Cornas is the last big-name red wine cru of the northern Rhône before the 50km break in the vineyards around Montélimar. So if you want one final infusion of 100 per cent pure Syrah, it's a good place to stop for your fix.

Jean-Luc Colombo is a local leading light – a sparky self-publicist with unshakeable self-belief who's injecting life and energy into the area. Every November his winery puts on a food and wine festival – 'Les Automnales' – with local produce, tastings and input from top names in food. Mostly it's for visiting chefs and sommeliers, but you can join in on the Friday night – tickets are amazing value.

Visit the wine shop adjoining his newly refurbished winery and the team there will lay on a tasting for you, though it's sometimes necessary to book in advance. If you want somewhere to stay, Jean-Luc's daughter, Laure, has two *chambres d'hôtes* just down the road in St-Péray. Surrounded by forests and wild meadows, they're a beautiful place from which to savour the region.

SOUTH

CHÂTEAU LA NERTHE, CHÂTEAUNEUF-DU-PAPE

Château la Nerthe has a bit of a back story. It was first officially mentioned in 1560, making it one of the oldest estates in a region not short on history. The existing château is a relatively modern structure, merely dating back as far as the 1700s.

Apart from the fact that it looks fantastic, one of the beauties of Château la Nerthe is that it is an estate: the winery's vineyards are all around the residence, rather than scattered across the region. They're also planted with all 13 grape varieties permitted in the appellation's wines, which is not that common either.

Visitors get a chance to see the beautiful old cellars and carry out a tasting of six wines. Pay a bit more and you get a tasting in a private room with an extra two wines, a selection of food, and a glass engraved with the château's coat of arms.

VIEUX TÉLÉGRAPHE, CHÂTEAUNEUF-DU-PAPE

The terroir of Châteauneuf-du-Pape is all about the 'galets' – big flat pudding stones that litter the landscape. And nowhere are they more of a feature than on the La Crau plateau, home to Vieux Télégraphe. Surprisingly, given that this is one of Châteauneuf's best producers, when Henri Brunier gifted his son Hippolyte the land in 1891 it was considered practically unusable, and it was only the fact that vines had been planted here centuries before that led the young man to put a few in.

They haven't done too badly. The average age of the vines used in the estate wine is an impressive 65 years – and even for the second wine it's 45 years. Nowadays, the family-run estate is 'organic raisonnée' and sustainable, which means it uses as little intervention as possible without going full-on organic. Sadly, there are no official tours, but the shop is always open for free tastings and sells all the current vintages.

CHÂTEAU GIGOGNAN, SORGUES

Not all estates in the Rhône have been in the same hands for generations. Château Gigognan was bought by a local back in 1996, and what was then a run-down property has been brought back to life. It's less than 10km from Avignon, making its on-site accommodation a great base for exploring the area. The rooms are beautiful, with a terrace and shared pool – and a cellar visit and tasting included.

If you're just passing through, the tasting room is open throughout the day and they arrange a tour every morning, which includes a look round the cellars and can also take in a trip into the vineyards if you let them know in advance. Make sure you do. The estate has been practising organic principles since 2003 and talking to the team about what organic means for plants, land and wine, while surrounded by the vines, is a chance not to be missed.

THE SOUTH OF FRANCE

It's odd that the typical tourist clichés for the South of France – beaches, yachts, Van Gogh cornfields baking in the heat – don't tend to include wine, because vineyards are absolutely everywhere.

The sun-drenched stretch within 100km or so of the Med is, in a sense, the heart of French wine. Bordeaux, Burgundy and Champagne might be the regions that make the headlines, but the wines of Provence, Languedoc and Roussillon are the ones that sit on millions of midweek dinner tables in France and across Europe, month after month, year after year.

The South is France's biggest wine-producing region by a stretch, and there remains a slight whiff of another era about it – and not just because it's still possible to fill up your *bidon* from a giant pump at the local co-op in places. In general the whole wine industry here is free of bling – people might be growing grapes, but few of them are getting rich doing it; it's just what they do.

Sadly, there are too many of them. Wine consumption in France has been falling for decades – specifically of the kind of 'lunchtime reds' that are the South's stock in trade – and this has led to general overproduction.

The government has now removed some of the subsidies it paid to growers who were producing too much (cue tractors on motorways, burning tyres on roads) and started offering money to those who pull up vineyards and grow something else. This has gone some way to lowering production. But it has also seen the removal of a lot of magnificent old vineyards with ancient vines.

On one level, this is logical. Old vines, after all, have low yields, so healthy, vigorous young plantings of Cabernet Sauvignon might make more commercial sense. On the other hand, it's impossible to escape the feeling that the South has been complicit in selling off its heritage.

That said, the area is so massive that, even after all the grubbing up of unproductive plots, there is no shortage of old vineyards still being managed. And the good news is that a growing number of committed practitioners are getting the most out of them.

Your typical southern wine will be a) red, b) gutsy and
c) a multi-varietal blend, probably permed from a combination
of Grenache, Syrah, Mourvèdre, Cinsaut, Carignan, Cabernet
Sauvignon and Merlot. Whites, generally, are less important
down here – though if you head to the South's western
edges, up on the hills south of Carcassonne, particularly in
Limoux, the influence of the Pyrenees and even the Atlantic
combine to create a place cool enough to make genuinely
good sparkling wine. In fact, there are records of this place
producing 'traditional method' fizz 100 years before
a certain Dom Pérignon – the father of champagne – was
even born.

If you love rosé, there's only one place to go: Provence.
The pale pink style, mostly made with Grenache, Mourvèdre,
Cinsaut and Carignan, has become immensely popular all
round the world now, spawning countless imitators, from
Rioja to Australia. Some producers are even oak-ageing it
for added weight.

Fans of sticky or fortified wines, meanwhile, should head
to Roussillon. Around Perpignan, which enjoys over 300 days
of sun a year, there is no shortage of super-ripe grapes, and
they're used to make Vins Doux Naturels (aka VDNs – rich
sweet wines).

For the wine tourist, therefore, this huge area has every
style and quality of wine you might want – from dry white
fizz to rosés and powerhouse reds, from cheap and cheerful
to genuinely top-class.

It would require an impressive effort to cover the whole
region on one visit, though Provence and the eastern
Languedoc can be easily added in after a trundle down the
Rhône. Similarly, the craggy loveliness of Limoux, St-Chinian
and Minervois on the western edges might be worked into
a trip taking in the fortified majesty of Carcassonne or a
westside wine exploration of Bordeaux and the Loire.

Whichever way you fit it in, your wine knowledge –
and cellar – will most surely benefit.

EAST OF MONTPELLIER

DOMAINE DE TRÉVALLON, BAUX DE PROVENCE

If you're heading towards the Med from the southern Rhône, this is one of the first estates you'll come to. Domaine de Trévallon is in the most westerly of Provence's wine appellations, 20km or so south of Avignon.

It's a small estate in a lovely spot – the kind of place that on cold winter evenings all wine lovers dream of owning: vines gently folded into the countryside, the surrounding forests and southern French 'garrigue' scrub perfuming the night air.

The estate was bought by the artist René Dürrbach in the 1950s and is now worked by his son, Eloi, whose highly regarded estate wine is a Cabernet Sauvignon/Syrah blend. Though it's officially in the Baux-de-Provence appellation, Eloi prefers to keep his wine a humble Vin de Pays. This despite the fact that it's recognised as one of the best wines in the whole of the south, the limestone soils giving it a real elegance.

Visits are by appointment and during the week only, but do make the effort. Not only are the wines excellent, but there's also art everywhere, from sculptures in the grounds to myriad pieces that René drew for the labels before he died in 1999. One word of warning: if you want to visit the cellar, don't wear perfume… they won't let you in.

CHÂTEAU D'ESCLANS, PROVENCE

Probably the best-known of all the top Provence rosés, Château d'Esclans' Whispering Angel has become something of a cult classic among the cognoscenti. The estate certainly has plenty of history. As Sacha Lichine, who bought it back in the 1990s, puts in: 'We don't own this château – it owns us. We're just operating it during its lifetime.'

The first ever château was built here in the 12th century, though only the cellars of that remain. The vineyards, meanwhile, are renowned for their plots of old Grenache vines. The oldest are 90 years old, and give small yields of highly concentrated fruit – one of the reasons D'Esclans' wines are so good. Another is the influence of winemaker Patrick Léon, who spent 20 years with Baron Philippe de Rothschild, overseeing among other things, the Bordeaux First Growth Mouton Rothschild and Californian super-wine Opus One.

D'Esclans is one of the first to make a go of creating a genuinely good top-end rosé that's been fermented in oak. But Léon is careful to ensure that the woody influence is in no way dominant, adding texture rather than flavour behind the fruit.

Situated less than ten minutes off the A8 motorway, the winery's shop is open all week in peak season and just weekdays the rest of the time. Tours are possible, though must be booked in advance. Even if you just go to taste, this is a fabulous chance to see just how good Provence rosé can be.

CHÂTEAU DE BERNE, PROVENCE

If you're looking for a bit of Provençal luxury, Château de Berne is for you. More or less halfway between Nice and Aix-en-Provence, the five-star hotel/wine estate/spa is a sumptuous – and handy – stop-off point mid-region, provided your wallet can take the strain.

The wine estate, in the hills to the north of the Côtes de Provence appellation, is an almost picture-perfect example of a southern-French château: vines, orchards, beehives, slopes and a few brooding crags in the distance. It's a place absolutely designed for summer evenings and a cool glass of Provence rosé.

As you might expect for such a slick operation, it offers an impressive range of wine tours, from simple 'visit the cellar and taste a few bottles' versions to ones involving cooking, spa days, classes and vertical/blind-tasting workshops. The shop is open all year round bar Christmas and New Year, and offers a tempting array of local foodstuffs alongside the wine.

This is not a cheap visit, but it's a good one that places a high premium on offering 'experiences' rather than just tastings. It's also just 40 minutes from uber-rosé producer Château d'Esclans (p53), which offers great wines but less creativity, so you could combine the two for a five-star day.

CHÂTEAU DE BELLET, NICE

Nice is best known for its people-watching, sunny climate and pavement cafés – plus, of course, *that* salad. But it also used to have an enviable reputation for wine – Thomas Jefferson was a fan, apparently. And if you're in the city, Château de Bellet, situated on the high limestone hills at the northern edge of town, is a definite must-visit.

Named after the Barons of Bellet, the Bellet appellation is one of the oldest in France, having started in 1941. And the château that mirrors its name also has one eye on the past – at least when it comes to grape varieties. The playfully aromatic white Vermentino might be widely planted across the south, but red grapes Braquet and Fuella Nera are far rarer these days.

Just 20 minutes from Nice's bustling centre (and the same time from the airport), the château offers tours that start with a walk through the vineyards and continue to the striking semi-circular cellar. Built into the land to allow the transfer of juice from the winery by gravity rather than pump, it's proof that new can be just as impressive as old.

Finishing up with a tasting in the château's chapel – built in memory of a family member who died at a young age – it all makes for a wonderfully memorable exploration of a little-known appellation.

Note: summer and winter tours vary, and if you want to visit at the height of the tourist season, book ahead.

WEST OF MONTPELLIER

CHÂTEAU DE FLAUGERGUES, MONTPELLIER

There are plenty of wineries in France carrying the name 'château' that distinctly lack the kind of glamour you'd expect from the title. Château de Flaugergues is emphatically not one of them. Even better, in the summer months, owners Brigitte and Henri de Colbert (who still live on the property) let you come and poke around the 300-year-old tapestries, art, furniture, and aristocratically manicured gardens of their grand 17th-century house. And if you like a grandiose staircase, this is definitely the visit for you: the *escalier* at Flaugergues takes up a quarter of the building.

You can enjoy a guided tour of the vineyard and cellar, which offers a peek into a part of the world that was knocking out decent volumes of wine in Roman times and is also famous for its 'grès' stones – big rounded river pebbles that might remind you of Châteauneuf-du-Pape.

Despite the history dripping from every pore of their property, Brigitte and Henri are also not averse to a bit of forward thinking – all the estate's wines are bottled under screw-cap to avoid issues of cork taint. The whole range is on offer at the château's restaurant, which serves fresh and seasonal dishes – though isn't open at weekends.

This is a visit for people who want to do a bit of everything (not just view vineyards) – a good half-day out if you're based in nearby Montpellier.

PRIEURÉ SAINT JEAN DE BÉBIAN, PÉZENAS

If you need proof of just how good the wines of the South can be when they're made with care and ambition, put this estate on your itinerary.

This one-time abbey, just north of the charming town of Pézenas, has been growing grapes for centuries thanks to its Roman and religious past. But it's only in the last 40 years, since a succession of owners with real ambition have come on board, that it's made an impression.

Its stony vineyards have been planted with all 13 grape varieties that you'd find in that other rock-fest, Châteauneuf-du-Pape, and the red wine that comes out of them is similarly muscular, ambitious and age-worthy. This is one of the South's top estates.

Many of its wines are available for tasting in the shop's oenomatic machine, which ensures they're always in perfect condition. Be warned, though: once you've tried a few, you're sure to want to take home a few cases.

LES DOMAINES PAUL MAS, PÉZENAS

The Mas family bought their first vineyard – a manageable nine hectares – near Pézenas in the 1890s. Various generations added a few hectares here and there, before a sizable expansion in the 1950s and then again under the stewardship of its current dynamic owner, Jean-Claude Mas. Now, the company has 12 wine estates of its own, covering a whopping 650 hectares of vineyard across the Languedoc-Roussillon region and has dozens of growers who supply it with fruit.

If it sounds like a big operation, it is: during harvest, around 40 different grape varieties come into the winery and are used in everything from high-end wines for restaurants to quirky supermarket labels such as Arrogant Frog. Molière, who lived in Pézenas for a bit, would doubtless have appreciated the irony of that name.

Mas is often credited with leading the birth of the 'new Languedoc', dragging the region out of making cheap but not always cheerful wine and into something more modern and outward looking. His USP is the concept of 'Le Luxe Rural' – celebrating simple, but high-quality food and drink – and it's the driving principle behind everything at his Côté Mas estate.

A sybarite's play park, it has a good restaurant, a wine bar, a bistro and suites to stay in. The wine shop stocks over 50 wines and offers five- or eight-bottle tutored tastings with a sommelier, as well as themed evening tastings, while the chef and head sommelier of the Côté Mas restaurant put together regular themed wine and food pairing dinners.

If you want to savour the region, though, I'd suggest getting out into the vineyards – not least because it's very easy to do. These are classic southern French vineyards, sandwiched in between the higher, craggier hills to the north and the glinting oyster beds of the Bassin de Thau in the Mediterranean, and there are a variety of walks, horse rides and quad-bike trips to enjoy.

CHÂTEAU RIVES BLANQUES, LIMOUX

Limoux is one of the most beautiful of the southern French appellations. Running up into the foothills of the Pyrenees, the altitude and the growing influence of the Atlantic mean it's cooler here, despite the Mediterranean sun. As a result, Limoux is well known for its elegant whites (Chardonnay in particular) and high-quality sparkling wines. Indeed, there are written records of bottle-fermented fizz being made here in 1531, well before they properly got going in Champagne.

At an altitude of 350m, Rives Blanques is cool even by the standards of the appellation, and there's a fine-boned elegance to its wines that wins over critics. Beyond the beauty of the location and a simple tasting room with stunning views out to the mountains, there's no tourist bling on offer here. Just a weekly, free and incredibly informative 45-minute tour of the vineyards and cellars with a tutored tasting attached. But make sure you book in advance, and wear 'vineyard tramping' footwear.

DOMAINE GAYDA, BRUGAIROLLES

Ever felt your wine knowledge isn't quite where it should be? That with just a little bit of training you'd be off and running? Well, perhaps a visit to Gayda is what you need. Admittedly, since it's in the Malèpere appellation, it's not exactly local to anyone bar, perhaps, residents of Carcassonne. But this small estate has a splendid range of courses on offer, run by a thoroughly engaging Master of Wine, Matthew Stubbs, and covering everything from wine weekends and official Wine & Spirit Education Trust qualifications to two-hour introductions to the subject. And if you're there over the weekend, there are gîtes to stay at on site, with tennis court, pool and (essential for the South of France) a *pétanque* pit.

CHÂTEAU L'HOSPITALET, NARBONNE

Former rugby international Gérard Bertrand acquired his first vineyards upon the untimely death of his father in 1987. By his own admission it took him a while to find his feet, but having consistently bought new properties since, he now has a truly exciting range of 11 small wine estates under his belt.

From the high slopes of the Domaine de l'Aigle in Limoux to the 100-year-old bush vines of Domaine de Villemajou in Corbières, they make up a fascinating collection of diverse characters. One thing unites them, however: biodynamics. Eight of the estates have already converted to this zero-chemicals way of growing grapes that relies heavily on lunar cycles and natural treatments, and they're working towards the whole lot being certified.

Sadly, only one estate is open to tourists, but it has a fabulous array of wine-centred activities. Château l'Hospitalet, just to the south-east of Narbonne, within spitting distance of the Mediterranean, is the centre of Gérard Bertrand's 'L'Art de Vivre' philosophy and celebrates food, wine, art and music.

Not for nothing has it been named a European Winery of the Year by *Wine Enthusiast* magazine. As well as a restaurant and a 38-room hotel, there's jazz every Friday (including a jazz and wine matching!) and a truly impressive annual jazz festival at the end of July that pulls in some big names.

There are the usual cellar-plus-tasting visits, but in summer it also has free guided tours every day that are impressively comprehensive, taking in the vineyards, winery, cellar, tasting and explaining its biodynamics philosophy. If you ever wanted to find out why burying cow horns full of manure helps grapes, here's your chance.

ITALY

Welcome to the biggest wine-producing country in the world. With vines running almost unbroken from the Alps to the southernmost shores of Sicily, it's no wonder Italy is home to such an immense array of wine styles and grape varieties (350 are authorised by the Ministry of Agriculture but perhaps as many as 1,000 are grown here). You'll need more than a few visits to reach expert standard but, along with the likes of Barolo, Chianti and Soave, the country has plenty of hidden gems waiting to be uncovered.

NORTH-EAST

For the wine-curious tourist there's probably no more stimulating area to visit than Italy's north-eastern corner. From the broad-shouldered heft of Amarone through the ethereal purity of an Alto Adige Riesling to the simple bonhomie of prosecco, the sheer variety on offer is extraordinary. The biggest issue is knowing where to start.

So, let's begin with a few of the big names from the region. Verona – a lovely place to visit in itself – makes a good base, since it has two of the best-known names in Italian wine right on its doorstep. Soave, to the east, produces an awful lot of wine, much of it of no great distinction. Crisp and palate-cleansing, yes; interesting, not so much. It's a shame, because for those who put the effort in with the Garganega grape, the rewards are there. It can give wines that are refreshing but with charming citrus flavours and a tantalising hint of bitterness on the finish. They're whites of texture and mouthfeel, tailor-made for food. Pick your visits with care.

Valpolicella is the other big beast of this area. From the hills running broadly north of Verona towards Lake Garda, it produces an extraordinary range of styles. Basic Valpol is (or should be) fairly light and fragrant, a burst of slightly sour cherry fruit with a brisk whip of acidity. It's the perfect midweek wine, and until recently represented great value for money. The original heartland of Valpolicella, nearest to Lake Garda, is now called Valpolicella Classico and the wines from here tend to be a bit more ambitious – with more concentrated fruit flavours, and a bit of time ageing in oak.

But if it's sheer size you're after, you need to look at Amarone. Made from super-ripe grapes, some of which are dried out in special lofts to concentrate their flavour even further before fermentation, these reds are among the most powerful in the world and demand both rich food and a strong constitution on the part of the drinker.

Just the other side of Lake Garda, near the town of Brescia, is Franciacorta, Italy's best sparkling wine-producing region. While you'll see it on the odd wine list, it rarely makes it on to retailers' shelves abroad, so a visit is the best chance you'll have of trying a lot of it. It's worth doing so, particularly if you're a fan of blanc de blancs fizz: over 80 per cent of the vineyards are planted to Chardonnay.

Franciacorta is a genuinely world-class wine style, and one that's usually compared to champagne. But if you're in the north-east, you should also head to the heartland of the drink that launched a thousand nights out: prosecco. Vast swathes of the Veneto are planted with the Glera grape – a verdant carpet of party juice waiting to happen. But the place to go for the good stuff is up round Valdobbiadene. A beautiful area in the foothills of the Dolomites, its slopes produce proseccos that are significantly more elegant and interesting.

Those are two words that also neatly describe the northern valleys running up into the Alps. Trentino and, particularly, the Alto Adige are two of the most beautiful parts of the entire wine world, with towering limestone peaks, medieval castles and vineyards clinging to the steep slopes and valleys. They're lovely areas that also make lovely wines: the cool mountain air adds an effortless lift and freshness to the whites in particular.

With so much to look at, it's best to consider basing yourself in four separate places if you want to get the most out of this north-eastern corner: round Lake Garda for Franciacorta, Valpolicella and Soave; in the Venice area for prosecco; Gorizia at Italy's eastern border with Slovenia for the increasingly impressive vineyards of Friuli (home to the kind of Pinot Grigio you'd actually want to drink); and then three or four days trundling up through the mountains towards the Austrian border.

VERONA

PIEROPAN, SOAVE

If you want to see just what Soave should be all about, you have to visit Pieropan, which has been setting the benchmark for the region for at least the last 30 years. The winery was set up in 1880, in the Palazzo Pullici in the heart of the medieval village of Soave, and (like most of the best ones) is still family owned and run, now on its fourth generation.

They have vineyards across the Soave Classico area, mostly south-facing (to ensure good sun exposure), but on differing soils and at varying altitudes. The family farm organically but don't bother putting it on their labels since, as they put it, it's an ethical choice, not a marketing tool.

If you get the chance, try to compare a couple of their single-vineyard Soaves. There's a world of difference between the typically Soave-like perfume of La Rocca (limestone soil) and the savoury, saline punch of Soave from the volcanic soils of the Calvarino vineyard. The latter translates as 'little calvary' because the soil is so hard to work, and the path to get to the vineyard so narrow, steep and tortuous to navigate.

There are four visits each weekday, but weekends are out. The reasonable price includes a look at the winery plus a tasting of the main wines, but they need to be booked at least two weeks in advance and numbers are limited. Booking windows open three months prior to the prospective visit date, so get in touch nice and early.

ALLEGRINI, VALPOLICELLA

The village of Fumane lies pretty much smack in the heart of Valpolicella Classico, just over 10km from the eastern edge of Lake Garda. It's home to one of the region's best producers, Allegrini, which has created a fantastic experience for the myriad tourists who flock to the area each summer.

The Villa della Torre, in the foothills surrounding Fumane, is a magnificent Italian renaissance villa, scattered with quirky design gems. It's possible just to visit the villa, but with so much quality wine on offer, that would be perverse – go for a tour and tasting at the very least.

If you're visiting between September and mid-January, you'll also have the chance to see the Terre di Fumane, the drying area, where the grapes are laid out in racks to shrivel and concentrate – the key process behind making Amarone.

But the best visit without a doubt is the vineyard tour. It's pricey and numbers are limited, but provided you have transport, you will get to see five of Allegrini's most important vineyards – a great two-hour crash course in the topography of the Valpolicella denominazione from one of its best producers.

Oh, and if you're looking for a base in Verona, it even has a B&B – also called Villa della Torre – in the centre of the city.

BELLAVISTA, FRANCIACORTA

When Vittorio Moretti took over Bellavista in 1977, it was a small family wine business with a few hectares of vineyard. In the 40 years since, it has been transformed into a sparkling (ahem) example of what Franciacorta can be.

Bellavista means 'beautiful view' and it's aptly named. Looking out towards the foothills of the Alps, you get a feel for the combination of warm sun and cool air that allows Franciacorta to make great fizz.

Over the years, Bellavista has steadily acquired more vineyards, and now has over 100 on a variety of terroirs, from flat to steeply terraced. Unusually for a sparkling wine producer, some of its base wines are fermented in oak for added richness – a practice that isn't even that common in Champagne. Interestingly, non-vintage Franciacorta needs to spend more time ageing in the bottle before release than non-vintage champagne.

The winery has an impressive range of visits available, though given that it's within striking distance of Lake Garda, it's perhaps unsurprising that none are free. On the plus side, the tours include an element of interactive tasting to help you understand the different flavours in a glass.

The cheapest involves a cellar visit and a standard two-wine tasting. A bit more also gets you a look round the vineyards, though the tasting features three still wines. If you want sparklers and vineyards, you'll have to splash out on the full Bellavista Experience, which includes vines, cellar, a food pairing seminar and three fizzes to taste with posh nibbles.

VENETO & FRIULI

CARPENÈ MALVOLTI, CONEGLIANO

If you're a fan of prosecco, this visit needs to be on your bucket list, since it's where it all began. Inspired by spending five years in Champagne, Antonio Carpenè was the first person to make sparkling wine from the Glera grape in this region back in 1868 and the family are still at it four generations later.

They're in Conegliano, which forms the eastern border of the best prosecco-growing vineyards (Valdobbiadene, about 20km away, forms the western boundary). The slopes, varying aspects and multiple soil types give wines of far greater ambition and complexity than those from the flatter lands to the south.

Don't believe me? Well, these guys are real specialists, so a visit allows you to taste a huge variety of different expressions. They have a range from the best DOCG vineyards around Conegliano and Valdobbiadene that runs from dry through to well off-dry. It also includes a wine from the fabulous (and tiny) Cartizze cru on top of the hill in Valdobbiadene, which shows you just how good prosecco can be when it's grown in the right place and vinified by people who care.

But they also have simpler, more cheerful wines, grown in cheaper areas and made differently, so you'll be able to decide whether you get what you pay for when you move upmarket. The winery tours explain all the variations in terroir and production methods, so by the end you'll be a real expert.

JERMANN, FRIULI

If the name Jermann doesn't look very Italian to you, that's because it isn't – though that's not uncommon in this part of the country. In the 19th century, Anton Jermann left Burgenland in Austria and, after a spell in Slovenia, finally settled between Udine and Gorizia on the Italian side of the border. And things have worked out well: the family now own almost 200 hectares of vineyard – a lot for this part of the country, where there aren't many big players.

The majority of what they produce is white wine – particularly the light, aromatic styles so typical of this part of the world. There's a solid range of single varietals, but the most interesting is the Vintage Tunina – a high-class (and unusual) field blend from a vineyard planted with Sauvignon Blanc, Chardonnay, Ribolla Gialla, Malvasia and Picolit. There aren't many Italian whites that improve with time, but this one does.

While the family do occasionally open the doors of their old winery at Villanova di Farra, visits usually take place at their modern installations in Dolegna del Collio. Before heading to either, you first need to contact them, so find out which is open then. Lasting 90 minutes, tours take in the vineyards, cellar and a tasting of three to six wines, though you can tailor the bottles in advance if you want.

PICÉCH, FRIULI

The far north-eastern corner of Italy is different. As the surnames start to become more Slavic, so the grape varieties change, too: Ribolla Gialla, Malvasia and Tocai Friulano bring a decidedly Balkan flavour to the country. It remains a largely unvisited region, and so is the place to come if you're looking for warm welcomes from the family, rather than shiny visitor centres.

The Picéch family have been growing grapes and making wine up on the slopes of Pradis, near Cormòns, for almost 100 years. They use no herbicides on their vineyards, yields are kept low to ensure concentration of fruit, and the wines, made by Roberto Picéch and his wife Alessia, are high quality.

As well as visits, which include a tour and a tasting plus matching with the excellent local ham and cheese (book in advance), they also rent several double rooms. They're mostly B&B, though there's also an apartment (sleeps two to four) if you want to do a little self-catering. The room up in the tower, with a 360-degree view out over the vineyard (and nearby Slovenia), looks the pick of the bunch. This is also possibly the only winery in the world with a hedgehog as its logo.

RUGGERI, VALDOBBIADENE

There's no shortage of prosecco-sceptics among wine traditionalists: people who've watched the northern Italian fizz's tsunami-like advance since the millennium with a baleful eye, and refuse to accept any good will come of it.

There is, to be sure, a good deal of highly average pop from this part of Italy, but you won't find any of it at the Ruggeri winery. Set up by the Bisol family (who already had a lucrative stake in the world of prosecco) in the 1950s, it makes only superiore wines and those from the very top of the prosecco quality tree, from the tiny sub-region of Cartizze.

These are elegant, structured wines in a variety of styles that show you just how good prosecco can be. The family do like to receive guests, but they're not massively set up for them – numbers are limited to about ten at a time so you'll need to contact them in advance and see if they can fit you in. Visits take in vineyard, winery and wines, helping you understand the best area of Prosecco, and prices vary depending on the wines you taste.

ALPS

FERRARI, TRENTINO

The wine world is full of mavericks who felt that current thinking didn't apply to them and went off to do their own thing. Such a man was Giulio Ferrari, who decided there was no reason why Champagne should have a monopoly on elegant cool-climate sparkling wine, and set about proving that Trento was perfectly capable of making something similar.

That was back in 1902, and led to Signor F planting large amounts of Chardonnay specifically for making high-quality fizz. And it worked – as, logically, it should have. After all, the vineyards round Trento are pretty cool, with the grapes retaining the natural acidity so critical to making good sparkling wine. Ferrari's blanc de blancs have established a fine reputation for themselves over the years – and the company was instrumental in getting a special appellation for the region's sparkling wines, Trentodoc, established in the 1990s.

Ferrari runs a range of tour-plus-tasting options, going up in price depending on what you elect to sample at the end. It also offers a tour plus lunch/dinner at its Locanda Margon restaurant, though oddly any wines you have with lunch aren't included in the cost.

If you're on a 'fizz tour' of north-east Italy, and have already ticked off Franciacorta and Prosecco, this place should be on your radar.

CANTINA TRAMIN, ALTO ADIGE

It's hard to be neutral about Gewürztraminer – it's one of those 'love it or hate it' varieties. The team at Tramin are unequivocal: they love it to bits. Of course, it helps that their particular part of the Alto Adige is well suited to growing it – indeed, this might have been the grape's birthplace. The clue's in the name: Gewürztraminer means, roughly, 'spicy grape from Tramin' (though it sounds better in German).

Here the plentiful sun on the south-eastern slopes allows Gewürz to develop its characteristically perfumed aromatics, but up in the Alps the temperature also drops rapidly at night, helping it retain an extra lift and freshness that often escapes it in the suntrap of Alsace.

The winery, with its floor-to-ceiling windows and outer shell of green struts looking like a verdant spider's web, gazes down on Lake Kaltern and the surrounding vineyards with the quiet complacency of a parent who knows their children have turned out all right. Even though it's a co-operative, with many growers contributing fruit from their smallholdings, it's regularly cited as one of Italy's best white wine producers.

With so many growers contributing fruit, it's perhaps not surprising that Tramin has a large range of wines in its portfolio, and this is a great opportunity to try varieties you might not know too well as well as ones you do – such as Chardonnay and Cabernet Sauvignon – grown in a slightly unusual climate. The tastings include three wines and are in Italian or German, though English can also be accommodated if you give some advanced warning.

FRANZ HAAS, ALTO ADIGE

The Haas family have been growing grapes in the Alto Adige for generations, but their wines' quality has taken a significant leap forward since the latest Franz Haas took over.

The winery is famous for two things: its love of Pinot Nero (Pinot Noir) and its truly funky labels, courtesy of artist Riccardo Schweizer – a contemporary of Picasso, Chagall and Cocteau.

Until recently, the family's vineyards went from 240m to 850m above sea level. But climate change has allowed them to buy land even higher, and their vines now span an almost unbelievable 900m of altitude, giving them an incredible range of styles and soils to play with.

Just across the valley from Cantina Tramin, this place makes an interesting counter-visit, providing a range of red wines to compare with the predominantly white offerings from the co-op on the western slopes.

ABBAZIA DI NOVACELLA, VALLE ISARCO

Bolzano (Bozen in German) lies at the spot where three rivers converge: the Adige from the north-west, the Talvera (Talfer) from the north and the Isarco (Eisack) from the north-east. This is Italy's northernmost wine-growing region and it looks about as Italian as, well, Austria, which owned this land until 1919.

The abbey, known as Kloster Neustift in German, lies upriver on the Isarco near Brixen, surrounded by terraced vineyards at altitudes of 600m to 900m. It gets pretty chilly at night here, and the abbey relies on autumnal sunshine to ripen the grapes. Even so, there isn't much in the way of red grapes (which mature later) round here – the winery's reds are grown in the lower, warmer vineyards round Bolzano.

The shop is an absolute gem. As well as a full range of wines, it sells other products from monasteries across Europe – a kind of ecclesiastical Walmart, full of excellent food and drink. The wine selection provides a good chance to compare a Grüner Veltliner grown on this side of the Alps with the Austrian version, and also to try the rarely seen Kerner white.

On top of that, there are also tutored tastings and tours/tastings at a good price, and you should make time to visit the 900-year-old abbey itself. You don't even need a car – nearby Brixen is a permanent stop on the main Munich/Innsbruck/Verona train line.

NORTH-WEST

There's a different feel to Italy's north-west corner. The terracotta roofs of southern France might lurk just on the other side of the Mont Blanc tunnel, but Piedmont is a place that's better captured by the faint tang of autumnal woodsmoke than the crack and fizzle of barbecued fish.

Maybe it's the snow-capped immensity of the Alps looming to the north, or the dense umami-laden scent of truffles – so much a part of this region – influencing my judgement. Or maybe it's just that the most famous wines of this area of Italy cast such a long stylistic shadow.

One Barolo producer describes his wines as having 'ethereal beauty, like a sweetly whispered poem', which is rather like how devotees of Burgundy talk of their beloved Pinot Noir. Certainly, there's a similar romantic wistfulness to the best Barolo and Barbaresco that calls to mind banks of golden leaves, damp earth and a sweet autumnal melancholy. The perfect reward for a bracing winter's walk, they demand plates groaning with truffles and game.

The wines are made from the Nebbiolo grape. Almost suicidally late-ripening, it gets its name from the fact that it's usually picked in the heart of autumn, a time of mists, mellow fruitfulness and fog (*nebbia*). Traditionally, Barolo got long fermentations of four weeks, which would give wines with a lot of tannin. All-but undrinkable in their youth, they would be aged for several years in oak barrels that imparted no overt flavour but allowed the tannins to soften.

However, the modern school of thought sees grapes picked slightly riper, fermented for less time and aged for a shorter period in smaller, newer barrels. Unsurprisingly, there's been no shortage of opinions on whether these fruitier and oakier modern-style Barolos are worthy of the name. If you want to hear a barrage of excitable Italian, ask any local winemaker their opinion on the issue. The debate was even documented in a film: *Barolo Boys: The Story of a Revolution*.

In both Barolo and Barbaresco the vineyards are draped across south-facing slopes. On these curved suntraps, away from the sludgy soils and spring frosts of the valley bottom, thick-skinned, late-ripening Nebbiolo gets the rays it needs to reach full ripeness.

Barbaresco, east of Alba, is the smaller of the two appellations. The hills are slightly lower, the grapes ripen a little sooner and the wines tend to be somewhat more approachable when young. Barolo, while larger, is still small: its famous '11 villages' are packed into a roughly 10km by 8km area, so it's easy enough to get round them in a few days.

If you're thinking that sounds like rather hard work for your gums, bear in mind that nearly all of the producers also have wines from other parts of Piedmont and, unless you pay extra (or pre-arrange something in advance), you won't get to taste half a dozen Barolos as part of your visit.

If you're keen to try more of these less challenging styles while in the region, there's no shortage of them on offer. The soft-fruited Barbera, in particular, is a good red option if you want a break from tannin, though Dolcetto runs it close. Both are grown in vineyards around Alba and Asti.

Gavi, to the east, is probably the region's most famous white wine, but if you'd like to stay round Alba (after all, it's one of the best food towns in Italy), Arneis from the Roero hills just north of the town is arguably a better bet. It doesn't quite have Gavi's soft charm, but is capable of hitting greater heights – and how can you pass up the opportunity to taste a grape whose name means 'little rascal'?

Finally, if you want the polar opposite of lofty, serious, challenging Barolo, you should consider a visit to one or two wineries in the Asti denominazione. These wines are fresh, fruity and cheerfully unsophisticated – glugging a glass of exuberant, perfumed Moscato is like watching a sitcom after three hours of *Hamlet*. You'd need a heart of stone not to drink it with a smile.

Alba and Asti are linked by a motorway, but elsewhere the hills of Piedmont can make for slow travelling. Many good vineyards are accessible from a base in Alba, including Barolo and Barbaresco, but if you want to explore further east, you'll want to relocate.

BAROLO/BARBARESCO

FONTANAFREDDA, BAROLO

If you think the Wood of Thoughts sounds like something out of Narnia, you'd be wrong. In fact it's an ancient woodland on the Fontanafredda estate, and the winery has created a guided wander through it, complete with thought-provoking quotes. Benches are considerately supplied for those who grow weary of pondering...

Eccentricities aside, this is a fantastic visit. There aren't many big wineries in Barolo, which also means there aren't many visits that can detain you for more than an hour. But this one has plenty going on. Not for nothing was it named 2017's European Winery of the Year by *Wine Enthusiast* magazine.

Vineyards surround the winery and you can visit them unaccompanied to see the hallowed Barolo slopes and soils close up. There are free wine tastings in the shop, but if you're happy to part with some cash, you can also get a tour round the 19th-century cellars, which includes a tasting of three wines, one of them a Barolo. Stuffed full of the typical large *botte* used in the region, they're well worth a look.

If you want to make a day of it, there are informal lunches in the winery's Disguido eatery, and Michelin-starred finery in the Guido restaurant. You can even stay at the hotel, which could make a good base – particularly if you decide to rent an electric bike and zip around some of the denominazione's famed 11 villages.

MARCHESI DI GRÉSY, BARBARESCO

If you want to try a wide range of Piedmont wines in one visit, the Marchesi di Grésy, which lies just south of the village of Barbaresco, is a good place to go. The winery is based in Martinenga, site of the first Roman settlement in the area, called Villa Martis. The Marquis acquired this lovely estate in 1797, though the family had vineyards in the region over 100 years before that.

Martinenga's natural amphitheatre of broadly south-facing vineyards is good for soaking up the sun that late-ripening Nebbiolo needs to mature. And to experience the nuances the grape is capable of in these limestone/clay soils, try the three Barbarescos that Marchesi di Grésy makes from just one 24-hectare site – its various elevations and exposures create a trio of distinct wines.

For a break from Nebbiolo, there's also a range of softer, more easy-drinking Dolcetto, Barbera and Merlot reds, plus some palate-refreshing whites. The winery is open six days a week most of the year, but you'll need to book.

BRUNO ROCCA, BARBARESCO

In the prenuptials Francesco Rocca had drawn up ahead of his marriage to Luigia Cheinasso back in 1864, he is described as 'a farmer born and living in Barbaresco'. This seems fitting. Several generations later, the Roccas still see themselves as growers rather than winemakers and view wine as a product created by the land rather than people.

This isn't a big operation, so there are no swanky tourist facilities. But any tasting (which should be pre-arranged) will probably involve a chat with one of the family, and can be adapted to include more, should their time and your budget permit. The winery, for instance, is always available for visits provided no actual winemaking is in progress.

The four-wine tasting involves a mix of one or two Langhe reds and whites plus one wine from the core of what they do: Barbaresco. These come in varying levels of rarity, volume and prestige, and while you're unlikely to get the very limited Riserva wines, it's worth trying to buy a couple of them to taste on your own later.

Comparing the wines from the family's two different Rabajà and Currà sites is fascinating. The latter is lighter, charming and more perfumed – a good example of a softer style of Barbaresco; the former, from one of the top sites in the region, is dark, intense and complex.

GD VAJRA, BAROLO

On the western edges of the Barolo denominazione, the Bricco delle Viole is a classic Barolo vineyard. A jutting south-east to south-west curved hillside, it absolutely makes the most of the day's sun from when it rises in the east with the first espresso to when it disappears to the west at grappa time.

Interestingly (and possibly uniquely), this is a winery that grew less out of generations of farmers than out of a teenager's misplaced rebellion. Back in 1968, Turin was aflame with student protests, and a somewhat naive 15-year-old, Aldo Vajra, joined them. His horrified father found out and packed the youth off to his grandparents' farm in Piedmont. The rest, as they say, is history.

Aldo enjoyed working in the winery and, essentially, never left, with his grandparents eventually asking him to take over the business. If you think that's a good story, the one behind the winery's famous (and quirky) stained-glass window is even better. It was commissioned from a Franciscan monk in a fetching blue hat after a series of misunderstandings that would make your average blockbuster novelist think twice about their plausibility. Get the full tale when you visit. The tour also gives you four wines to try of whatever the family think is showing well.

REST OF PIEDMONT

CANTINE ASCHERI GIACOMO, BRA

Barolo and Barbaresco, to the south-west and east of Alba respectively, might be the two heavyweight denominazione in Piedmont, but there's plenty worth exploring in other directions, too.

Due west lies Bra, where the Ascheri winery lives up to the town name by providing a truly uplifting visit. If you're only planning to visit one winery in the region, this should probably be it. Ascheri makes all the key styles of wine from Piedmont. Ideal if you want to compare a Nebbiolo from Barolo with one from the nearby Langhe hills, or see whether you prefer Gavi, Arneis or Moscato.

The company also owns an *osteria* specialising in traditional (ie hearty and simple) Piemontese cuisine, where all its wines are available by the glass. Since so much of the charm of wines from this part of Italy is their ability to match with food, this is a great opportunity to experiment.

BRAIDA, ASTI

If you've developed a taste for Barbera during your visit to the north-west, head to this winery in Rocchetta Tanaro. It was on these slopes that Giacomo Bologna first began to prove what the variety could do back in the 1960s. With attention in the vineyard and barrel-ageing in the cellar, he elevated it from wannabe into a grape to be taken seriously, never more so than in his Bricco dell'Uccellone wine.

From the best vineyards on the hilltops of Rocchetta Tanaro, its name means (roughly) 'the big bird's vineyard', after an old lady who always dressed in black and presumably looked like a large crow as a result. Either way, it remains one of Italy's must-taste wines, and was a game-changer for the variety.

Barbera can come in all manner of types – dark, pale, serious, playful – and Braida has a range of versions from different soils, altitudes and so on across Piedmont to sample, as well as one where it's blended with Cabernet Sauvignon, Pinot Noir and Merlot. There's even a lightly sparkling 'cheeky girl' – La Monella. Lucky, then, that the winery is big on tours and tastings, with various options led by a sommelier.

MICHELE CHIARLO, ASTI

Making wine is often described as an art, and there's certainly plenty of that on offer here. Midway between Alba and Acqui Terme, in Castelnuovo Calcea, it's an invigorating mixture of vines, wines, sculptures and conceptual pieces.

The art theme carries on to the winery's labels, which are designed by artist Giancarlo Ferraris. There's a good range to try, too. If you like Nebbiolo, there are versions from Barolo, Barbaresco and a Nebbiolo de Langhe, as well as (softer, cheaper) Dolcettos and Barberas. If you prefer white, all the main styles of this part of Italy are here: Gavi, Moscato and Roero Arneis.

Those after a typical tour (rather than an art experience) will need to visit the winery at Calamandrana.

CENTRAL

As Bordeaux is to France and the Napa Valley is to California, so Chianti is to Italy. It's a place that's come to stand for more than itself – shorthand, almost, for 'Italian wine'. Even the casual wine drinker has heard of Chianti – in spite of various attempts down the years by the region to shoot itself in the foot.

For instance, the region's vinous boundaries – in the spectacularly lovely hills between Florence and Siena – were first drawn up in 1716 by Cosimo III de' Medici. But as the wine grew in popularity so the borders also expanded, allowing producers from far-less-impressive vineyard areas to produce 'chianti' as well. The original vineyard area, home to the best estates, was renamed Chianti Classico in an attempt to preserve (or reinstate) its integrity. But despite the added presence of a black rooster on the label of Classicos, it's a distinction that passes too many wine drinkers by.

Chianti is all about Sangiovese. The most Italian of grapes, it can charm and infuriate in almost equal measure, capable of elegance, poise and perfume in good years or in the hands of a sensitive producer, and of being grumpy, mean-spirited and downright unpleasant in tough vintages or from a less caring *coltivatore*.

Sangiovese's Achilles' heel is its tendency for its light colour and herbal, savoury characters to cross the dividing line into pale, thin and gutless when unripe. Which is why it was so incomprehensible that until relatively recently wineries were allowed to add up to 30 per cent white grapes to their red wines, while 'interloper' varieties such as Cabernet Sauvignon and Merlot were banned. This despite the fact that, for most neutral observers, they brought an added dash of elegance and richness that supported rather than masked the local hero.

Some producers simply turned their backs on the denominazione rules and produced what they wanted, bottling their wines as Indicazione Geografica Tipica – IGT – the Italian equivalent of Vin de Pays. This marked the birth of the Super Tuscans, which often attract far higher prices than actual Chianti, and were a key driver in the rules belatedly being changed. Now, white grapes are out, and small amounts of 'international varieties' are allowed. The region is better for it.

Many of these Sangiovese/Cab/Merlot blends come from out in the flatter lands towards the coast – the Maremma – a region that's well worth a visit. Though if you're on a budget, areas such as Carmignano, just outside Florence, have been blending Sangiovese with Cabernet and other grapes for longer than Chianti has.

There's no shortage of wine regions to visit throughout central Italy – on both sides of the Apennines. In general the best wines are on the warmer western side, though don't overlook the taut, appley Verdicchios from the hills west of Ancona. Vino Nobile di Montepulciano (60km south-east of Siena) is an established aristocrat, making intense plum and cherry-flavoured wines from Sangiovese. Just 30km further west in Montalcino the same grape gives brooding, powerful wines that can (and sometimes need to) comfortably age for decades. These two powerhouse red regions would make for a good, if gum-stripping, mini-tour.

But without doubt the best place for visitors to the middle of 'the boot' is Chianti Classico. It's not an especially big region – barely 250km² – so you can legitimately expect to cover it from one end to the other – and it's easy to get to from Rome (250km to the south) or, particularly, Florence on its northern edge. What's more, the wineries are brilliantly set up for tourists, with myriad tours, tastings, matchings and even places to stay thrown in.

But perhaps the best thing about the heart of Chianti is that, while it's easy to get to via motorways, it still seems gloriously cut off once you're there. Narrow roads twist and turn down valleys and round hills, and spectacular views, bars and wineries seem to lurk past every corner, demanding an hour of your time and making a mockery of your day's schedule.

It's a popular destination with touring cyclists – although it has plenty of hills, there's nothing too extreme and there are lots of places to stop en route for photos and refreshment. Hopping on a bike will also help you burn off some of the calories of the region's justly famous *bistecca alla Fiorentina*.

CHIANTI

ANTINORI NEL CHIANTI CLASSICO

There's no shortage of impressive architecture in Chianti. Most of it is centuries old, but the Antinori winery, finished in 2012, is every bit as jaw-dropping as the plethora of medieval castles. From the elegantly curved ceilings of the barrel cellar to the tessellated walls, it seems to have been designed as a work of art as much as a functional building – a beautiful ochre-tinged combination of wood, steel, glass and terracotta, all soft sweeps and light. The curling spiral staircase is a standout.

If that makes this place sound like a showy flash in the pan, it isn't. The Antinoris have been growing grapes here since 1385, and the Marchese's three daughters are the 26th generation to work in the family business. This is a company that has kept its roots and its commitment to wine, but has never been afraid to move forward, either.

As well as ventures in the New World and around Europe, the family have wineries elsewhere in the country and you'll get to taste some of their Italian output as part of the basic tour, providing a kind of 'family's-eye view' of Italy. If it's chianti you're after, there's no shortage of good stuff in the winery's shop, including their famed game-changing Super Tuscan, Tignanello.

The winery itself is set into the hillside, which means that its roof is at ground-level and (a nice touch) planted with vines. The vineyard is still young, so not contributing much to the family's wine production in the grand scheme of things, but with a range of tours available (as well as custom-made options) and a rather good restaurant on site, this is a must-visit for anyone who wants to experience modern Chianti. And because it's only five minutes off the main Florence-Siena motorway (Bargino exit), it's easy to swing by if you're just passing through.

CASTELLO DI AMA

'The hills and valleys surrounding the castle of Ama are the most beautiful in all of Chianti.' So wrote Grand Duke Peter Leopold in his 18th-century report on Tuscany. Sadly, beauty wasn't enough, and the hamlet of Ama went unloved until it was bought by Lorenza Sebasti and her husband Marco Pallanti in the 1970s. They set about creating a great winery from its crumbling walls, and have succeeded to an extraordinary degree: in 2005 it was named winery of the year by Italian wine magazine *Gambero Rosso*.

Its wine is fascinating, moving up from Chianti Classico to Gran Selezione, and including single-vineyard expressions and chiantis made from new clones of Sangiovese. If you want to see how international grapes do here, try the likes of Haiku – Merlot and Cabernet Franc blended with Sangiovese – or L'Apparita, Tuscany's first 100 per cent Merlot. As tastings go, this is a good one.

As well as the wines, Castello di Ama has a traditional restaurant and hosts work by some of the world's leading artists – think Anish Kapoor and Roni Horn. You can stay in the plush 18th-century rooms and get a guided tour of the winery, oil press, art and a meal. It's a stimulating, fascinating visit and, situated towards the south of the Chianti Classico, is accessible from Siena, too.

CASTELLO DI BROLIO

It's fair to say that the Ricasoli family don't like to move around much. The Baron's ancestors first started making wine at this estate in 1141 and production has never moved anywhere else in the intervening 875-plus years. Mind you, if you go there to visit, you'll understand why.

With its aristocratic heritage, this, in the denominazione's south-eastern corner, is the biggest estate in Chianti Classico, and almost ridiculously beautiful, with rolling hills and oak forests. The enormous castle itself is ringed by deferential ranks of bowing cypress trees. Since it's still a family residence (albeit a large one), the castle isn't widely open to the public, though if you opt for the top Privilege Tour, you get a look round, as well as a tasting in the armour room.

As you'd expect from such a large estate (some 235 hectares of vineyard), there are major shifts in soil types, from sandstone to shale and river pebbles. Over the last 20 years, it has been busy replanting its vineyards to ensure that it gets the right varieties in the right places, which wasn't always the case.

The two-hour Cru Tour takes in all of this, focusing on the ground below your feet rather than the cellars. Explaining the difference between the estate's various terroirs, it comes complete with a tasting outside in the vineyards. The Vineyard Tour is a little longer and is more nature- rather than grape-driven.

Those less interested in land and more into history will likely prefer the Classic Tour, which takes in the gardens, the family chapel and museum, plus the winery and a tasting. You can also go for a posh picnic with food prepared by a chef, wine from the estate, and lovely views.

And if you'd like to stay in the heart of the countryside, Castello di Brolio has a lovely Tuscan farmhouse to rent complete with pool and similarly winsome vistas.

CASTELLO DI GABBIANO

In the 12th century, this was no more than a square, fortified tower designed to protect the main route between Florence and Siena. There was little love lost between these two principalities, so when the wealthy Bardi family from Florence took ownership, they set about building walls and battlements around the tower with gusto.

Fast forward 800 years and this winery, in the north-east corner of Chianti Classico, is an altogether more tranquil place. With 140 hectares of vines, it's one of the larger estates in the region. Sangiovese, naturally, is top dog, though there's a little Cabernet and Merlot to add seasoning. The vineyards range in height from 150m to 350m above sea level, which gives winemaker Federico Cerelli different fruit styles to play with.

The owners have put a lot of effort into making the estate tourist-friendly, and there's a good range of activities, tours and courses – plus top levels of Chianti, Cabernet and Merlot IGT blends and even a rosé to try. If you get the chance, make sure you taste the (sweet) Vinsanto. With a restaurant, self-catering apartments and a few rooms, it could be a handy option if you want to stay in the vineyards and remain half an hour from Florence.

CASTELLO VICCHIOMAGGIO

Thirty kilometres south of Florence is the bustling market town of Greve in Chianti. It found itself incorporated into the Chianti wine region in 1932 and appears to have barely been able to believe its good fortune. As the largest town in the DOCG, it's a real centre for food and wine lovers.

To the north of it, on top of a hill, is Castello Vicchiomaggio. Its 32 hectares of vineyards spreading out on the galestro (clay/lime) slopes are all south-facing, which helps the Sangiovese get fully ripe, even in tricky years.

The winery operates sommelier-run tastings all week, which for a very reasonable price gives you the chance to try the 'five classic' styles of the region: Chianti Classico, Riserva, Gran Selezione, Sangiovese/Cabernet Sauvignon blend and, er, extra virgin olive oil. I'd be tempted to upgrade to the marvellously named Count Agostino's Wine and Gastronomy Lunch option, though. You get a tour of those south-facing vineyards, the cellar and gardens, and (the best bit) four wines paired with a couple of classic dishes. It is the easiest introduction to Tuscan food and wine you'll ever get.

CASTELLO DI VOLPAIA

Just to the north of the medieval walled town of Radda in Chianti – worth a visit in itself – is the ancient *borgo* (hamlet) of Volpaia. An old fortified village right on the Siena/Florence border, it was once abandoned (as many of these remote settlements have been), but has now been renovated into a quirky, characterful tourist destination.

This, quite literally, is a wine village. As you approach, you pass the winery's vineyards on both left and right, with wine production facilities and cellars scattered around the hamlet's various dwellings and former churches. With

The legend of the black rooster

The black rooster logo on bottles of chianti is the symbol of the region – and how it came to be so is something every wine lover ought to know. Go back 800 years and the two city states of Florence and Siena hated each other as only powerful neighbours can. In the 13th century, they decided on a method to define where the frontier between their two territories would lie: knights would set off from each of the cities at cock-crow and where they met would be the border. It was fair in theory, but the Sienese reckoned without the untrustworthiness of their brethren to the north. While the former fed their white rooster well so it was happy and relaxed, the Florentines starved their *gallo nero*, disorientating him still further by leaving him locked in a box for several days. Unsurprisingly, the bird woke up in the middle of the night, crowed loudly and the Florentine knight got a head start of several hours on his Sienese rival.

Instead of meeting halfway, the two horsemen met less than 20km from Siena, ensuring that Florence had vast swathes of land under its control that it probably shouldn't have had. Florentines see this as an example of their street smarts; Sienese as proof of their rivals' deviousness. For wine lovers, the black rooster is nowadays just proof of genuine Chianti Classico.

barrels, bottles and production equipment jammed into whatever space is available, it's almost a complete takeover. This is guaranteed to be one of the quirkier winery visits you'll ever make, though you need to pre-book.

And for those who like food as much as wine, it's a particularly good stop, even by Tuscan standards. First, the shop (in the main tower of the old castle) sells estate honey, a range of vinegars and fabulous extra virgin olive oil, as well as wine. Second, the oldest part of the village houses a thoroughly modern kitchen that's home to cookery and food and wine matching classes.

VIGNAMAGGIO

Drive north/south or east/west in the Chianti Classico, and you're likely to be within striking distance of Vignamaggio. It's pretty much smack in the heart of the appellation, equidistant from Siena and Florence and about halfway between the two most famous Chianti stops, Greve and Radda.

The villa is thoroughly lovely in a very Italian kind of way: effortlessly beautiful and classy without making a song and dance about it. Once, supposedly, the home of the Mona Lisa (who knew a thing or two about being effortlessly and enigmatically beautiful), it has more recently served as a temporary residence for the likes of Graham Greene and Marc Chagall, as well as the setting for Kenneth Branagh's 1993 film version of *Much Ado About Nothing* with Keanu Reeves.

If you want to follow in the footsteps of Ken, Keanu et al, there are a range of tours and tastings available, ranging from free to reasonable, though the real value looks to be in combining a visit with food. The two-hour Tour and Sunset Dinner includes four wines and four courses made from seasonal, organic produce. But the view from the terrace at sunset justifies the outlay in itself.

Since it's not a good idea to drive after four glasses of wine, it's handy that Vignamaggio also offers a range of attractive apartments, suites and villas. If you stay on site, take a morning to explore one or two of the trekking trails that wend through the countryside and vineyards. It's a restfully beautiful part of the world, and you can imagine yourself following in the footsteps of La Gioconda herself.

Super Dario

A few kilometres to the south of Vignamaggio is the town of Panzano, which has become famous for one man: Dario Cecchini. At his butcher's shop/restaurant he estimates that he's cooked enough pork chops to circle the planet several times, though since he's an inveterate showman, it's hard to tell. Dario believes that an animal should have four things: a good life, a good death, a good butcher and a good cook. If you visit, go the whole hog and order the Officina della Bistecca restaurant's fixed menu – a five-course steak-fest perfect for the Gran Selezione you bought earlier that day. With no corkage fee, you can eat and drink like a king on a shoestring.

TUSCANY

CAPEZZANA, CARMIGNANO

Nowadays, the practice of blending the local Sangiovese grape with Cabernet Sauvignon is relatively common. And if you talk to producers of Super Tuscans, you could be forgiven for thinking they invented it. But in fact the growers in Carmignano, 20km west of Florence, were blending the two grapes together long before the likes of Tignanello arrived on the scene.

Capezzana does make a full-on Bordeaux blend that comes, fittingly enough, from a Graves-like pebbly ex-river bed, but its two staple wines are both Sangiovese/Cabernet blends with Bordeaux varieties. It has vintages of its Villa di Capezzana going back to 1925.

The tour and tasting will fill you in on the history of the estate and the region, and in spring and summer, there are also tours with lunches of varying complexity. A good stop if you're heading out of Florence but away from Chianti.

CASTELLO BANFI, MONTALCINO

The Montalcino region, centred on the fortified hilltop town of the same name, has become the Tuscan version of Barolo: a place making dense, tough, age-worthy wines that spend a long time in the barrel before release.

Castello Banfi's large estate lies in the far south of the region and it's a beauty: a combination of vineyards, olive groves, plum trees and forest, with a feeling of space and silence. The Castello itself is now a refined hotel (complete with a very good restaurant) and many of the former village houses have been converted into rooms and suites.

Within walking distance of your bucolic accommodation, you have access to the Enoteca, which organises tastings and sells all the Banfi wines, as well as the Balsameria – a tiny artisanal facility producing minuscule quantities of 12-year-aged *salsa etrusca* (supercharged balsamic vinegar) every year. Check out the difference between the simpler, more accessible Rosso di Montalcino and the more concentrated Brunello di Montalcino wines: same grape, different sites, different treatments and different levels of concentration.

While the vineyards themselves are scattered around the Castello and form a lovely panorama for afternoons flaked out by the pool, the winery itself is a 5km drive away. It's very civilised, with a high-level walkway that lets you see the whole facility easily. Make sure you ask about the estate's 'winery within a winery' concept and its research into different clones of Sangiovese. It sounds nerdy, but it's work that has been of huge benefit to improving the quality of Italian wine as a whole.

CASTELGIOCONDO, MONTALCINO

Just 10km or so west of Montalcino town lies Castelgiocondo. A 900-year-old-plus estate that's been neatly refurbished, it's owned by the Frescobaldis, one of the biggest wine families in Italy, with estates scattered across Tuscany.

Castelgiocondo is relatively small but has that nice feeling of a classic wine estate – of vineyards and winery all gathered in the one place, the dark galestro soils combining with the Sangiovese grape and 300–400m altitude to create pretty classic Brunello di Montalcino.

Visits need to be booked in advance, and include trips to the vineyard, the bijou winery and a tasting. There isn't a huge range to try here (which is, in itself, rather nice), but there's a great opportunity to compare the estate Brunello (from a range of vineyards) with the tighter, spicier single-vineyard Brunello from the Ripe al Convento site.

Light and VIP lunches for visitors are available, though both need to be booked well in advance. While there are catering facilities, Castelgiocondo doesn't have an actual restaurant, though plans to create one are in the pipeline.

COSTANTI, MONTALCINO

The Costantis are an old Sienese family who have been politically and professionally active in the southern edges of Tuscany for over 500 years, and engaged in the production of Brunello since the 1700s. Indeed, in 1870 Tito Costanti was among the small group of producers to show their wares at an exhibition in Siena that marked the first record of Montalcino's wines being called Brunello.

On top of a series of ridges, the estate is relatively small at 25 hectares, and only half of it is planted to vines. With south-facing slopes and barren, stony soils, it's perfect for the local Sangiovese, which dominates plantings. Visit the winery and you should ask about the barrels: the tendency is to use larger, older casks that have less direct influence on the flavour of the wine. This is the more traditional winemaking style for the region, allowing the sometimes tough young wine to soften gradually without imparting any active flavour from the wood. The result is, if you like, a purer expression of the grape in this area.

Visits take place in the afternoon, last about an hour and include some time in the vineyard, so you can see the galestro soil (and maybe a few fossils) for yourself. A word of warning, though: the winery sells out its production by late autumn and stops tours until the new vintage comes on stream after the winter, so it's best to schedule your visit for spring or summer.

PETRA, MAREMMA

The Maremma – the flatter lands west of Chianti towards the sea – has mushroomed in popularity over the last 30 years, with dozens of companies planting vineyards and building wineries. But even within that rush towards the coast, the Petra winery stands out.

A spectacular split disc, tilted towards the heavens, you simply can't miss it. The building looks like a modernist Mayan temple, or something that's landed from Dune, but in fact its design is at least partly practical: grapes go in at the top, and are processed downwards by gravity, from crushing to vinification to barrel cellar to bottle. No pumps are used, making for a gentler, more efficient process.

While Chianti relies on altitude to temper the sunshine, the Maremma uses the breeze. Little more than 10km from the Tyrrenhian sea, on the iron-rich soils of the Val di Cornia, Petra's vineyards are right in the sweet spot between sun/heat and wind/freshness.

The grape mix here is very Maremma – Cabernet Sauvignon, Merlot and Sangiovese are all made as single-varietal wines, and blended together in Petra's Hebo label. The tastings offer three wines, which come after vineyard and winery visits. Neither the regular nor the 'with lunch' options are especially cheap – but you wouldn't expect a winery like this to do 'budget'. The views from the top of the tilted disc out over the vineyards towards the sea are great for getting a feel for this corner of Tuscany.

ROCCA DI MONTEMASSI, MAREMMA

While Tuscany has tightly packed (and steeper) hillsides, the Maremma is wider and more open, making it feel more untamed and less manicured, despite the often impressive wine estates that have appeared in recent times.

Maybe it's this that lends the vague feel of a large New Mexican hacienda to Rocca di Montemassi. Or maybe it's the immensely imposing white, long-horned local cattle… The chance to see and learn about the latter is part of a recently introduced tour, which takes in everything from crops and vineyards to cows and kitchen gardens. The visit culminates in a trot round the museum dedicated to the Maremma's rural life, which is stuffed full of country craft and farming equipment from the last 400 years.

If you think that all sounds a bit too bucolic, and fancy a bit of gritty real life with your home-grown rosemary, the tour also explains the region's strong history of metal mining, which used to take place in areas now peacefully swathed in vines. A monument in the Montemassi vineyards at the former mouth of a mineshaft provides a sombre reminder of a terrible day in 1954 when 43 miners lost their lives.

EAST

UMANI RONCHI, MARCHE

If you're heading east of the Apennines, you can get a flavour of these somewhat less-heralded wine regions with a visit to one producer. Umani Ronchi has vineyards throughout the Marche and Abruzzo and is keen to help visitors understand what it's all about.

The heart of its operation is its barrel cellar – La Bottaia – in Osimo, 20km south of Ancona. Built into the hillside, it's a modern building but a sensitive and attractively designed one, and its well-lit tasting area surrounded by 500 barrels is an atmospheric place to try wines from across the company's portfolio.

If you're a fan of the appley, nutty Verdicchio dei Castelli di Jesi whites you should probably consider staying at its Villa Bianchi country house to the west of Ancona. Once a small winery, it combines food, accommodation and tastings from May to September, though you can still visit the vineyards outside of that time. Oh, and there's a pool, too.

SOUTH

It's impossible to visit vineyards in the south of Italy and not feel the pull of history. After all, this was the beating heart of wine production for the Roman Empire and, before that, it was a vine-filled western edge of ancient Greece. The latter's influence is still felt today: both the white grape Greco and the red Aglianico take their names from adaptations of words meaning 'Greek'.

If you were being unkind, you might be tempted to say that these long-gone civilisations represented the region's vinous heyday. Unkind, and also wrong. It's true that most of the last 100 years have not been exactly glorious for the south. Much of its decent wine was trucked to Tuscany, Piedmont or the Veneto to add weight and colour to underpowered northern Italian counterparts. The cheap stuff that was left didn't really excite anybody. Much was sold in bulk to northern European supermarkets for their bottom-shelf cheapies.

The unwanted influence of the north did not stop there. There were also unsuccessful attempts to plant cooler-climate grapes such as Sangiovese and Trebbiano. As anyone who's ever spent an hour broiling in the Mezzogiorno summer sun can attest, this is not a climate that plays to their strengths. They ripen far too early to have any character.

Fortunately, the last 20 years have seen a shift. The region has learnt to love what it has, discovered how to make the best of it, and grown in confidence as a result. Today there's way more decent wine coming out of this part of Italy than ever before.

With one or two exceptions, such as Chardonnay, the key to most good wine in the south is nearly always the use of indigenous local grape varieties – particularly if they're tied in to old vineyards. From Aglianico to Zibibbo, they're an exciting voyage of discovery for the wine-curious visitor.

Yes, reds like Nero d'Avola or Negroamaro can be big and powerful, with back-slapping tannins, but that's not a blueprint that's followed across the board. Nerello Mascalese on the slopes of Mount Etna and, especially, Frappato in Sicily's windy south-east corner make red wines of elegance and precision.

So how do they do it? What's the secret to creating good, rather than so-so wines in this scorching climate? Well, sometimes it's the soil – both the limestone that lifts Greco to another level in the hills east of Naples and the smoky pumice on Etna add a distinctive minerality to the wines. Sometimes it's altitude – like everywhere in Italy, there's no shortage of mountains here, whether in the form of Etna or the slopes of the Apennines, which stretch all the way down south, run under the Strait of Messina and reappear in Sicily. Higher vineyards cool off quicker at night, and the big day/night temperature shifts help preserve freshness in the grapes.

And sometimes it's as simple as the cool breeze. You're never far from the sea in Italy, and its influence can have a big impact on stopping wines from becoming hot and baked. The furthest corner of Sicily is close to the north African coast, yet the non-stop wind can give wines of a freshness and purity that your palate will tell you belong hundreds of miles further north.

One of the joys of the south is that there are also so many non-wine-related things to see and do, so winery visits can be worked into a wider schedule.

In Sicily, a good tour involves starting at Palermo, dropping down to Marsala, going along the south coast to Vittoria and then swinging back up to Catania via Etna. But be careful with your planning. Sicily is the biggest island in the Med, almost the same size as Albania, and since many highways seem to have missed out on the EU road-sign budget, you should schedule in a bit of 'driving around aimlessly' time. Should your tour finish in Palermo, you can catch a ferry up to Genoa and the vineyards of Barolo.

On the mainland, you can start at Naples/Pompeii, take in some wineries in the Fiano/Greco di Tufo/Taurasi area en route to the eastern side, before swinging down to the UNESCO heritage site of Alberobello and the heartland of the Primitivo grape. After that, head off on a ferry from Bari to Greece.

Don't rush it, though. Not only is there plenty to see, but there's a pace of life down here that can seem itinerary-proof. Far better to go with the flow and see less, but see it better.

MAINLAND

FEUDI DI SAN GREGORIO, CAMPANIA

There are three good wine areas 50km east of Naples, specialising, respectively, in Greco di Tufo and Fiano di Avellino whites and the powerful Aglianico red. You can try them all if you visit Feudi di San Gregorio.

The winery is up in the Campanian Apennines, a succession of mountains, hills and plains, criss-crossed by streams and rivers. A place of Mediterranean latitudes and mountain viticulture, with cold snowy winters and long, mild summers, it's a long way from the typical image of the south as a baked suntrap.

This alone makes it an inspiring visit. But San Gregorio has also worked with top international designers to create everything from its winery to its bottles and labels, and there are exhibitions and installations to view throughout.

The firm likes to see its winery as a 'workshop of ideas' – a place for people to come to learn, taste and swap views, so no surprise that it's well set up for tourists. The cheapest package, which lasts one-and-a-half hours and provides three wines to try, is good if you're in a hurry, though you can pay a bit extra if you want to taste a different selection.

But if you're serious about food, and your wallet can stand it, the three-hour tour with lunch/dinner gets you a lot more for your money, with a guided tasting session and special matching of wines to a four-course meal at its Michelin-starred restaurant, Marennà.

A MANO, PUGLIA

This is winemaking as Hollywood would have it. Husband and wife team Mark Shannon and Elvezia Sbalchiero met 20 years ago while working for another winery, and joined together not just in marriage, but in establishing A Mano. The name means 'hand-made', and while there's nothing fancy about the operation, there's a real heart and warmth to the set-up.

Neither Mark nor Elvezia is from Puglia. He is from California, she is from Friuli in Italy's far north-east. Yet they chose to base themselves in Noci, 50km south-east of Bari, because they loved the pace of life here and felt that Puglia would give them a chance to make wines that were both good and affordable. 'Great wine', says Elvezia, 'should be available to everyone who wants to enjoy a glass.' Amen to that.

Certainly, their decision has been vindicated. A Mano's wines regularly pick up medals in competitions, outscoring competitor bottles at twice the price.

They're best known for their work with the Primitivo grape, and their Imprint, made with part-dried grapes in the style of an Amarone, is an unusual, voluptuous style that's worth a look, as is the wine made with the rare Susumaniello variety. It means 'little donkey' in the local dialect, so-called because it's apparently a stubborn and awkward grape to work with.

A tasting in their tasting room, tucked away in the narrow alleys in the centre of Noci's old town, is a great chance to chat face to face with the people who make a living growing the grapes and making the wine – go ahead and ask Mark or Elvezia yourself about donkeys and *appassito* Primitivos when you meet them. There is a charge for the tasting, but it gets taken off any purchases you make.

Although there's no tour of the winery (which is out of town and not equipped for visits), this is a great stop-off if you're visiting Albarobello and its amazing conical-roofed *trulli* 10km to the east.

CANTINE SAN MARZANO, PUGLIA

Back in 1962, 19 growers from the village of San Marzano di San Giuseppe came together to form a co-operative, pooling their grapes to make and sell the wine together. In the last 50 years, it's safe to say that it's grown a fair bit, and now a staggering 1,200 local growers contribute the fruit from their vineyards.

In the heel of Italy, San Marzano is near Manduria, which is famous for two things: the Primitivo grape and Salice Salentino. The latter is a combination of the powerful, structured Negroamaro and the softer, more carefree Malvasia Nera. Unsurprisingly, given the number of growers contributing grapes, this co-op does impressive things with both styles.

While there are some strong examples of small-volume, expensive wines – the Collezione Cinquanta, a blend of different Puglian varieties from old bush vines, is a red of rare concentration – the mid-priced bottles probably represent the best value for money. Working your way through a few tasting glasses of them here is a great way to understand two absolutely classic southern Italian red wine styles.

You can't try them in the winery itself – while it does do tours (which need to be booked a week in advance), it doesn't sell any products directly. But all of the wines are available in the shop out front, which also arranges tastings that are free for the entry-level and mid-range wines.

SARDINIA & SICILY

SELLA E MOSCA, SARDINIA

The fact these vineyards exist at all is incredible: they are lined with sandstone monoliths, rocky sentinels that had to be painstakingly removed from the land before planting. It would be a big job now, let alone 120 years ago.

Sadly, visits here don't include trips into the vines, but they do take in the old cellar, plus a scoot round the small museum that gives you the full family history from 1899 to the present. The best bit about the visit, however, is the tasting. Typically, over a dozen wines are available to try in the shop – you pay as you go – so it's a great chance to get to know some native Sardinian grape varieties. Sometimes these come on their own, sometimes they're blended with the likes of Cabernet and Merlot. While Cannonau (aka Grenache) and Carignano (Carignan) might be familiar from elsewhere, they have a distinctive spin to them on Sardinia, with the former in particular expressing a certain exuberant wildness that seems to sum up the island nicely. This is also probably the best place to come if you're a fan of the aromatic floral explosion that is Vermentino.

AZIENDA AGRICOLA COS, VITTORIA

Cerasuolo means 'cherry soil' and the red clay/sand over a limestone bedrock combines with the constant sea breezes to create a unique environment perfect for growing the pale, aromatic Frappato grape, and for putting a new spin on the darker, fruitier Nero d'Avola. Both grape varieties are made separately, but can be brought together to create Cerasuolo di Vittoria. This is the only DOCG on Sicily and it's a beguilingly mid-weight wine, with perfume, structure and class.

This, in itself would make Cos worth visiting, but it's a highly distinctive winery in its own right. Founded by three friends in 1980, it's a long-term practitioner of organic farming. And for a couple of decades now, Giusto Occhipinti and his partners have also been experimenting with ageing the wine in amphorae rather than oak barrels. 'You rediscover elegance this way,' he says.

Visits are by appointment only and take in the vineyards, winery and a tasting.

FLORIO, MARSALA

Marsala – like sherry – is born in the production process. This is, to put it mildly, a bit different, relying on oak ageing, fortification with grape brandy, and gentle oxidation. You should check it out for no other reason than it will help you appreciate an underrated – indeed, almost forgotten – style of wine.

Founded in the 1830s, Florio is one of the biggest producers of Marsala, now making around a million bottles a year. Mussolini and General Garibaldi have both stayed here – perhaps it's a wine that appeals to power.

Certainly, it's not simple. There are 30 or so wine styles, classified by age, colour and dryness. A visit to Florio's wonderful wine warehouses – kept cool using a Moorish method – and a tasting with food should help you start to get your head round them. And if you buy one, you can open it and keep it – it won't go off.

DONNAFUGATA, MARSALA

While you're in Marsala, swing by Donnafugata. It's a high-quality producer of Sicilian wines which, counterintuitively, doesn't make Marsala. Ethically, it does lots of good stuff that puts it ahead of 99 per cent of other wineries – sustainable viticulture, lighter bottles, monitoring its carbon footprint, promoting clean energy and biodiversity in the vineyards. It's also well set up for tourists, so might serve as a crowd-pleasing stop if your fellow travellers aren't as into wine as you are.

Even though the cellars are attractively photogenic, the real opportunity here is to take advantage of the superb range of food and wine matching options available afterwards. Ignore the half-hearted ham, cheese and biscuits offer and dive into the Mediterranea or Donna Gabriella packages. They really help you understand how to use Sicilian wines at the dinner table.

OCCHIPINTI, VITTORIA

Lovers of Frappato – and it's very easy to love, particularly if you like lighter, more elegant styles of red – should be sure to visit here. And if the name looks familiar, it's because Arianna is the niece of Giusto Occhipinti from Cos (p87). Although she was born in Marsala on the other side of the island, it was her visits to Cos that inspired her to enter winemaking. And the nature-friendly way of creating wine adopted by Giusto is also in evidence in Arianna's philosophy – she's been certified organic from the start.

Her wines are wonderful, with a lift and purity, and the excitement you feel on tasting them is only amplified by her obvious love for the region and what she's doing. Get in touch at least a few days before to check she will be free to take you through the vineyards and winery.

PASSOPISCIARO, ETNA

Andrea Franchetti is a man who likes a challenge. He set up his first estate in Tuscany from scratch before embarking on an even tougher task: restoring some ancient terraced vineyards on the slopes of a live volcano. While the lower levels of Mount Etna are dotted with forests and flowers, the 1,000m northern slopes where Passopisciaro sits have been repeatedly singed by lava flows, creating an eerie landscape with the grey, pumice soil providing a pungent smoky backdrop.

Based here since 2000, Franchetti now makes eight wines, six of them from the noble Nerello Mascalese variety. Taste a few and you'll see why wine enthusiasts are coming to view this location as Italy's answer to Burgundy: the wines have a wonderful light-footed fruit with spice, smoky minerality and structure.

Visitors to the 'contrade' (cru) in Guardiola get to visit a combination of new and old vineyards, the latter showcasing some superbly gnarled 100-year-old Nerello Mascalese vines. The tasting takes in a 1,000m-altitude Chardonnay, an old-vine Nerello Mascalese and a single-vineyard wine made from the same variety.

PLANETA, MENFI

Planeta is not the largest producer on Sicily, but it has done more than anyone else to drive the quality revolution on the island. Its calling card is Chardonnay, which it has been making from its base in Ulmo (near Menfi) in the west since 1994. But over the last 20 years, it has quietly acquired a string of small estates across the island, creating a wonderful portfolio of interesting classic regional styles. If you did nothing but tour the Planeta vineyards, you'd still get a clear snapshot of the different terroirs and varieties of the island.

All are visitable (though Vittoria and Capo Milazzo both need to be pre-arranged), and all offer a variety of options from tasting and vineyard/winery visits through snacks to light lunch. In a nice touch, the food at each winery is local to that particular part of the island. The visits themselves are free, though there's a charge depending on which wines you try.

The minimum impact estate in Noto has some characteristic *case sparse* – traditional rural houses – to stay in. But for something a bit fancier, Planeta's La Foresteria wine resort in Menfi is hard to beat. Relaxing in an infinity pool surrounded by vineyards and looking down towards the Med is the kind of interpretation of 'terroir' that even non-wine lovers can appreciate.

TASCA D'ALMERITA, CENTRAL SICILY

The Tasca d'Almerita family have been key players on Sicily's wine scene for generations, acquiring a portfolio of estates, from which they make head-turningly good whites, fizz and dessert wines. They have estates from Etna (Tenuta Tascante) to the dreamy island of Salina (Tenuta Capofaro), between Sicily and the mainland. But if you only visit one of their properties, it should be Tenuta Regaleali. Lying in the Madonie mountains in the middle of Sicily, it's a tranquil place, with 360 hectares of vineyard and over 3,000 olive trees. This is the heart of their wine operation, with dozens of experimental grape varieties planted on the rolling hillsides. There are also hikes and bike rides through the vines, a cooking school, and an awful lot of silence to be enjoyed.

TERRAZZE DELL'ETNA, ETNA

Since they started in 2008, the Bevilacqua family have reclaimed 36 hectares of abandoned land on the slopes of Europe's highest and smokiest volcano and turned it into a functioning estate. The vineyards run from 650m to 900m above sea level, and while there are plantings of Chardonnay, Pinot Noir and Petit Verdot, they concentrate on Etna's finest: Nerello Mascalese. And they've really experimented with what it can do. It's made as a single varietal, blended with the lesser-known native Nerello Cappuccio and also with Petit Verdot. Though you'll need to call ahead, this is a stellar visit in an unforgettable location.

SPAIN

The third 'big beast' of
European wine, Spain
is a stimulating mix of
modernity and tradition
– which makes it a great
country for the wine
lover. It has no shortage
of native grape varieties,
but it's often open to
non-local ones, too.
It also merges both
multi-million-euro
wineries with centuries-
old vineyards and
arcane techniques with
tourist-friendly facilities.
It's big, though, so unless
you're on a month-long
tour you'll need to pick
your areas with care.

RIOJA

There aren't many wine names that are recognised by wine lovers from Beijing to Buffalo, but Rioja is indisputably one of them. For many, it's practically shorthand for 'Spanish red'. It's easy to see why, too. The wines gained their reputation for being soft, medium-bodied, and smoothly approachable – as comforting and reliable as a favourite pair of slippers.

Rioja is in the north-east of Spain, poised between the heat and dryness of the country's central plains and the windswept mists of the Atlantic coast. Not for nothing is Spain's northern edge known as the Costa Verde – the Green Coast.

In theory, this betwixt and between location gives Rioja the perfect combination of heat and sunshine to get grapes ripe and cooler influences that prevent the fruit from getting too baked and jammy. In reality, every year an intriguing battle plays out between the warmer and cooler factions, which is complicated still further by the influence of altitude up in the vineyards of the Sierra de Cantabria foothills.

But if this sounds like the region might be difficult for wine tourists, you can breathe easy. Producers do a great deal to make life easy for their fans.

Traditionally, Rioja has been famous for two things: blending wines from vineyards across the region, and ageing wines for a long time in oak barrels. Both practices were predominantly carried out for reasons of consistency and approachability: pan-regional blending allowed wineries to gather different styles of grape to minimise the effects of vintage variation, while leaving wines for months – or years – in oak gave time for any unruly tannins to soften. Not that the latter is as big a problem in Rioja as it is in, say, Barolo. Tempranillo, the region's superstar red grape, is a relatively approachable customer.

Besides, modern grape growing and winemaking techniques have rubbed off any rough edges that existed in the first place, creating a very different style: wines with riper fruit, deeper colour and aged, not for years in ancient barrels, but for shorter blasts in newer oak.

Unsurprisingly, the growth of 'modern-style' riojas has not been welcomed everywhere. Some critics feel the region has lost some of what defined it, arguing that the paler, more oxidised 'old-style' riojas offered a point of difference that their more garnet-coloured, fruity versions lack. Fortunately, there are versions of both styles out there, with some producers (López de Heredia Viña Tondonia for instance – p97) wearing their old-fashionedness like a badge of honour.

Logroño is the biggest city in the region – and has a fantastic street (Calle Laurel) stuffed with restaurants that is an absolute must for a tapas crawl. But Haro, at the northern edges of the region, is the most atmospheric place to stay. Not only is it an attractive old town, but it's home to many of the region's best (and oldest) wineries, which set up around the town's train station in the latter half of the 19th century – the quickest way to ship wines out of the region at the time.

It's probably the best concentration of superb wineries in the world. Here Muga, La Rioja Alta, Roda, CVNE, López de Heredia, Gómez Cruzado and Bilbainas are all within a few hundred metres of each other. The Barrio de la Estación (Station District) is only about 1km from the town centre, so if you stay in Haro and walk down, you won't have to worry about swallowing the fantastic samples you'll be given to try.

Rioja might be a region with a big reputation, but it's fairly compact, barely 100km from east to west, and the main motorway chews up the distances with ease. There's also no shortage of places to visit, both large and small, particularly in the cluster of villages in the region's western third, from Fuenmayor, San Asensio and Elciego to the grand old wine town of Haro.

CASA PRIMICIA, LAGUARDIA

There is no shortage of old buildings across Spain, but not many of them are still a functioning winery. This 11th-century building, where the Church used to collect its tithes (ten per cent of the whole harvest), was the first place in Laguardia to make wine back in the 1400s, so though Casa Primicia was only set up 30 years ago, it comes with a fair whack of history attached.

With 45 hectares of vines that stretch from the foothills of the Sierra de Cantabria towards the plains near the River Ebro, it's a small but captivating visit. Its fabulous ancient cellars are 9m below street level, and the winery is quirkily shoe-horned into the medieval spaces. For that reason, it can't accept large touring groups, so best book well in advance.

Outside is a treat, too, with the mountains forming an imposing backdrop to the beautiful garden, with fine views out over the organic vineyards. A rare lagoon, surrounded by vines, attracts all manner of birdlife and, possibly uniquely, Casa Primicia offers not just tours of vineyards and cellar, but a Days of Wine and Birds experience that adds a spot of birdwatching into the mix. Spring (in particular) and autumn are the best times to visit for all things avian as the lake, which is filled entirely by rainwater, dries up in summer.

CONDE DE LOS ANDES, OLLAURI

Another of Rioja's classic wine villages, Ollauri lies 4km south of Haro. Its so-called 'barrio de bodegas' (winery neighbourhood) is home to several 19th-century producers, who excavated the high ground in the upper area of the village to build their cellars.

The Conde de los Andes examples, known as the Calados, are wonderfully atmospheric: three traditional old buildings with cool grey-stoned subterranean vaults. More than 1km in length, they were hewn out of the rock over several centuries and are some of the most impressive cellars in the whole of Rioja. They are also claimed to be the oldest.

A tour of these and the winery takes two hours and includes the chance to try a gran reserva by candlelight in the vaults, and sample a further two wines in the shop. The latter has several exclusive bottles that are no longer available commercially elsewhere, some dating back 30 to 40 years.

CONTINO, LAGUARDIA

The Compañía Vinícola del Norte de España is, given its mouthful of syllables, usually shortened to CVNE (pronounced koo-nay). It's one of the best small groups in the region, and a fantastic one for visitors. The firm has three premises: CVNE in Haro, plus Viña Real and Contino, both more or less next door to each other north of Logroño.

All are well set up for visitors (the first two even have special workshops for children) and each is worth a look for different reasons. CVNE is down in the historic Barrio de la Estación in Haro, while architecture fans will enjoy Viña Real's amazing avant-garde winery. But if, like me, you like small, old wine estates, Contino is the pick of the bunch.

As most wines in Rioja are blended from fruit across the area, the fact that this is an estate – the first in the region, apparently – instantly makes it unusual. Its 63 hectares wind round the Cerro de la Mesa hill, gently shelving down to the slow-flowing River Ebro, and produce wines that are consistently excellent – it does nothing below reserva level. A visit is a good chance to try (or buy) not just the typical Rioja multi-varietal blends, but also a couple of single varietals. The Graciano – quite rare within Rioja these days – is one of the best you'll ever have.

VIVANCO, BRIONES

Vivanco might not have the lengthy pedigree of some Rioja wineries, but it's done more than most to make itself an attractive tourist destination. Its Museum of Wine Culture in Briones should be a must-visit for anyone interested in wine.

An impressive array of antique vineyard tools, winemaking equipment and artworks is permanently on display, while further halls are regularly filled with temporary exhibitions. The enormous collection of corkscrews, which range from old-style and classical to the frankly bizarre, is worth half an hour of anybody's time.

Outside, the Garden of Bacchus pays homage to the world of the vine, containing over 200 different grape varieties all planted in one place. Here you can see everything from Riojan classics such as Tempranillo and all-but extinct varieties like Maturana Tinta to global superstars such as Cabernet Sauvignon and Pinot Grigio.

And once you've reached information overload, the restaurant isn't a bad place to sample the traditional local cuisine and let it all soak in. An interesting half-day visit celebrating all things vinous.

BODEGAS FRANCO-ESPAÑOLAS, LOGROÑO

If you're staying in Logroño and fancy a visit that doesn't require taking the car, wander over to Bodegas Franco-Españolas.

As its name suggests, the winery came about as a merger between French and Spanish companies, back in the 1890s. At that time, vast swathes of France's vineyards had been destroyed by phylloxera, and many of the country's wine growers were heading over the Pyrenees to Spain. A good many settled in Rioja, so it's not too far-fetched to describe the very existence of Franco-Españolas as a bit of living history.

Located just over the Puente de Hierro (Iron Bridge), a five-minute walk from the old town, it might be one of the easiest winery visits you'll ever make. And if you're there on a Saturday, you can add a spot of lunch to your tour, setting you up nicely for a Calle Laurel tapas crawl that evening.

VIÑA IJALBA, LOGROÑO

If you get tired of musty cellars and centuries of history, Ijalba makes a nice counterpoint. Just north of Logroño, it's one of the new wave of Rioja bodegas, set up by local businessman Dionisio Ruiz Ijalba , who, having made his money from quarrying stone, in the 1970s hit upon the idea of turning the open-cast mine workings into vineyards.

It's been really well done. The winery is as modern as the bottles' funky labels, and not only has the old industrial landscape been regenerated, but the firm is big on recycling and sustainability as well.

Visits are reasonably priced and explain the whole process, while the tasting – of wines that are unashamedly 21st century in style – makes an interesting contrast to ones at the region's more traditional bodegas. The winery also produces a couple of wines from near-extinct varieties that are now slowly being revitalised – Maturana Tinta and Maturana Blanca – though you'll have to buy in order to try as they're not part of the tasting. Ijalba's Garnacha was the first single-varietal version to be made in Rioja, back in 1994.

LA RIOJA ALTA, HARO

Set up by five local families in 1890, La Rioja Alta is one of the region's great old wineries and makes some of the most beautiful expressions of classic rioja in existence. These are wines that talk intelligently, rather than loudly; as sheer and shimmeringly sensual as silk.

La Rioja Alta's most famous wine is its Viña Ardanza Reserva, which celebrated its 75th anniversary in 2017, and remains a benchmark example of the traditional style, beloved by experts and amateurs alike.

Prolonged oak ageing is the key (few wineries age their wines for longer) and a tour of the cellars, where the magic happens, is fascinating.

LÓPEZ DE HEREDIA VIÑA TONDONIA, HARO

There have been many changes in Rioja over the last 100 years, but few, if any, have infiltrated López de Heredia. It remains proudly, defiantly traditional – a tribute to the man who founded it in 1877, Rafael López de Heredia. Something of a romantic, he built its extraordinary winery, whose observation tower (known as the birdhouse – *txori toki* in Basque) is as famous as the turrets of Château Lafite.

Though it owns over 170 hectares of vines (including the famously beautiful Tondonia vineyard), López de Heredia's wines are defined more by what happens in the cellar. This is one winery visit where you really don't need to head out among the vine rows to get the big story. Of course, you can't make good wine with bad grapes, but what really sets López de Heredia apart is the length of time its wines spend sitting first in old oak barrels, then in bottles in the bodega.

Unsurprisingly, the cellars are pretty busy. Inside you'll find 14,000 barrels and goodness knows how many bottles, all ageing under a soft black covering of mould, spiders' webs and dust. Provided you don't mind a bit of intentional fustiness, this is a fantastic, unique visit. And the chance to taste three of its reds afterwards (including Tondonia Reserva) is also not to be missed.

One warning: you'll need to contact the winery a long way in advance to visit. Tours are run around the availability of staff, and there's no shortage of demand.

MUGA, HARO

Muga loves wood. Its wines are fermented as well as aged in it, and it employs three full-time coopers to create barrels to its own specifications, as well as a *cubero* – an all-but extinct profession responsible for making the fermentation vats that are so much a part of its calling card.

Muga also loves eggs. Despite technological advances, all its wines are still fined with egg white, just as they were when it was established in the 1930s – worth bearing in mind if you're vegan. This is a winery that adheres strongly to tradition – but is also happy to give things a modern twist.

The reds are excellent (the Prado Enea Gran Reserva remains one of the region's most respected wines), but the whole range is sensitively made – right down to the two rosés. And if you've ever wondered what a cava made in Rioja might taste like, here's your chance.

With no stainless steel tanks in sight, the basic guided tour is a real oaky love-in, and even gives you a chance to take in the working cooperage along with winery and cellar. The five-wine tasting includes both Torre Muga and Prado Enea, but as it needs a minimum of eight participants, might not be guaranteed. The vineyards visit has the same eight-person-minimum caveat, though provides the opportunity to have some of the region's best terroir explained to you by an expert. If you're feeling sluggish, there are also Segway tours and – a real five-star option – a hot-air balloon ride. It's not cheap, but the memory of a one-hour drift over some of Europe's loveliest vineyards at sunset will be priceless.

MARQUÉS DE RISCAL, ELCIEGO

Riscal, as it's often known, is a winning combination of tradition and modernity. On one hand, its wines are some of the finest and most elegantly classical in the region; on the other, it's never been shy to look forward.

It was one of the first wineries to introduce modern techniques from Bordeaux in the mid-19th century and then, in the 21st century, it built its quite extraordinary hotel in Elciego. Designed by renowned architect Frank Gehry – the mind behind Bilbao's famed Guggenheim art gallery – this striking building has become, as its creators hoped, a 'city of wine'.

There's food from casual dining up to Michelin-star level, a spa featuring grape-based vinotherapy treatments and, as you would expect, a pretty nifty wine bar.

Right in the heart of the old winery and surrounded by vineyards, it's a brilliant place to stay if you want to visit the Marqués de Riscal cellars – which date from 1858 – not to mention a striking contrast of old and new that sums up this Riojan powerhouse quite beautifully.

BODEGAS VALDELANA, ELCIEGO

Wineries like to talk about their history, but few of them go to the extent the Valdelana family does. Visit this small winery in Elciego, roughly halfway between Logroño and Haro, and you get far more than the usual cellar-plus-tasting tour. Not only is there a wine museum featuring all manner of equipment from days gone by, but also an ethnographic museum full of finds from the region dating back as far as Jurassic times. By these standards, the 14 generations of Valdelanas who have been making wine in the village since 1615 look but the blink of an eye...

If you prefer to look forward, the family have also created a rather good Tunnel of the Senses out of old fermentation tanks, which is designed to help you get your head around the sights and smells of wine. Striking and interactive, it provides an easy and effective introduction to wine tasting.

The tasting takes in four wines encompassing all the main Rioja styles – a white, a young red, a crianza and a reserva – as well as a crash course in how to sample the estate olive oil. It's great value and also one of the more child-friendly experiences in the region.

You might also want to consider a stay in one of the 12 rooms, since the full winery experience is included as part of the tariff.

FINCA VALPIEDRA, FUENMAYOR

The Martínez Bujanda family of wine growers are one of the best-known in Spain and have a fine track record for producing reliably good bottles. Back in 1999 they built a winery on one of their best vineyards, turning it into a single-vineyard estate (or *pago* in Spanish) in the process. Finca Valpiedra is in a wonderful spot, right in the middle of a loop in the River Ebro. Its 80 hectares of vineyard – almost all Tempranillo with just eight hectares of Garnacha, Graciano and the rare Maturana Tinta – are unusually pebbly for Rioja, and give the wine a distinctive mineral core.

This is a proper estate concept, and the three terraces sloping down to the river produce just two wines: the younger crianza, Cantos del Valpiedra, and the Finca de Valpiedra *gran vino*. Aged in a combination of French and American oak, they need a few years to loosen up, but mature nicely with time.

It's a tremendous place to explore – not just because genuine estates in Rioja are a rarity, but because the team have put together a wide range of programmes. The basic visit is decent, offering wonderful views over the estate, a tour, some nibbles and a tasting of both wines. But if you go for that, the very least you should do is taste a couple of extra vintages of Valpiedra, or compare 'old-style' and 'new-style' rioja.

You can also try wine and cheese, have a picnic in the vineyards, ride a Segway through the vines and try six different Spanish grape varieties. But if you want to make an afternoon of it, the Grandes Pagos of Spain Tour gives you a lot for your money, with vineyards, winery, tapas-pairing and a bottle of the estate wine to take away at the end.

YSIOS, LAGUARDIA

When the wine group behind Ysios hired Spanish architect Santiago Calatrava to design its winery and gave him *carte blanche*, it was a brave move, but it's paid off handsomely. The elegantly rippling wave design creates a roof-line as sympathetic to the peaks of the Sierra de Cantabria in the background as it is striking. If you're an architecture aficionado, a visit to this iconic building just north of Laguardia, along with the two Frank Gehry works (the Guggenheim in Bilbao and the Marqués de Riscal winery – p98) should definitely be on your radar.

From the curvy cellars to the striking central tasting room with its enormous window, this is a visit that will linger long in the memory. It also helps that the wines are good, too. The flagship winery of a large drinks company, it produces nothing below reserva level.

CATALONIA/
NORTH-EAST

Wine probably isn't the first thing that comes to mind when you're asked for a defining image of Catalonia – it's more likely to be beaches, Gaudí or Barcelona FC.

Yet this is also a stimulating and hugely varied region for vineyards. While it does have five-star producers and a world-famous wine style, Spain's north-eastern corner is also a rewarding place to go looking for surprises – small producers in remote villages, beautiful views and oddball grape varieties, sometimes mixed with French classics such as Cabernet Sauvignon. Given the proximity to France, such commingling isn't surprising.

The combination of sea, mountains, different exposures and plentiful sunshine gives Catalonia an incredible range of regional climates and, within them, local microclimates – and that's even before getting into the effects of soil type.

Such complications suit the can-do spirit of the locals – Catalans are famously entrepreneurial and independent (some might say bloody-minded) – and the region makes a vast range of wine styles, from ethereal whites to some of the biggest reds you'll ever taste.

But if you had to pick one style that defines the region wine-wise, it would be cava. Although it's possible to make it elsewhere in Spain, in reality almost all of it comes from Catalonia. In fact, three-quarters of it is made around Sant Sadurní d'Anoia, just west of Barcelona. The small town is to Spain's famous sparkler what Reims is to champagne or Beaune is to Burgundy.

Like champagne (and unlike prosecco), cava is created by a secondary fermentation in the bottle, with a bit of ageing in the cellar afterwards. This allows the wine to take on some bready character from the dead yeast cells, but as it usually spends less time 'on the lees' than champagne, it tends to be fresh rather than toasty in style.

The biggest difference between champagne and cava, though, is the grape varieties. The French use Chardonnay, Pinot Noir and Pinot Meunier; the Catalans, by contrast, have stuck defiantly to their native grapes: Xarel·lo, Macabeo and

Parellada. Chardonnay is permitted (as is Pinot Noir), but both are planted in small quantities. In general red grapes only play a minor supporting role.

Having said all that, I feel I owe the Catalans an apology. It must be hugely annoying for them to have their wine constantly set against something that is very different. Yes, both have bubbles, but would you compare Bob Marley to Duke Ellington just because they're both musicians? Anyway, the point is there's lots to explore in Catalonia and you should go and do so for yourself.

The other big-name wine region in this neck of the woods is Priorat, and it's hard to think of a place (or wine) more different. If cava is affordable, approachable and joyfully frivolous, the wines of Priorat are intense, serious and brooding. They're also some of the most expensive in Spain, though if you visit the region, you'll understand why. A mountainous, remote and unforgiving place, every drop of wine has to be positively coaxed from its glinting, slatey *llicorella* soils. Prices might be high, but yields are also low, and the people who work here are believers on a mission, not dropouts in search of a lifestyle.

You might need a certain amount of commitment yourself if you're planning to explore the area's wine regions in any detail. While some parts (Costers del Segre and Conca de Barberà, for instance) are handily close together, the mountainous terrain can make for slow driving – particularly if you're visiting when there are likely to be lots of tractors on the many secondary roads.

Penedès and cava country are doable by day trips from Barcelona (traffic notwithstanding), as are Montsant and, to a lesser extent, Priorat from Tarragona, depending on your tolerance for early starts and late finishes.

This is a region where there's no shortage of interesting places to go that, moreover, you're unlikely to know much about beforehand. Get ready for a real voyage of discovery. But if you're only going to visit two areas, I'd suggest Priorat and (to the north-west) Somontano. Both are among the most spectacular wine regions in Spain.

ALODIA, SOMONTANO

At the foothills of the Sierra de Guara, Alodia was set up in 2005 by the Labata family, who have lived in the region for over 500 years. Unusually for Somontano, its focus is not on international grape varieties such as Cabernet Sauvignon, but on reviving native Somontano ones: Parraleta, Moristel and Alcañón (Macabeo). Even more unusually, it makes three sparkling wines (two whites and a rosé) using the same 'second fermentation in the bottle' technique as champagne – the only place in the DO to do so.

At just 17 hectares, it's also one of the smallest wineries in Somontano, and makes for a quaint, personal (and free) visit that has not just interesting wines, but also stunning views across all the villages in the region. Perched on a craggy outcrop, the spectacular Alquézar with its 12th-century walls is a local highlight.

There are visits at the weekend, with 50-minute tours plus the chance to match wines and food in the family's 100-seater restaurant, Alcañón.

PERELADA, EMPORDÀ

Give most 25-year-olds a bit of success and they'll probably buy a car. Miguel Mateu bought a castle. The Castillo Perelada estate had been making wine since the Middle Ages, and it was Mateu's dream to restore it to the kind of glory that it once enjoyed when the resident Carmelite monks were wowing travellers with their vino.

Nowadays, it has 130 hectares of vines, spread over five vineyards. The jewel in the crown is Garbet, a particularly beautiful site on the steep, slatey foothills of the Pyrenees overlooking the Mediterranean, which makes Perelada's top single-vineyard wine.

There's no shortage of things to do here. As well as the standard vineyard/cellar/tasting tours, there are also options to add in the castle museum, complete with a wide art collection, or do tastings in a couple of their vineyards. The three-hour Garbet tour would be my pick. If you fancy indulging yourself afterwards, this is also one of the few wineries in Spain that can offer you two hours in a spa after your tour and tasting – and has an (ever-so-discreet) casino on site.

The Gratallops pioneers

In the 1980s a group of winemakers bought vineyards in the high slatey hills of the Siurana Valley in Priorat. Their intention was to ignore the costs involved and do whatever it took to make exceptional wine in the region. Today, the producers working these unforgiving slopes are some of the best-known names in Spanish, indeed global, fine wine. Álvaro Palacios, Sara Pérez at Mas Martinet and René Barbier Jr at Clos Mogador make magnificent wines at eye-watering prices. If you're a fine wine fan, you'll want to come to these high, remote hills. But contacting the wineries, let alone arranging a time to come, can be painful. Clos Mogador is the best set up for visitors.

CODORNÍU, CAVA

If you're interested in ticking off wine-world icons, Codorníu has to be on your list. Though people had been experimenting with sparkling wine in the region for a while, it was the company's former head, Josep Raventós, who managed to produce it a) reliably well and b) in sufficient quantities to make it financially viable.

By 1895, things were going so well that he commissioned Josep Puig i Cadafalch, a contemporary of Gaudí's, to enlarge his winery. It's in the cava capital of Sant Sadurní d'Anoia, and the spectacular Art Nouveau building is an understandably popular tourist attraction

This is a hugely worthwhile visit even before you consider the wines. The standard tour alone is impressive, including a video, explanations of Puig's architecture, the lengthy family wine history (they've been growing grapes since the 1500s, making them one of the oldest wine names in Spain), the winery gardens, press room, 'table of aromas' (to help you identify flavours), and a look round the cellars, complete with bottles ageing photogenically for the cameras.

But there are also a number of add-ons to this basic package, from cheese and cava pairing to touring the vineyards by e-bike. If you're only spending one day in this region, however, it's hard to beat the combo that takes in both the Codorníu winery and a trip to the 1,000-year-old Benedictine monastery under the iconic jagged peaks of Montserrat.

ENATE, SOMONTANO

While it sometimes seems that every other winery in Italy has a hook-up with the art world, it's not so common in Spain, which is just one reason why Enate, with its 100-strong collection of contemporary artworks, stands out.

The winery, built in 1993, is modern, too – an attractively designed place, with plenty of space and light. And if you're popping in here on your way from Rioja to Catalonia or France, it makes an interesting counterpoint to the procession of predominantly 19th-century edifices.

There are big differences between daytime and night-time temperatures in Somontano, which allow Enate to grow varieties rarely found in Spain, such as Syrah and (even more unusually) Gewürztraminer.

Its best-known wine is, justifiably, the barrel-fermented Chardonnay – a well-balanced mix of ripeness, freshness and toasty oak – and you can try it with local food if you go for the three-course 'tour and lunch at the winery' option, which is a fun (and indulgent) way of filling three hours on a Saturday.

If you happen to be there on the first Saturday of the month, you can upgrade to the Expert Tasting and Tour beforehand, which adds in a visit to the art gallery and a tasting of five wines conducted by the winemaker. The basic tour covers winery, tasting and gallery.

If you want to buy one wine after your visit, the Uno Tinto is a powerfully silky Cabernet/Merlot/Syrah blend, featuring original artwork on the label.

JEAN LEON, PENEDÈS

To describe Jean Leon's life as 'unusual' is a bit like saying that Shakespeare could write a bit. It's not untrue, but barely does the subject justice. Leon's story is one of family tragedy, draft evasion, midnight flits, jumped ships, vagrancy, celebrities, glamour, Hollywood's golden age and, finally, wine.

Long story short: having stowed away on a ship to the States and (eventually) made good money serving Hollywood celebs in his Beverly Hills restaurant, La Scala, Leon bought himself a sizable wine estate in Penedès in 1962. His intention: to make a five-star wine with his name on it that he could serve to Sinatra, Brando et al. To that end, he planted it not with local grape varieties, but with French heavyweights – Cabernet Sauvignon, Cabernet Franc and Chardonnay – a decision that sent shockwaves through Spain's wine scene.

As you'd expect from a winery with a far-from traditional backstory (few winemakers, you can assume, have personally delivered a plate of pasta to Marilyn Monroe's apartment), this is a fun place to visit.

It's not that unusual for a winery to offer short (two-hour) courses on how to taste wine, but here you can also have a go at blending different wines together to create your own cuvée. As elsewhere, there's the opportunity to take a gentle ramble through the vines, but you can also work up an appetite by cycling, Nordic walking or, if that's a bit much, riding a Segway down the rows. The 'dramatised tour' where Jean Leon (all right, an actor) tells you his life story and winery dream is a wonderful touch, too.

CLOS MOGADOR, PRIORAT

René Barbier was one of the Gratallops pioneers (p102) – a group of idealists who moved into Priorat (in his case from France) in the 1980s with the intention of making extraordinary wine in this remote, inhospitable corner of Spain.

It's not been easy. Yields are suicidally low and in this tough climate on such poor soils the vines need a lot of work. Barbier calls it an act of love, and having worked for a while at Pomerol icon Pétrus, he knows all about wines demanding their pound of flesh.

But the results can be spectacular and his terraces on the steep slopes overlooking Gratallops village produce a wine that, along with the likes of Pingus in Ribera del Duero, is regularly cited as signalling the birth of the modern Spanish fine wine scene.

Visits may seem pricey, but they're worth it. Partly because they take in not just the winery and cellars, but also a drive out into the vineyards, which are always impressive in Priorat. And also because the tasting includes a white, plus the Clos Mogador and Manyetes reds – two of Spain's finest tintos. Just make sure you book early.

RAIMAT, COSTERS DEL SEGRE

What sets great people apart is often the ability to see things that nobody else does. Back in 1914, Manuel Raventós, head of cava giant Codorníu (p103), came across what is now the Raimat estate. Then it was little more than an unloved moonscape with the abandoned bones of an old castle. But Raventós believed that, with irrigation, this woebegone land could be coaxed back into life, and set about proving it.

To do so he had to build 100km of canals to fetch water, and the workers had to battle salty soil, voracious rabbits and mosquitoes, so it wasn't exactly a quick win. But, bit by bit, the vineyard established itself and in 1988 Raimat built its glorious new winery. Set into the side of the hill, architect Domingo Triay's 'temple of wine' manages to be both sympathetic to the environment and strikingly space age at the same time.

All in all, it's a 100 per cent interesting visit from start to finish. The stroll through the vines gives you the chance to discover how Raimat made the transformation from Lear-esque blasted heath to vineyards now certified sustainable. The winery itself is still jaw-dropping 30 years after it was opened, and the wines (you get to taste three) are an idiosyncratic mixture of local, international and Spanish varieties.

CASTELL DEL REMEI, COSTERS DEL SEGRE

This spot, it seems, has always been popular. There have been people living here since Roman times (there's a Latin gravestone on display), and evidence of winemaking as far back as 1780.

But in wine terms, it properly took off in the latter 19th century when phylloxera started to destroy vineyards in France. The Girona family, who owned the place at the time, knew an opportunity when they saw one and brought in a load of unemployed Frenchmen to sort out the vineyards and winery. In celebration of their cleverness, they added four crenellated towers at each corner of the building: instant castle!

OTT architecture notwithstanding, this is a lovely spot. At one time 50 families lived here, and there are a good number of buildings to poke around: a workshop, distillery, flour mill and olive oil press. There's also a lake (good for birdwatching), a chapel with painted ceilings, and a restaurant serving local food at lunchtimes.

And, of course, there's a tour – but if you're feeling a bit cellared out, you can just potter aimlessly and spend a bit of time in the shop. Castell del Remei is part of a group that owns several other wineries in Costers del Segre and Conca de Barberà, and since all their products are on sale here, you can taste your way around a fair bit of Catalonia without leaving the building. From high vineyards (700–800m above sea level) with hot summers and cold winters, the reds are particularly excellent. The Gotim Bru is a real bargain.

CELLERS SCALA DEI, PRIORAT

There's no shortage of drama in Cellers Scala Dei. Most obviously, there's the landscape, which is impressive even by the high standards of Priorat – a series of towering mountains, jagged bluffs and arid vineyard terraces. It doesn't look much like somewhere that humans would choose to settle, but the early inhabitants, to quote *The Blues Brothers*, were on a mission from God...

Legend has it that a shepherd boy awoke one night to see angels descending to earth down a heavenly ladder. He told the local priest and in 1163 an order of Carthusian monks duly came and established a priory, which they called Scala Dei – God's staircase.

The monks are long gone, but a tiny village, Escaladei, remains, with the winery itself on the site of the old monastery. It's best known for its opaque Garnacha/Carinena blend, Cartoixa Scala Dei, a wine of head-spinning concentration and alcohol that, if you drink a bottle, might well make you see angels descending a ladder, too.

Not all the wines are so rich, however. As well as the typical glinting dark *llicorella* (slate/quartz) soils of Priorat, Scala Dei also has some vines on limestone. Grown at 700m above sea level, these can have a freshness unusual for this DO.

There are daily tours that involve a tasting of three wines, though if you have an implacable hatred of oak barrels, you can just do the tasting.

TORRES, PENEDÈS

There's a big tradition in Catalonia of building human towers – *castells*. Google it – it's terrifying: you'll find yourself peering at the screen through your fingers with morbid fascination, waiting for the tottering spire of humanity to come crashing down in a tangle of limbs.

The pastime is particularly popular in Vilafranca, just south-west of Barcelona, which is fitting, because this is also the home of Torres, where the concept of adding extra layers of achievement to solid foundations provides a nice metaphor for its wine success.

In a country not well known for wine brands of any description, Torres stands out – a truly global name, with good wines and a hearteningly progressive attitude to the environment. It shows no sign whatsoever of tumbling down, but keeps on adding layers around the world, with estates in Chile and California as well as across Spain.

Penedès, though, is its homeland and has been for five generations, during which time it has been an early adopter of modern winemaking techniques and has sensitively used both French and native grape varieties.

The Pacs del Penedès visitor centre is an hour from Barcelona and the Selection tour is decent value for a two-hour visit, taking in a scoot round the Mas la Plana vineyard (home of the single-vineyard wine of the same name), a cellar visit and a tasting of five wines. There's also no shortage of add-ons if you fancy something more educational: wine and cheese/ham pairings or a two-and-a-half-hour wine-tasting workshop.

The food thing is done in more depth at the company's farmhouse restaurant, Mas Rabell, which offers eight courses of tapas or a tapas/main course/dessert combo plus wine. If you fancy something genuinely different, there's also a blindfolded tapas and wine tasting aimed at challenging your palate. Rest assured that it's less messy than it sounds.

MIQUEL OLIVER, MALLORCA

It might seem odd including a Balearic winery in a section that's predominantly Catalan, but the islands are easily accessible from Barcelona by ferry. And in any case, if you're heading out that way, you should make the effort to visit a non-mainland winery – not least because, according to the locals, California's first vines came from here. Mallorcan priest Fray Junípero Serra founded 20 missions on America's west coast, and every time he went over, he took some vine cuttings along in his luggage, which he'd then plant in the gardens.

If you want to see the kind of wines these vines might have made, you should try Oliver's Mont Ferrutx red, a blend of the local Callet, Fogoneu and Manto Negro grapes, or the white Son Caló Blanc, made from Prensal. Reds are the main focus here, and there's a strong range of wines made from Cabernet, Syrah, Merlot and other 'international' varieties.

Four tours are available that take in varying combinations of vineyards, old cellar, new cellar, tasting, tapas and food. Importantly, for this most touristy of islands, the place is also well set up for children.

NORTH-WEST/ GALICIA

If you're looking for a quick way to hustle some money from your friends, you could show them a photo of Spain's north-west corner and promise them £20 if they guess where it is – the only caveat being that each guess costs them a fiver. You're guaranteed to be up on the deal.

Partly it's because not many foreigners come to this north-western corner of Spain. There are, of course, hardy trekkers walking the Camino de Santiago, the pilgrims' path that pulls in hikers from all over Europe and beyond, but the Costa del Sol this isn't.

Mostly it's because Galicia doesn't conform to any of the images that we typically associate with Spain. With its crenellated coastline, sentinel pine forests and mighty sea lochs, its geography is more like that of Scotland or Scandinavia. Visit Santiago de Compostela – the end destination of the aforementioned *camino* – and you'll find high stone buildings, grey flagstoned alleys and the skirl of Celtic bagpipes (*gaitas*) wafting out of open windows.

The climate is similarly more Caledonian than the rest of the country. Bathed by the Atlantic, it's a cooler, damper and softer place – one of the reasons that so many sun-battered Madrileños flee the summer *infierno* for the north coast in July and August.

It's little wonder, then, that the wines made here are so different from those produced elsewhere in Spain. Galicia is home to the country's best blancos and it's no coincidence that so many big names from Rioja have bought vineyards out here in the last 20 years – they recognised they could produce something that they just couldn't back home: a genuinely world-class white wine.

Albariño is the star variety – a grape that treads a hugely likeable spectrum of flavours from peachy to zesty. Traditionally, it's a wine made without any time in oak, but a growing number of wineries are now experimenting with barrels. As a variety, it goes brilliantly with the region's seafood, which is exceptional even by the standards of Spain.

Albariño is mostly grown in the Rías Baixas (pronounced Ree-as Bye-shas) – the most westerly edges of Galicia and the region's best-known denominación de origen. Santiago de Compostela and Pontevedra are good bases from which to explore.

As you head away from the sea, where Rías Baixas starts to merge into Ribeiro, you'll find a heady cocktail of grapes more usually found in Portuguese whites – mostly Treixadura and Loureiro but also Godello. The latter has established a name for itself as Spain's second great white grape (after Albariño) and it's at its best in Valdeorras.

It's fitting that these shores, thrashed by the furious Atlantic, should be so known for their blancos, which are as refreshing as a blast of sea air. But it's not all about white wines, particularly once you head inland a bit.

Bierzo, about 150km from the coast, is sheltered from the worst effects of the ocean by hills. It's still relatively cool – certainly a lot gentler in climate than Castile to the east – with summer highs typically in the mid-20s. But it's also drier than Albariño country, and this combination has proved fantastic for the local Mencia grape. Fresh, almost crisp in style, it makes great summer/midweek reds at a decent price. No wonder it's much loved by sommeliers.

North-west Spain is a wonderful place to visit, with majestic scenery pretty much everywhere you look, and a less punishing summer climate than other areas of the country. Rías Baixas should be on every wine lover's list, but the magnificent Ribeiro and, particularly, Ribeira Sacra ought to be on your radar, too.

The only disadvantage? This isn't an especially quick region to get around, particularly once you're in the inland vineyard areas. Nor, stuck as it is above the top of Portugal, is it always easy to get to – Galicia is 600km from Madrid, and even further from Rioja.

So it pays to err on the side of caution when putting together your itinerary and add in a bit of dawdling time. Thankfully, there's plenty in this part of Spain to encourage you to do just that.

RÍAS BAIXAS

MARTÍN CÓDAX

Supplied by the fruit of some 300 families' vineyards, this is the biggest winery in the region, though with average vineyard sizes in Galicia decidedly Lilliputian, it's not particularly large by the standards of your average Spanish co-op.

What it is, however, is considerably more forward-thinking. The Salnés Valley is famous for being the birthplace (or rebirth-place) of Albariño, and Martín Códax showcases the grape in every format, from sparkling through its usual dry to off-dry and even late-harvest. Albariño is an easy grape to like, but with a line-up like this, you ought to find something to rave about.

Options for visitors vary from the super-cheap (for a tour and two-wine tasting) to the still-not-that-pricey (tour, four-wine tasting and visit to its top vineyard). The vines here are definitely worth a look. To keep the grapes away from the often-damp ground they're trained on high horizontal stakes, or *parras*. Oh, and in case you were wondering, the winery is named after a medieval Galician troubadour, who sang of love, loss and the sea.

PALACIO DE FEFIÑANES

Palacio de Fefiñanes is one of the oldest wineries in Galicia – and a benchmark producer of Albariño. If you want to see how good this white grape can be, pay a visit to its renaissance building in the centre of the town of Cambados. Fefiñanes was the first to bottle Albarino as a single-variety wine back in 1928, so it's had longer than anyone else to get the hang of it and its wines are subtly beautiful. As the urbane owner, Juan Gil de Araújo, puts it, 'An excess of aromas doesn't necessarily improve the wine. Will people still love it after the second glass?'

The range isn't extensive – just four wines – but each is vinified differently, and together they provide a fascinating example of how you can make a small line-up with one variety, from one region, and still create a selection that's distinctive.

The standard visit starts in the courtyard of arms, and takes in a small vineyard, some lovely bijou cellars and a tasting. A bit extra will get you three very different expressions of very good Albariño.

TERRAS GAUDA

Albariño might be the star player in the Rías Baixas, but it's not the only grape on show. If you head away from the sea, other varieties start to appear – and there's an ample selection of them at this winery in the Rosal Valley.

All Terras Gauda's tours take in the vineyards (by minibus in the summer months, walked the rest of the year), which gives you a chance to see two things that influence the flavour of its wines: the soil, which is schist rather than the granite you'll find in the Salnés Valley, and the way the vines are strung up on wires rather than hung high off the ground in *parras*.

REST OF THE NORTH-WEST

ADEGAS AMEDO, RIBEIRA SACRA

This modern winery, founded in 1997, might not have the heritage that others do in the region, but in a DO as stunning as Ribeira Sacra that's not necessarily an issue. The sweeping curves of the hillsides and vine-dotted slopes tumbling down to lazily ambling rivers will have you snapping photos till your memory card bursts.

Of course, there's the basic tour-plus-tasting option. But for a very reasonable price, you can follow one of the winery team in your car to the vineyards – and all the best views. Those who prefer something more 'winey' can pay a bit more for a tutored tasting of the entire range. The place is well set up for kids, too, with two different activities available. If you fancy doing the 'vineyard drive' as part of a more adventurous day, you can tie it in with a one-hour paddle along the River Sil by canoe. Available through Enoturismo Galicia, it's probably the most spectactular (and peaceful) way to view this most beautiful of Spanish DOs.

CASAL DE ARMÁN, RIBEIRO

Ribeiro butts up against the eastern edge of Rías Baixas, straddling both sides of the Miño river. Further to the west, it marks the border with Portugal, and the latter's influence is clearly seen in Casal de Armán's wines. The standard white, for instance, is 90 per cent Loureiro with a dash of Godello and Albariño thrown in. You wouldn't find wine like that in the Rías Baixas' Salnés Valley, just 50km to the north-west.

Built in the 1990s by a family who've been growing grapes in the region for four generations, Casal de Armán has a nice personal feel. You can get to know the whole portfolio of half-a-dozen wines very easily, and there's a good chance you'll run into at least a couple of the family – particularly if you stay in their hotel. Located more or less in the middle of the Ribeiro DO, this attractive 18th-century stone farmhouse is a great place from which to explore the whole region.

RECTORAL DE AMANDI, RIBEIRA SACRA

Visit Ribeira Sacra and it's easy to see why monks and hermits settled here in the early days of Christianity. It's stunningly beautiful: lush hills, plunging valleys and forests. And where there are monks, there are vineyards. It's reckoned that wines from here were shipped across the Empire back to the togaed bigwigs in the Roman senate.

Housed in a converted 16th-century rectory, this winery is the beating heart of the region. Not only is it the biggest producer, but it was also the driving force behind the creation of the Ribeira Sacra DO in the first place.

The ancient walls house a modern setup that makes only Mencia. It does take visits from the public, but during the week it's tastings only. If you'd like to see the vineyards or more of the winery, or visit on a weekend, arrange it in advance.

PEIQUE, BIERZO

You wouldn't come to Valtuille de Abajo for the nightlife. With less than 200 houses, it's not exactly downtown New York. What it is, however, is surrounded by vineyards, 40 hectares of which belong to the brothers-and-sister team of Luis, Mar and Jorge Peique who built a small winery to vinify the crop from vineyards planted by their grandparents.

There's a little Godello (white) and an old-vine Garnacha Tintorera (aka Alicante Bouschet), which you don't see every day. But this is mostly about Mencia, the local Bierzo red, and on old bush vines like these, it shows depth.

There's nothing too fancy about this place – the joy is in spending time with a family born and brought up in the area who had the guts to back their dream.

As well as the cellar and tasting, the two-hour visit takes in the vineyards, giving you plenty of opportunities to photograph gnarly old bush vines. You can upgrade to the Winemaker Tour, which includes the chance to taste not-yet-available wines from barrel and tank, plus three different vintages of the same wine over lunch in the village. It's a great, personal way to understand a little-known but increasingly fashionable region.

PITTACUM, BIERZO

Now part of the same group that owns Terras Gauda in Rías Baixas (p110), Pittacum was originally set up by six friends aiming to rescue the local Mencia grape variety. Upon excavating the land to build the winery, they found a Roman amphora called a *pittacum* and liked the way it tied into the region's wine-growing past. Boom – they had a name for their new venture.

It's a small operation, so visits only last an hour or so, which is more than enough time to take in the old winery, barrel room and the bottling line. The star attraction is the tasting, which gives a chance to try two Mencia reds from different sites: Pittacum from the warmer vineyards, and the Petit Pittacum, from cooler, clay soils in the north and east of Bierzo with a more Atlantic influence.

It's a nice example of the effects of terroir, and you can add extra wines for a small supplement. The cost of the tastings is taken off any bottles you buy.

VIÑA MEÍN, RIBEIRO

This is the kind of winery that people dream of retiring to in order to get started on that novel they've always intended to write. A small estate folded away into the hills of Ribeiro, surrounded by forests, it's a truly inspiring spot. It's possible to rent a room in its 'Casal' country house and each one backs onto the vineyards, so you can feel at one with nature.

There's a lovely walk through the vineyards to the nearby village, though if literary inspiration still proves elusive, you could try kick-starting it with some of the wines. Viña Meín's speciality is whites, specifically the Ribeiran blends of grapes such as Treixadura, Godello, Loureiro (and others), and they're wonderfully fresh, aromatic and complex. It only owns 16 hectares of vineyard, and doesn't export a great deal either, so this may well be your best chance to taste them.

DUERO VALLEY

As Frank Sinatra almost sang: they've got an awful lot of castles in Castile. They're scattered right the way across this high, dusty region; crumbling monuments marking the limits of the Moorish invasion of Spain over 1,000 years ago. And some of that stubborn resistance of the frontier-land still remains. With its big skies, never-ending horizons and lazily swirling dust clouds, it's the sort of place you expect to run into a poncho-clad Clint Eastwood riding an equally taciturn nag.

This is a region of big contrasts: of bitterly cold winters and broiling summers (the famous description of Madrid as 'nine months of winter, three months of hell' applies just as well here, too), while the wines run the gamut from head-spinning reds to lip-smacking whites; cheerful rusticity to some of the most expensive bottles in Europe.

The star red region is Ribera del Duero. Only 100km or so west of Rioja, there's a kind of football team-style rivalry between the two denominations over which is Spain's top dog for tintos. Rioja might have the heritage, but Ribera increasingly has the attention of the collectors, critics and sommeliers. The aristocrat versus the arriviste – it's a little like the tussle between the châteaux of the Médoc and the garage wines of Pomerol.

What's extraordinary about Ribera is how quickly this reputation has been created, and how close the region came to withering away completely. When the denominación de origen was established in 1982 there were only seven producers. Today, there are nearly 300.

The star grape is Tempranillo – here called, rather dismissively, Tinto del País, or 'country red' – though Merlot and, particularly, Cabernet Sauvignon are sometimes used (and blended) to good effect as well, most notably at the region's most famous winery, Vega Sicilia. Sadly, it doesn't accept non-trade visitors so you'll have to worship from afar. The key to all wine production in this area is the altitude: the Castilian plain is around 700m above sea level. Take slopes into account and some vineyards sit almost 900m up. As they're a long way from the coast, there's no moderating sea influence and the mercury climbs relentlessly during the day. But the altitude means it also drops quickly at night, allowing grapes to retain their freshness.

The effect is to give Ribera del Duero's wines a winning combination of weight and brightness, of sweet fruit and fresh crunch, and it's why the best ones from the best vintages are so sought after – they retain this glorious balance for years, while also acquiring extra layers of complexity.

If Ribera is all about reds, Rueda is its blanco counterpart. Like Ribera, it was on its knees in the 1970s, but has dragged itself up off the canvas to become a serious rival to Galicia as Spain's number one white wine region. The key grapes here are the local Verdejo and the French interloper Sauvignon Blanc. They can be mixed together or made as separate single-varietal wines. Verdejo, with its combination of lift and gentle bitterness on the finish, is the kind of wine that sommeliers love and is great with food.

If you want a wine with serious historical chops, you should probably make an effort to take in Toro, too. Columbus was a big fan of the region's wines and took some with him on his voyages of discovery. Locals (perhaps mischievously) claim that he nicknamed one of his ships La Pinta after the region's means of measuring wine. And if you find some of the prices in Ribera del Duero a bit eye-watering, these should come as a relief.

One of the beauties of Castile for the wine tourist is the plethora of great cities to stay in within striking distance of vineyards: Valladolid and Burgos are both fantastic places for lovers of history. It's not far from Burgos to Rioja, either (Haro is only 90km away), so you could potentially use the city as a base to explore both Rioja and Ribera del Duero.

RUEDA/TORO

CAMPO ELISEO, TORO

The name François Lurton might not sound very Spanish, and it isn't. Nor are Michel and Dany Rolland, his equally French partners in this venture. But the team who founded Campo Eliseo two decades ago in the Toro DO know a thing or two about picking promising wine spots, having done so all around the world.

They were attracted by the region's untapped potential. This was a place that had old vines, great terrain and a reliable climate, but for the most part seemed to be content making cheap and cheerful table wine. Their ambitions ran far deeper.

On these stony, alluvial soils, the 40-year-old-plus Tinta de Toro vines produce grapes of real concentration and depth, the big shifts in temperature between day and night preserving natural acidity and freshness in the wine and giving it elegance and structure along with its ripeness. They make only two Toro wines – the approachable Campo Alegre and the estate Campo Eliseo, which is produced for mid- to long-term ageing – though in 2016 they also started making white wines in neighbouring Rueda.

There are a range of visits, all taking in the 18th-century ancestral home. The pick of the bunch is the 'Oeno-Road in Vineyards'. At four hours, it's great value, with a guided tour of the vines, pine forests and winery, plus a tasting.

BODEGAS MOCÉN, RUEDA

Restaurateur José Luis Ruíz Solaguren came to Rueda with two friends from Madrid and a head full of dreams about setting up a winery. But when they arrived, they found a place of abandoned cellars and desperation. José Luis's two friends promptly thought better about the whole thing and high-tailed it home. But he stuck to his guns and bought some tatty 16th-century cellars.

To describe it as an act of faith barely does it justice. The world was not falling over itself to drink Rueda in the late 1980s. But José Luis's commitment (you could say contrariness) has paid off. The subterranean maze of cellars, 3km of narrow passageways, Moorish arches and side-alcoves full of resting bottles, is beautiful.

FARIÑA, TORO

Ask locals who's the main man in Toro and they'll say Manuel Fariña. It wasn't just that he was quick to dispense with old ideas that he thought were damaging and introduce modern technology, but also because he was a vocal advocate of the denomination's wines all round the world. It was largely his efforts that led to the creation of the Toro DO in the first place in 1987.

Given the weight of achievement behind it, you might expect a visit here to be a bit po-faced. But not a bit of it. Despite all that Fariña has done for the region, there's no sense of portentous self-importance. As well as a series of pre-set offerings for visitors – including a wine-tasting class and a pricier option that takes in an art exhibition and a hearty lunch – it's sufficiently relaxed to allow visitors to cherry-pick different elements to create their own tailor-made tour.

RIBERA DEL DUERO

AALTO

If you were looking to create a five-star winery from scratch, you'd be hard pushed to improve on the blueprint followed by these guys.

Aalto is the partnership of the one-time head of the Ribera del Duero wine council, Javier Zaccagnini, and Mariano García, former winemaker at Riberan heavyweight Vega Sicilia. They have 32 hectares of top-class vineyards across Ribera, plus access to another 90 hectares of very old vines, farmed by trusted growers whose efforts they oversee.

There is no messing around with 'accessible' or 'affordable' here. They never make more than two wines: Aalto and (in the best years) Aalto PS, their top creation. The accolades from wine critics, sommeliers and magazines have been continuous, and it is very much one of Spain's finest reds.

Visits are available on request and by prior booking. Amazingly, there's no charge – they consider guests to be 'friends of the winery', but they would expect a degree of knowledge, interest and respect on the part of any visitor. Anyone committed/intelligent/tasteful enough to be reading this book ought to be fine.

Tasting-wise, you get to try the two current vintages, though they're not averse to opening something older if you're prepared to pay for it. It's worth considering, for sure.

ABADÍA RETUERTA

Officially, the wines from this one-time abbey are marginally outside the Ribera del Duero denominación de origen. But what this large estate of mostly Tempranillo (with a little Cabernet and Syrah added for good measure) proves is that you don't always need to be in a five-star appellation to make five-star wine.

It's got one heck of a history, too, with the original building having been part of a 12th-century plan to shore up Christianity across the region – a kind of front line in the battle against the spread of *los moros* from north Africa. Like all monks, those of the Premonstratensian order planted vines – with one unusually forward-thinking abbot the first person to bring French grape varieties into Spain.

Its best-known wine, the Selección Especial, is still a blend of Tempranillo and Cabernet Sauvignon, but it also has some fine, silky, single-vineyard (*pago*) wines on offer that are, variously, 100 per cent Cabernet, 100 per cent Syrah and 100 per cent Tempranillo.

It has an amazing range of visit options, too, taking in everything from helicopters and horses, to bicycles, barrel-tastings and even bees. None are especially cheap, but this is a special place, so you can't begrudge it charging for 900 years of history.

Its hotel is one of the best on the Iberian peninsula, no question, but if the tariffs are a bit steep for you, Abadía Retuerta is only a short hop (30km) from Valladolid and 20km from Pesquera (p118), so you could make it part of a day touring Ribera del Duero's western edges.

ARZUAGA

The life of the wine tourist is tough. Long days, lots of standing around in cold cellars and hot, dusty vineyards – to say nothing of bottle after bottle to be forced down. So if it's all getting a bit much, Arzuaga is a perfect place to stop for some recalibration.

It has put together a thoroughly attractive hotel and spa complex, which offers several wine-related activities. If a wine jacuzzi is too left-field (though it's not as weird as it sounds), there's always the more classic sauna or hot-stone treatments.

Arzuaga is a huge estate – 1,400 hectares, only 150 hectares of which are vineyard – and its Thematic Morning package makes the most of everything it has. As well as cellar tours and a tasting, visitors get to stroll through a game reserve full of wild boar and deer, learn to tell one grape variety from another in the vineyard, taste grapes direct from the vine and, er, hug an ancient oak tree.

Obviously, some of these activities are a) weather dependent and b) seasonal, but pick the right time of year and it could all add up to a fun three hours.

The restaurant serves venison (*ciervo*) and wild boar (*jabalí*) and you get an enticing discount if you've done anything more than the basic 45-minute cellar visit. As for tasting, try comparing the difference between its crianza – where Tempranillo is blended with Cabernet Sauvignon and Merlot – and the reserva, which is almost entirely Tempranillo.

PAGO DE LOS CAPELLANES

Pago de los Capellanes is, in a sense, the Spanish wine story in microcosm. Its name means 'estate of the chaplains', referencing the fact that the land (like so much of Spain) used to belong to the Church, and its wines are 100 per cent Tinto del País, which has been grown in the region for centuries. Stylistically, though, there's a juicy sleekness to the wines that marks them out as thoroughly modern expressions of Ribera.

Visit its Pedrosa de Duero winery and winding corridors and 18th-century architecture are conspicuous by their absence. This is a place of art exhibitions and big windows, rather than dusty tapestries and medieval coats of arms.

Pedrosa is the heart of the appellation and produces some of Ribera's best wines. The clay/gravel/sand soils (think St-Émilion in France) are excellent for vines since they drain brilliantly. You might not be able to pick out the detail in the soil if you take one of the balloon flights it sometimes offers, but, lifting off at dawn, they're an unforgettable way to get a perspective on the whole region.

If they're a bit beyond your budget, the other two visits are no slouches, either: both include a tasting of the Godello white from the owners' estate in Valdeorras – handy if you've not made it over to the north-west. And the Picón Tour allows you to explore the growing and vinification of one of the region's best single-vineyard sites, which comprises just two hectares of low-yielding vines. The cost might seem steep, but since you get to taste a wine that retails for three times that price per bottle it's not bad going.

PESQUERA

If there's one man who's responsible for the resurgence of Ribera del Duero, it's probably Alejandro Fernández. And yet, amazingly, he had no formal wine education at all when he set up his winery (named after his home village) in 1972. Fernández had made a decent living redesigning beet harvesters (!) and brought the same creativity and single-mindedness to bear on wine.

Along with a healthy disregard for fashion, Fernández had a rare affinity with Ribera's signature red grape variety, Tinto del País (Tempranillo), and before long his wines were attracting the attention of critics everywhere – not least the super-influential American Robert Parker, who dubbed it 'the Spanish Pétrus'.

Perhaps because he has no formal wine education, or perhaps because he's wonderfully bloody-minded, Fernández rarely follows the herd. His wines are unfiltered, and his vines are strung up on wires and irrigated when necessary. Famously, he's quoted as saying that 'no one gets a headache from drinking Pesquera' – a theory you could put to the test if you stay at its Pesquera AF Hotel in Peñafiel. Tours of the winery and cellars last 90 minutes and need to be pre-booked. At weekends they're in Spanish only.

ISMAEL ARROYO

A family-run winery not far from the small valley village of Sotillo de la Ribera, Ismael Arroyo (aka ValSotillo) is one of the most respected wineries in the region. The family had been growing grapes for over 400 years before they threw their weight and influence behind the creation of the Ribera del Duero denominación de origen in 1982, and some of that heritage comes through in their winery: bottles are aged in a magnificent 16th-century cellar, with getting on for 1km of underground passageways carved out of the stone.

Like many wineries in Ribera del Duero, they only use one grape – Tinto del País (Tempranillio) – and they do great things with it. There is an affordable Mesoneros de Castilla range, but the flagship ValSotillo wines (which take in crianza, reserva and gran reserva) are what it's all about – supple, complex examples of how good this grape can be in this location.

Ismael Arroyo runs tours all year round at set times of day, and they're pretty reasonably priced, especially if you speak Spanish – the foreign-language versions are a bit more. They include a tasting of the crianza, but it's worth paying a bit extra to try the reserva as well.

Off the main road south out of Burgos, it's easily doable as part of a day trip from the city.

SOUTH

It might seem odd gathering together the entire southern half of Spain into one section. La Mancha is, after all, the biggest wine-growing region in the country – and one of the biggest areas for vineyards anywhere in the world. But while there's unquestionably a great deal of wine produced on the scorched plains south of Madrid, not much of it is worth going out of your way for. A good place if you're tracing the tragi-comic footsteps of Don Quixote, not so good if you fancy tilting at vineyards rather than windmills.

Southern Spain is not an easy place to be a wine tourist. Distances are huge, quality patchy and the climate unforgiving: searingly hot in the summer, freezing cold in the winter and blasted by strong winds pretty much all year round – the reason, of course, for all those windmills. April–June and September–November are probably the best times to visit. The Canary Islands, off the west African coast (also mentioned in this section), have a more accommodating climate.

Much of La Mancha is planted either with Tempranillo (called Cencibel here), a workhorse white called Airén that's of little interest, or international varieties such as Cabernet Sauvignon and Merlot. If you're in search of something different, the Canaries (again) is a good bet. The two best mainland regions are Utiel-Requena, west of Valencia, and Jumilla, west of Alicante. Both of these denominaciónes have overcome hardships – Jumilla, for instance, got clobbered with phylloxera as recently as the late 1980s – but both also have attractions for wine-curious visitors.

For Jumilla it's Monastrell. The grape is known as Mourvèdre in France, but at these latitudes and on these sandy soils, it is capable of something different and, frankly, better: a supple richness balanced with an attractive lift and perfume. The revolution is some way advanced and it's worth trying to visit some wineries to see for yourself if you can.

Monastrell's equivalent in Utiel-Requena is Bobal. Big, deep-coloured and powerful, it was traditionally used to add colour and muscle to more anaemic wines in the region and further north. Producers are waking up to the idea that its perceived lack of finesse was less to do with the grape and more about how it was grown and vinified, and there are a growing number of fine examples coming out of the DO.

The Sherry Triangle, between Jerez de la Frontera, Sanlúcar de Barrameda and El Puerto de Santa María in the south-west, is the one part where it's hard to go wrong.

As a drinks category, sherry might be between high points (he said tactfully), but there's no denying the wealth of heritage in this corner of Andalucía. There are world-famous names with quirky old buildings and ancient cellars pretty much everywhere. The sherry-making process is different from that of table wine, and relies heavily on techniques that have barely changed in hundreds of years. Key to it all are the cellars full of ancient barrels that are scribbled with the cryptic chalk marks of the *capataz*. Visits to sherry bodegas are as atmospheric as they are educational, and you can guarantee coming out with a newfound respect and love for this classic wine style.

Sherry is a food wine par excellence, and the best way to sample it is over a classic lengthy Andalusian meal. The city of Jerez has any number of good restaurants plus, it sometimes seems, a big-name wine company round every corner.

If you're coming down this way, a couple of days in Jerez, followed by a day in each of the other two sherry towns would be the minimum. Oh, and make the effort to take in some of the Pueblos Blancos. Arcos de la Frontera – its whitewashed buildings clinging to a limestone crag above the Guadalete river – is a spectacular visit.

ANDALUCÍA

FERNANDO DE CASTILLA, JEREZ

If you're even halfway interested in sherry, this is a must visit. It spent many years just making brandy, but in 2000 decided to branch out into the wine side with a simple brief: to make the best sherries in the region. It's succeeded, too.

This magnificent set of wines regularly wins gold medals in competitions across its entire range. With standards this high, it's hard to pick out a star, though the palo cortado shows the classic combination of fino-like zip and freshness with a long, complex oloroso-style finish.

Based in Jerez's old town, the winery runs a tour and tasting where the wines are drawn directly from the cask, and finishes with a civilised *copa y tapa*.

GONZÁLEZ BYASS, JEREZ

He's the most famous uncle in the wine world. Tío Pepe – uncle Joe – was a relative of the company's founder, Manuel González, and a sherry connoisseur who was buying and blending finos when the young Manuel started out. Rumour has it that he had a special fino solera of his top wine, which he kept for his friends and best customers, and became known as the Solera del Tío Pepe. When Manuel's sherry business began to grow he kept the name in tribute to his uncle.

For a big, globally recognised brand, Tío Pepe is still ridiculously good – a benchmark against which most fino is still judged today. Its name is as recognisable as the jaunty jacket, hat and guitar in which the bottle is dressed on billboards and neon-lit façades across the country.

As visits go, this is about as good as it gets, with wonderful, slightly quirky architecture, great products and as many dine-out stories as you care to mention – all just a sherry-spit from the cathedral. The barrel room, with its layers of ancient casks, signed in chalk by everyone from Margaret Thatcher to Pablo Picasso, radiates history, while younger (and young at heart) visitors will enjoy being driven around on a mini train. Uncle Joe's old tasting cellar has been preserved since his death in 1887.

There are also more specialised tours. If you want to get to understand the vineyards of Jerez as well as the production process, the one that takes you to the heart of Jerez Superior with the *capataz de la viña* (head of the vineyard) looks a real opportunity. Check out the famous chalky *albariza* soil as you follow up your visit with breakfast, lunch or dinner.

GUTIÉRREZ COLOSÍA, EL PUERTO DE SANTA MARÍA

Fino sherry is often described as having a briny whiff of the sea about it, and if you want to test this out in situ, you can't do better than visit Gutiérrez Colosía. At the mouth of the River Guadalete, it's the closest of all the region's bodegas to the Atlantic. This means perfect conditions for the development of the essential flor on the sherry and a light, nutty, fine-boned fino as a result.

Gutiérrez Colosía was set up in 1838, and the high ceilings, Moorish arches and gentle patina of mould hint at the timelessness of its production techniques. Apart from the tourists taking selfies on their smartphones, it's easy to imagine things haven't changed much here in the last 180 years.

The winery recently set up a restaurant next door, selling decent modern interpretations of classic Andalusian tapas. With a large sherry list (natch) and a wide range of craft beers, it's an excellent place for a snack, lunch or dinner. The tasting menu, which includes a different wine with each dish, seems a particularly good idea.

HIDALGO LA GITANA, SANLÚCAR DE BARRAMEDA

If Tío Pepe is the world's most famous fino, La Gitana, with its iconic Gypsy girl label, is its manzanilla equivalent – a standard of elegance and reliability against which all competitors measure themselves.

It's been on the go since 1792 and is now run by the eighth generation of the Hidalgo family, who have pushed for quality throughout. Their Manzanilla Pasada Pastrana (from old vines, single vineyard and aged for 12 years) is a startlingly good wine, and if you discover that you like manzanilla on your visit, this is the bottle to take home as a treat.

The basic guided tour is decent, featuring a tasting of five wines, one of which is manzanilla straight from the cask. But if you want to try some special sherry, it's worth shelling out for the Manzanilla and VORS wines option. VORS are sherries that are over 30 years old, so getting to try three of them (an amontillado, an oloroso and a palo cortado) along with a couple of top-class manzanillas is a real treat. It's a two-hour visit and requires prior reservation.

OSBORNE, EL PUERTO DE SANTA MARÍA

The Osborne group has a history going back to the 1770s, and is best known for its black bull logo – still silhouetted against mountain sides all around Spain. Its bodega is a few blocks back from the river in El Puerto de Santa María, not far from Gutiérrez Colosía (p121), and has managed to combine the 'history plus characterful old buildings' aspect with an attractive modern shop and some great food matchings to create a well-rounded visitor experience.

The pairing of different tapas with various sherry styles is only available in the summer, but if you're a fan of five-star Spanish ham, the stand-out opportunity is to try its range of VORS (30-year-old) sherries with Cinco Jotas *jamón*.

Once you've finished, you can buy some bull-branded clothing to fit your newly expanded waistline.

Take in a 'tabanco'

Even without dozens of bodegas to visit, there's no shortage of activities to demand your attention in Jerez, from ancient buildings to world-renowned riding schools. If you're there in early May, you can catch the riot of dresses, music and dancing that is the town's *feria* – all liberally washed down with more sherry than you ever thought possible.

But if you're visiting outside of *feria* time, content yourself with taking in a *tabanco*. These sherry bars are homespun, rough and ready, and utterly authentic, usually serving their wines straight from the barrel. The bijou Tabanco el Pasaje on Calle Santa María is a great example, and often has flamenco guitars and singers on its tiny stage.

WILLIAMS & HUMBERT, JEREZ

You might not have heard of Williams & Humbert, but rest assured it's a high-quality producer with a history every bit as long as its peers in the city. Set up in 1877 by two sherry-loving Brits, the winery was always focused on exporting, which explains the decidedly non-Spanish names of some of its most successful wines: Walnut Brown, A Winter's Tale, and, er, Dry Sack.

The latter is a serious fino (aged under flor for five years) – though if you visit, upgrade to try the eight-year-old Don Zoilo, which has always been one of the best finos in Jerez.

The barrel store is genuinely lovely, with striking Moorish columns and arches, and a classic sandy floor. As well as tastings and tapas, there are also equestrian demonstrations two or three times a week (depending on the time of year). Jerez is famous for its riding school, and this is a fabulous opportunity to see great horsemanship up close and for no extra cost. The show can be tied into wider packages involving various combinations of food, tastings and vineyard visits, too.

REST OF THE SOUTH

CASA DE LA ERMITA, JUMILLA

If you want to know just how many ways you can make wine with Monastrell, head to Casa de la Ermita. The grape appears on its own in its crianza wines, and is also blended with, variously, Tempranillo, Cabernet Sauvignon, Petit Verdot and Syrah. There's even a sweet red made out of it.

Casa de la Ermita has led the way with organic winemaking in this part of the world. Several parcels of its vineyard are already certified, and others are likely to join them over the next few years. The winery itself is gravity-flow, with grapes coming in the top and being processed down through the winery into the cellars without the need for pumps.

It's also in a truly lovely spot, at the heart of the protected Sierra del Carche regional park, so it's quite right that any visit includes some time in the vineyards – you might like to take a mountain bike for a spin through the vines.

If that sounds like too much hard work, at least take the trouble to check out the new 'experimental' area, where it's trying out 20 grape varieties. Some – Touriga Nacional, Gewürztraminer, Malbec – you might have heard of; others – Caladoc, Egiodola – you almost certainly won't have. Could one be the next Monastrell?

If you feel like exploring the area further, you can stay at its Casa del Labrador, which offers four double rooms, a shared kitchen, lounge and more. Totally surrounded by vines, it has views to die for.

EL VÍNCULO, LA MANCHA

Alejandro Fernández (of Pesquera fame – p118) is a man who likes a challenge, doesn't care too much for convention, and backs himself to pull off even the most apparently impossible victory – as this project proves.

Fernández bought this old Manchego homestead and converted it into a modern bodega around the turn of the millennium. But his goal was not to use the region to make affordable, exportable 'international' style wines. Oh no. What attracted him to the place was the vineyards of seriously old Tempranillo bush vines, from which he was convinced he could make great wine – and charge for it accordingly.

Somehow he's done it. The wine – made from grapes picked in August to ensure they still have some freshness – is intense but still elegant, and great value. Even so, the sight of Spanish wine drinkers paying so much for a bottle of La Mancha table wine still makes old boys do a double-take.

For visitors, it's near Campo de Criptana, home to lots of classic squat, white Manchego windmills. Twice the reason to make a trip.

FINCA ANTIGUA, LA MANCHA

You find the same names cropping up again and again in Spain's wine world – no doubt because the people who are good want to keep expanding their sphere of operation. This winery was set up by the Martínez Bujanda family (see Finca Valpiedra in Rioja, p99) early in the 21st century. Unlike Alejandro Fernández, their plan was to create a thoroughly modern winery (tick) that makes a decent amount of wine (tick) in a modern style (tick) at a good price (tick).

As you'd expect from this hot area, with wall-to-wall sunshine from mid-May to mid-September, their 400-plus hectare estate is mostly about red wine, with Cabernet Sauvignon, Garnacha, Merlot, Syrah and Tempranillo all made as single-varietal wines, plus a few more expensive multi-varietal blends.

For tourists, they're well set up, with quick 'visit, photo, tour and tasting' options for groups in a hurry, to leisurely strolls, more involved tapas and wine pairings and four-by-four rides through the vineyards. Many of these are pre-set packages, but they're quite flexible as well, and happy to put together a tasting or visit to your specifications. So if you wanted, for instance, to try their six single-varietal wines, to see how the likes of Cabernet, Shiraz and Tempranillo perform in La Mancha, they'll set it up for you.

Thoroughly modern but sensitively done, this place is a great example of 21st-century Spanish wine thinking – and reasonably close to El Vínculo (above).

VICENTE GANDÍA, UTIEL-REQUENA

Small isn't always better. This family-run winery is the biggest producer in the region, but it's also one of the best. It can claim to be one of the oldest, too. It was established in 1885 – a history that eclipses a fair few big names from Rioja – and is now on its fourth generation.

Gandía got into the kind of technology required to make technically perfect wines early on; it also cottoned on quickly to the potential of Bobal in Utiel-Requena. Its 300-hectare Hoya de Cadenas estate 90km west of Valencia is a good way to understand this renascent, but still relatively unknown denominación.

A visit here takes in the 17th-century farmhouse, thoroughly modern winery, vineyards, old cellars and an art gallery without a single canvas: instead, local artists have created their works on barrels.

If you visit, make sure to ask how the place got the name 'Hoya de Cadenas' – valley of chains. It's a good story, involving royal visits and rights of asylum.

BODEGAS MONJE, TENERIFE

The Canary Islands, it's safe to say, are a bit different. Off the west coast of Africa, and washed on all sides by the Atlantic, their climate is subtropical rather than Mediterranean, their black soils and steep slopes testament to a volcanic past that's not replicated anywhere else in Spain. Most of the tourists who flock here are sublimely indifferent to the unusual wine industry on the islands. Well, it's their loss…

The Monje family have been growing grapes and making wine round the northern edge of Tenerife for over 250 years, and a visit here should be on the bucket list of anyone who comes to the most 'winey' of the Canaries.

For starters, there's a decent restaurant with magnificent views out towards the looming crater of (the mercifully extinct) Mount Teide and down towards the Atlantic. But second, when you've finished gasping at the vistas, there's an extraordinary array of activities to get you right under the skin of the island's wine and food culture.

If wine/tapas pairing is all a bit meh for you, how about a 'sauce workshop' – three hours learning how to make the island's famous (and ubiquitous) mojo sauces? Alternatively, what about a tasting that compares bottles aged in a cellar with those stored on the sea bed? It could be the most unusual two hours you'll ever spend in a tasting room.

Failing that, there's breakfasts and lunches and a variety of tours and more conventional but eye-opening tastings as well. There are grape varieties and wine styles here that you just won't find on the mainland.

PORTUGAL

If Portuguese wine were a person, it would be a secret agent or, perhaps, a cat burglar. Certainly it's shown an amazing ability to slip under the radar when everyone is looking in the other direction. It's arguably the European wine country that's made the biggest strides in terms of quality over the last ten years, yet its story seems to be largely unreported, only picked up on by a few in the know.

It means you're in for a real treat if you visit. Not only has Portugal got a growing number of fantastic wineries and winemakers, it also has a head-turning array of native grape varieties and a staggering range of wine styles.

While it's true that lovers of fizz might be better off looking elsewhere, Portugal covers every other style from the slimmest, most saline of whites (thank you Vinho Verde) to the heftiest of reds and, of course, two absolute classics in madeira and port. The island from which the former takes its name probably wins the award for 'oddest wine-growing place on the planet' and the wine itself (heated, oxidised, apparently eternal) breaks all the rules, too. A kind of Jurassic World of wine, it's an extraordinary place to spend some time.

But if you want to follow the wine trail in only one part of Portugal, head to port country. Situated in the north, the Douro Valley runs inland from the city of Porto up through the mountains and into Spain (where the river becomes the Duero), and is a must-visit. Not just because it's home to a fascinating wine style with a seemingly endless array of great stories, but also because it's jaw-droppingly beautiful. Not for nothing is it the favoured destination of drinks writers, restaurateurs and wine merchants the world over.

Visits to the Douro split neatly into two parts. Opposite Porto, on the south side of the river, is Vila Nova de Gaia, where the port companies used to age, bottle and ship their wines. It's a wonderfully atmospheric, bustling sort of place, particularly at night when the skyline lights up with the neon signs and logos of the port lodges. This is where you'll get the full-on visitor experience, with tours, racks of barrels and towering wooden vats.

But you should also try to get upriver, too. You can drive from Porto to Régua in about an hour and a half, but the various tourist boats that amble inland are a stress-free, photo-friendly way of spending half a day. Less well-known is the train, which rattles its way erratically through the Vinho Verde region before hooking up with the river. The sudden appearance of the steep valley sides, scored by vines, tumbling down to the ribbon of dark water is striking, no matter how many times you see it. The route is acknowledged as one of the great train journeys of the world. And with the heat, silence and whitewashed port quintas clinging to the hillsides, this is one of the great wine regions of the world, too.

Dão and Bairrada, to the south of Porto, are areas with a growing reputation and the former, in particular, has a wild beauty that has barely been discovered by tourists. But if you prefer wide open spaces and recreation to history, the Alentejo provides a good 'alternative view' of Portuguese wine.

East of Lisbon, towards the Spanish border, the area has been rejuvenated over the last 15 years. If you want to make wine part of a holiday that takes in more activities or relaxation, it's highly recommended.

ALENTEJO

CORTES DE CIMA

There are times it helps to have a background in engineering, and setting up a vineyard in the middle of nowhere is definitely one of them. When Hans Jorgensen from Denmark and his American wife Carrie arrived in Portugal in 1988, having navigated their way across the Atlantic on their boat, they were looking for somewhere to set up home and raise children.

Growing grapes and making wine at the abandoned estate they'd bought seemed an attractive way to do it, but this southern bit of the Alentejo is exceptionally dry in the summer. So Hans built a dam. Engineer, you see...

In a region best known for its whites, they planted reds – and not always local ones, either. They found the French Syrah grape was particularly good – the only problem was it wasn't officially permitted. So they called the wine Incógnito and sold it as a non-appellation. The word 'ballsy' springs to mind.

Even without the great back story, this is a charming winery visit, with panoramic views and an interesting range of wines. Taking in multi-varietal blends and single varietals, it's an easy way to get to know the locals, so to speak.

HERDADE DO ESPORÃO

If you think corneal pelitic sounds like an eye complaint, you need to get to Esporão. It is, in fact, one of the seven types of soils on this 700-hectare estate, as recent research by the owners has shown. The survey was all part of a desire to understand their vineyards inside out, and ties in with a steady shift towards making them all organic.

So while it's perfectly possible to do cheaper tours and tastings here, you'd do well to upgrade to the van ride through the vines, where you'll learn all about their innovative work on sustainability, organics and diversity.

It's housed in the medieval fortified tower that appears on all the firm's bottles – a suitably defiant symbol for what is one of the best wineries in this part of Portugal. Made by garrulous Australian David Baverstock, its wines manage to be both accessible and typical.

HERDADE DA MALHADINHA NOVA

The Alentejo is a land of big, open spaces – and you'll get to see plenty of them if you come and stay here. A 450-hectare estate in the south of the region, not far from the Vale do Guadiana Natural Park, it's a place that luxuriates in the openness around it.

Malhadinha's vineyards were planted in 2001 and have grown steadily to take up 35 hectares of the property. It's a heady cocktail of mostly local grapes, supported by a few stalwart international varieties such as Cabernet Sauvignon, Syrah, Chardonnay and Viognier. There's no shortage of ambition – its top bottles cost well into double figures.

There are tours of the winery and tastings that vary in price depending on the number of glasses and the prestige of what's in them. But wine is only part of the experience here, and you'll get a lot more out of it if you stay over in the hotel. It's a thoroughly gorgeous place with a spa (including vinotherapy treatments) and cattle wandering around. And it offers enough activities to fill up a fortnight, from off-roading and canoeing on the Guadiana River to archery and parachute jumps.

HERDADE DO MOUCHÃO

If you're looking for something small and homespun, this is the visit for you. Mouchão was bought by John Reynolds around the end of the 19th century. The grandson of a Brit who'd moved here to work in the cork business, he set about planting vineyards in among the cork trees, adding an adobe winery a couple of years later as the crops came on stream. Surrounded by eucalyptus trees, it's an atmospheric spot that seems to have been barely touched by the 20th, let alone the 21st century. The red wines are still foot-trodden and aged in barrels, and the air-conditioning system consists of nothing more high-tech than leaving the windows open at night.

You're not going to get themed tastings, but you will get a lot of heart.

HERDADE DO SOBROSO

As you might be realising, this part of Portugal does relaxation well. Herdade do Sobroso doesn't quite have the bling of some of its counterparts, but it's in a lovely spot, with a more rural feel: hunting, canoeing in the lakes, and what seems to be the national pastime of flaking out by the pool, all come highly recommended.

Wine-wise, this visit is mainly about two things: the chance to wander in the vineyards and to get to know the local grapes. The whites, in particular, are nearly all made up of indigenous varieties. While the reds tend to mix Portuguese grapes with Cabernet or Syrah, the Barrique Select Tinto is made of entirely native varieties, majoring on Aragonez and Trincadeira, so you can see which style your palate prefers. It also uses quite a lot of Alicante Bouschet – which isn't that common – blending it with a wide variety of other grapes.

VILA SANTA

João Portugal Ramos is one of the stars of Portuguese wine. A consultant to seemingly half of the country's wine growers, he's made wine all over Portugal and has, over the last 25 years, set up small estates of his own, stretching from the Douro to this one, the Vila Santa winery in Estremoz, planted in 1990.

While there are a few international grapes – Cabernet, Merlot, Sauvignon Blanc et al – the overwhelming majority are the proven local performers that can tolerate the heat and drought of the country's deep south.

Because JPR makes wine across Portugal, there are some interesting tasting options available, featuring not just wines from this estate or even this region, but from a variety of DOs. The Reservas tasting might look pricey but there are some wines of serious ambition there, not least the Marquês de Borba Reserva – a mix of local reds and Cabernet Sauvignon from this estate that have been foot-trodden in an old stone Portuguese lagar.

If you want to appreciate how good a winemaker this guy is, you can have a go at stepping into his shoes for a few hours, getting to know the different grapes, then blending your own wine. Who knows? You might uncover a hidden talent.

TORRE DE PALMA

While it likes to think of itself as a wine hotel, I reckon it's probably most accurate to describe Torre de Palma as a hotel with a winery attached. It is, of course, possible to do a tour and tasting here, but there's a wider variety of food/matching options than just pure wine ones.

Still, this fabulous 14th-century homestead has been beautifully renovated and, just over two hours from Lisbon, has 'long-weekend' written all over it, with spas, pools and activities from falconry to horse-riding. If you've got the money, the two-night package discovering the region's signature wineries is a classy immersion in the food and drink of the area, and includes a tasting dinner at its Basilii restaurant and a visit and tasting at three wineries.

BAIRRADA & DÃO

LUÍS PATO

Known as the King of Baga, Luís Pato has shown a lifetime's dedication to the grape, convinced that it deserves to be spoken about in the same breath as the great Italian variety Nebbiolo. And since he has been experimenting with various techniques for most of the last 30 years, it's fair to say we ought to listen to what he has to say.

If you visit his winery in Amoreira da Gândara, you'll get the full story, plus the chance to try current releases and, if you're lucky, a few old gems pulled out of the library. Winery visits are by appointment, but the shop is open all the time.

MADRE DE ÁGUA

This is not so much a winery visit as a farm/hotel that happens to have vines, but it makes a great base for exploring the Dão. The hotel is well set up for visits to the countryside and the Serra da Estrela – mainland Portugal's highest mountain range – whether by bike, foot or four-by-four. In this high, silent, rocky region with granitic terrain the vines are used to surviving on slim pickings of both water and nutrients and there's a certain cool-hearted punch to the vinhos.

Guests can have a go at activities from cheese-making to sheep milking, vineyard work and, obviously, wine tasting.

MADEIRA

BLANDY'S

Madeira is one of the longest-lived of all wine styles (even after you've opened a bottle!), so it seems somehow fitting that the Blandy family have run their wine business for over two centuries and seven generations.

A vertiginous granitic chunk in the Atlantic, 700km west of Morocco, Madeira is nothing if not different. It's not an easy place to grow anything, and with space at a premium, vines are traditionally strung up on trellises to allow crops to be grown underneath. The country's famous *levadas* (narrow water channels) bring water from the peaks down to the farmlands and you can walk them.

The soils are chock-full of minerals, which give the wines their trademark acidic punch. Balancing the latter with a little sweetness is very much part of the skill of the island's winemakers. If this sounds a bit like producing champagne, tokaji or, indeed, any dessert wine, think again. Madeira has one of the oddest production techniques in the wine world, with the liquid exposed to both heat and oxidation – the reason it's so indestructible once made.

You can learn all about it if you visit Blandy's Wine Lodge, since the tour encompasses both 'normal' wine production features, but also its canteiro lodge where barrels are stored on rafters to warm up under the eaves. All old buildings, narrow corridors and spectacular views, this is a fabulously different winery visit.

DOURO

CÁLEM, VILA NOVA DE GAIA

Cálem was founded in 1870, which in the Methusaleh-like world of port makes it a relative newbie. Practically in the shadow of the landmark Dom Luís I Bridge between Porto and Vila Nova de Gaia, its visitor centre is one of the best, having recently been renovated to create a modern, interactive experience.

There are 3D maps – one of the best ways of understanding the topography, soils and climate of the Douro you'll come across – an interactive aroma zone, designed to train your nose to recognise the key port flavours; a brilliant liquid display of all the colours found in port, from pale yellow to the deepest ruby; and any number of other nice touches to help you learn without realising you're doing so.

The interactive element of the visit lasts around 45 minutes, and you can happily bring children. They should also be suitably awed by the towering wooden vats and stacked barrels in the old warehouse, which makes up the more traditional guided tour part.

There are tastings where you match port to different types of cheese and chocolate and even tours that include a 45-minute fado concert. Sitting with a glass of chilled tawny in a port lodge by the Douro while a singer wails about lost love is about as Portuguese as it gets.

The same group also owns Kopke, which sits next door and specialises in old colheita (vintage tawny port). If you're a fan, you might want to check your credit card limit before venturing into its shop.

FERREIRA, VILA NOVA DE GAIA

There's been no shortage of strong women in the world of wine over the years, but Dona Antónia Ferreira stands out. In the somewhat unenlightened environment of 19th-century rural Portugal, she acquired a reputation as a caring employer, feisty champion of the rural economy, and a shrewd businesswoman.

Having inherited the wine estates from her wealthy family, she ran them brilliantly after she was widowed at the age of 33, adding new properties bit by bit over her lifetime. Today, Ferreira remains the only port house that has always been Portuguese owned and run.

The visitor centre in Vila Nova de Gaia has a museum full of creaking ancient winery and vineyard equipment, barrels, wooden vats and as many bottles as you can shake a silver-topped ebony cane at. There's even a room dedicated to the lady herself, full of her accoutrements.

Ferreira makes table wine as well as port, so you can tailor your visit according to what you'd most like to try and learn about. Its Casa Ferreirinha wine is famous for making Portugal's best (and best-known) red wine, Barca-Velha. You won't get it as part of the tasting, but you can buy it in the shop.

QUINTA DO CRASTO, UPPER DOURO

Lying in an infinity pool halfway up hills striated with vineyard terraces, looking down the sleepy majesty of the Douro, a glass of port waiting for you when you get out... does it get much better than that? If you answered 'yes', you're a tough taskmaster.

Quinta do Crasto is, at 135 hectares, one of the larger estates in the Douro – and also one of the most beautiful. It makes both red wine and port – plus good olive oil – and while it's not a hotel, it can put up visitors in its rooms by prior booking.

Even if you don't get to stay over, there are tours and tastings that let you see the old stone lagares still used for foot-treading port and try four wines, all of them fantastic: three table wines and the LBV port. If you feel like splashing out, you can also turn the basic tour into a three-hour tasting-plus-lunch option (served with the four wines).

Sat nav isn't great for finding Crasto, but there are more romantic alternatives – if you take the train or a boat to Ferrão, the winery will pick you up if you ask. It can also arrange boat tours up the river.

QUINTA DO SEIXO, UPPER DOURO

This one-time run-down winery was bought by Portugal's biggest wine company, Sandeman, in the late 1980s and the group has spent a huge amount of money kicking it into shape since. It's really paid off. The winery is the epitome of a modern Portuguese installation, right down to the fabulously quirky 'robotic lagar' where automated 'feet' replicate the process of human treading.

Different tastings are available, depending on how many (and what quality of) ports you want to try. Unless you're a port agnostic, this is probably a good case of a small upgrade going a long way. But the standout is the visit out into the vineyards, where you get to do a quality tasting in an orange glade overlooking the languorous progress of the Douro.

It's a pretty unforgettable experience, but if for some reason you're left cold by the natural bounty of the countryside, the 100 Years Old Tawnies tasting (of 10-, 20-, 30- and 40-year old tawny ports) is a real treat for your palate, giving you a comprehensive overview of what many experts feel is the best port style of all. The same 100 Years option is also available at the Sandeman lodge in Vila Nova de Gaia (p135).

SANDEMAN, VILA NOVA DE GAIA

If you don't visit Sandeman's Quinta do Seixo estate in the Upper Douro, you can get a good idea of the company and its wines on the quayside in Vila Nova de Gaia.

Housed in a wonderful riverfront building, its visitor centre is well set up, with video tours in nine languages, cocktails, a shop and guides all dressed up as the port house's famous Zorro-like icon, the mysterious Don. The story's worth hearing, too. It's inspiring to discover how a 25-year-old with a £300 loan from his father managed to create what would become a globally famous wine brand.

If you're more interested in the history and the architecture, the Classic and Premium Tours are fine – though the wine selection (a ruby and a tawny for the former, with a white thrown in for the latter) suggests they're mostly for the uninitiated. Wine lovers will want to upgrade to the 1790 tour, which includes more information and five wines. And if you're a confirmed port nut, the 100 Years Old Tawnies tour (also available at Quinta do Seixo – p134) allows you to taste some exceptional aged tawny ports.

Port of cool

Porto has come a long way in the last 20 years, but it's still a bit short on genuinely excellent hotels. The one stand-out is the Yeatman. Set up by port house Taylor's in 2010, it's a luxury wine/spa hotel on the hills of Vila Nova de Gaia with spectacular views of Porto and the river. Walking down the narrow roads from here to the quayside for an evening of port visits is easy, getting back might be rather harder. The hotel has a superb wine list, weekly wine dinners and masterclasses – though given the venue's five-star credentials and Michelin-starred restaurant, they're understandably not cheap.

TAYLOR'S, VILA NOVA DE GAIA

It's easy to get inured to the weight of history in the Douro – the port houses have been operating for a long time. But to put Taylor's' longevity into perspective, it was established the same year as the Salem witch trials.

Plenty of port has flowed under the bridge since 1692 – some of it literally. One of the company's most famous figureheads, Baron de Forrester, was drowned when the *barco* full of barrels that he was travelling on capsized. Rumour has it that he was dragged down by his belt full of money. Dona Antónia Ferreira, who was with him at the time, floated to safety on her voluminous crinolines...

Taylor's has a lot of good port, but it's probably best known for its superb vintage ports and its late bottled vintages. You'll get to try one of the latter (along with its very good white port) as part of your basic tour of the atmospheric lodge in Vila Nova de Gaia. With audio-guides available in eight languages, there's no need to book, and if you want to upgrade the tasting to different styles (or just more) ports, that's easily doable.

You can also arrange customised additions to the tour, from dinner in the restaurant to private tastings, food matchings, and the chance to witness a traditional bottle opening with hot tongs.

QUINTA NOVA DE NOSSA SENHORA DO CARMO, UPPER DOURO

Quinta Nova, as it's usually known – understandably, given that its full name is more of a mouthful than a fork loaded with *bacalao* – is up there among the world's topmost wine tourism experiences. It regularly appears in newspaper, magazine and online 'best of' lists, and with good reason.

It's about two-thirds of the way between Régua and Pinhão on the north bank of the Douro. On the top of the hills, the winery affords stunning views, and it backs up the natural eye-candy with some pretty fine human-made attractions as well. Its Conceitus restaurant is one of the best in the region, and if you get to eat on the terrace on a warm Douro evening, surrounded by vineyards, it'll be a memory that stays with you for life.

This is a Douro winery that's more about regular wine than port, so if you're a bit fortified-out, you'll enjoy the wide range of table wines to go at here. It runs four tours a day, and they're pretty comprehensive, taking in vineyards, winery, warehouse, bottle room, wine museum, barrel room and tasting/shop.

If you want to make a day of it, there are 8km of walking trails over the hills and vineyards. The quinta will also help set up wine tours and tastings for you, perhaps including a boat tour from its pier.

It's not too far from Quinta do Crasto (p134) either, so the two could easily be combined into a day of thoroughly self-indulgent luxury.

QUINTA DO VALLADO, UPPER DOURO

Régua – easily accessible by motorway from Porto – is reckoned to be the start of the Douro proper, where the five-star vineyards and scenery begin. And with more bars, hotels and restaurants than anywhere further upriver, it's not a bad place to base yourself for dips in and out of estates.

Quinta do Vallado is within five minutes of the town, on its eastern edges. Fantastically, it mixes extreme history – the estate was founded in 1716 and once belonged to the famous Dona Antónia Ferreira (p133) – with extreme modernity.

You can stay in either the 18th-century manor house (where, presumably Dona A would have played as a child) or in its new Wine Hotel. The former has been neatly renovated to mix character with WiFi, while the latter's sleekly elegant 'letterbox' design is distinctive but not showy. Made out of local slate, it certainly makes a statement in a place as traditional as the Douro.

You can get out into the vineyards in a jeep or by bicycle, go fishing, boating or canoeing on the river, or just crash by the pool and take in the view. Less than two hours from Porto, it's a great stop-off – and it'll even arrange pick-ups and drop-offs at the airport.

Wine-wise, this is a good spot for testing out different styles. In table wines, for instance, you can compare how classic northern Portuguese red varieties such as Touriga Nacional, Sousão and Tinta Roriz fare in single-varietal wines and in more expensive multi-varietal blends. Port-wise, it's a chance to compare red ports such as LBV and vintage against comparably priced tawnies.

There are two tours a day and hotel guests get a complimentary private visit of their own, but it also offers some interesting feature events, too, from masterclasses and wine blending to vertical tastings. If you're there around vintage (you'll need to book way in advance), you might even be able to take part in its Harvest Experience, which includes grape picking, wine blending and grape crushing by foot.

Wild wild fest

If there's one time of year when the Douro is even more amazing to visit, it's during the festival of São João. Held on June 23, in honour of St John the Baptist, Porto's patron saint, it's a time for general chaos, with much partying, eating, waving stalks of garlic (really) or good-natured bopping each other on the head with squeaky plastic hammers (really really). The day after features the annual Barco Rabelo competition, where the various flat-bottomed port boats race – sometimes fast, usually erratically – from the river's mouth back to the iron bridge. It's quite a sight.

GERMANY

Had this book been written 30 years ago, this section would have been considerably more downbeat. German wine, not to put too fine a point on it, had a terrible time from the 1980s through to the early years of the millennium. This, after all, was when the world was moving from classic European countries towards the New World, from sweeter styles to dry and from whites to reds.

It wasn't, in short, a good time to be a European producer of off-dry white wine – and the country's output had become about as fashionable as a mullet haircut.

There are few sadder sights in the world of wine than abandoned vineyards – particularly when they're wonderful old vines that should be giving the best fruit of their lives. But go back 20 years and even great German sites were unkempt – older growers were simply unable to summon up the will or the effort to tend them given the prices they could charge.

But in these dark days others saw opportunity. There's a wave of young German growers who are determined to bring these old vineyards back to where they should be – right at the pinnacle of the world's wine pyramid. Energised rather than worn out by the challenge, they have merged wit, modernity and style with a genuine passion for heritage. Germany is a country that has rediscovered its mojo.

And thank goodness for that, because the wine world is all the better for it. The star grape, naturally, is Riesling. Often referred to as the Queen of white grapes, it's grown from one end of the country to the other, though it's at its best around the Mosel and the vineyards down the Rhine.

And if you're not sure whether you fancy visiting winery after winery that majors in the same grape, think again. Riesling is acknowledged as the most chameleon-like of all varieties (though Pinot Noir runs it close), changing its character massively from one terroir to the next. A tasting of five Rieslings from five different sites is a fascinating experience.

Even if you just honed in on the 25km between Ürzig and Piesport in the Mosel, you would find an extraordinary array of flavours and characters as the vineyards shift orientation with the haphazard meanders of the river. And the Mosel is almost all slate. Throw different soils into the mix (as happens in other parts of the Rhine) and you get a massive range of styles and flavours to choose from.

If you're touring Germany's wine regions, you'll get to know the Rhine well. An awful lot of the country's vineyards are within 10km of its banks. Most of the time it heads north to south with a very Teutonic decisiveness, though there is a 30km east-west midlife crisis between Bingen and Mainz, which provides a convenient plethora of south-facing slopes and is home to a frankly indecent number of really excellent wine estates.

If you fancy a break from Riesling, you probably want to be in the warmer areas, such as the Pfalz, Franken or, particularly, Baden. Here you'll get different white varieties such as Scheurebe, Silvaner and the Pinot twins, Gris and Blanc. But you'll also find some exceptional Pinot Noir. A combination of climate change and better vineyard management has seen its quality skyrocket. If you're a fan of the grape, you'll surely love the best German expressions – lifted, perfumed and complex, they're not often cheap, but they don't deserve to be.

For visitors, Germany is all about the Vinothek – the winery shop. Some estates (usually the larger ones) do run tours, but they're not especially common, and you're more likely to be offered a themed or tutored tasting in the store than a cellar tour. Other places might offer just a couple of visits a week.

So, themed Disneyesque wine parks might be out, but if you want to experience racy, uplifting wines, steep, stunning vineyards, and an industry with a tangible sense of regeneration, Germany is the place to come.

MOSEL

MARKUS MOLITOR

Markus Molitor is proof of both the journey that German wine is on, and also of what it is capable. He took over the family business in 1984, at a time when the world was moving away from the country's wines at some speed, and with a combination of intelligence, hard work and self-belief has created a high-quality wine business.

Studiously shunning anything to do with mass-market, labour-saving devices, he turned to the ideas of the past: trying to grow great grapes on great sites, however much effort it might take. In the Mosel, frequently, it takes a lot, since 'great sites' usually mean the steep slatey terraces that head down to the river, and to work them requires commitment, time, patience – and strong leg muscles.

On the west bank of the river, looking towards Zeltingen, the winery has views out over some of the region's most famous vineyards: Schlossberg, Himmelreich and Sonnenuhr. Built in the 19th century, the old building has been brilliantly restored, and the new Vinothek is particularly impressive.

You can't visit the winery, but a small fee gets you a tasting of eight wines in the Vinothek, and, best of all, it's not pre-set – you get to choose from over 40 that are typically available. There's Pinot Blanc and Pinot Noir, but if you've any sense, you'll home in on the Rieslings. There are wines from 20 grand cru sites across the Mosel, including vintages for some going back over ten years. It's a chance to see how well this grape can age.

If you want to visit vineyards, head to nearby Ürzig, where a quick clamber up the slopes will reward you with a fine panorama of the steeply sloping vineyards.

SA PRÜM

The Prüm family have been growing grapes in the Mosel for almost 900 years, so it's no surprise they're widely recognised as one of the heavyweight names in the region. They are all about Riesling, in all its variations, and have bottles from dry through off-dry to the ultra-unctuous Eiswein.

Their best vineyards are on the famous Wehlener Sonnenuhr – named after the square white sundial that sits on the hill. Designed by an ancestor in 1842, it gives you a clue as to what makes this place special. On these slatey inclines, vines soak up sunshine, while the rocky soil absorbs heat and radiates it gently back up on to the grapes. The result: long, slow ripening, despite a climate that's warm rather than hot.

Visits here include a cellar tour and a tasting of eight wines, though for added atmosphere, you might consider staying in the guesthouse next to the winery, which allows you to explore the terroir at your leisure. Breakfast on the terrace, with views out over vines and river should really get you in the mood for a day of Riesling exploration. There are any number of trails up into the vineyards, varying from gentle to calf-knottingly steep: the panorama is worth it.

If you'd rather cycle, there's a (hearteningly flat) cycle path that runs along the edge of the river that's ideal for a gentle day's pottering. But if even that's too much, head to the pier right by the winery from where you can hop on to a boat to quaff Riesling surrounded on the slopes by the vines that gave birth to it.

REICHSGRAF VON KESSELSTATT

The official descriptor of this region is the Mosel-Saar-Ruwer – the latter two rivers filtering into their big brother upstream around Trier. Unusually, Reichsgraf von Kesselstatt has vineyards in all three areas (only the Church can make a similar claim), and since it specialises in making single-vineyard wines, a visit here is a good opportunity to check out the stylistic differences from one region to the next.

This is one of the oldest estates in the Mosel – founded in 1349, with a long line of aristocratic and influential owners. The winery is based at its dreamy castle in the Ruwer, Schloss Marienlay, and if you book in advance, the staff will set you up with a tasting of seven wines, running all the way up to Auslese level. You can try your luck with a cellar tour – they do run them, but only if they have time, so if you visit during harvest, forget it!

A decent alternative to the winery is to visit its Weinstube (wine bar) in Trier. The town is interesting to explore and the entire range of Kesselstatt wines is on sale – with ten available by the glass. Make sure you try the Josephshöfer Riesling – it's a 'monopole', which means it's from a vineyard managed by this winery only.

WEINGUT PAULY

Axel Pauly is a great example of the young generation of German growers driving the country forward to greatness once again. Young he might be, but having taken over his family's vineyards he has looked to the ethos of the classic small growers of the Mosel for inspiration: a world of hard work and pride in diligence. It is, as he admits, not the easiest way to make a living, but there's a certain satisfaction to it – not least the reconnection with past generations.

His wines have attracted plaudits from across the world. For a small grower, he has an impressive range to try, including a Weissburgunder (Pinot Blanc), Spätburgunder (Pinot Noir) and a less well-known Kerner if you fancy branching out a bit. But as with most German Weinguter, this is really about different expressions of Riesling.

With big windows, surrounded by vines, the cellar door is, rather like the wines, modern yet sensitively done. It makes a statement by, effectively, not making a statement.

Between Piesport and Ürzig, Pauly lies in the heart of the Mosel's wine country and makes for a well-priced visit: a two-hour tour of the winery and cellars is complemented by a tasting of eight wines afterwards. Book in advance to make an appointment.

RHINE VALLEY

BASSERMANN-JORDAN, PFALZ

Anyone who knows about German wine will be aware of the names Forst, Deidesheim and Ruppertsberg; they're among the best vineyard areas in the country, and Bassermann-Jordan owns sites in all three. This being Germany, though, none of them are exactly enormous: their 20 plots cover just 49 hectares, though a third of them are classified as hallowed Grosses Gewächs (grand crus) – the highest German vineyard category.

The winery has history – Pierre Jordan bought the first vineyards in the Pfalz back in 1718 – but it's also laudably good at moving forward. It was Andreas Jordan who around 1800 pioneered the idea of planting vineyards to one sole best-suited grape variety rather than mixing them up – an idea that rather took off. These days, the company is working to introduce organic techniques into the vineyards, with an emphasis on minimum intervention and greater biodiversity.

There are two main ranges of wine. The historical range is classic German Riesling: spicy, concentrated and restrained, with a touch of sweetness to balance the grape's naturally tight acidity. The 100-year-old Probus range is drier and more fruit driven. All in all, a tasting here should guarantee you finding something you like and is certainly a better bet than a cellar visit. Tours are for a minimum of ten – and thus unlikely to suit passing tourists.

KLOSTER EBERBACH, RHEINGAU

This visit is a bit different. Kloster Eberbach is located in an old monastery (founded in 1136 but deconsecrated in the 19th century) and it gives this place a unique magic – not least because the film *The Name of the Rose* was shot here in the 1980s. The sights of barrels lining either side of the nave, as though in silent meditation, or bottles filling the arches where monks once prayed is not something you get on most winery visits.

The wines come from the monastery's own slopes. Say what you like about Cistercians, but they had an eye for a good vineyard – and weren't shy about acquiring them either. This was once Germany's largest wine estate, and at 250 hectares, is still pretty hefty today.

All its wines are available to buy and taste in the Vinothek, attached to the monastery. The shop also offers a nice view into the barrel cellar, which is just as well because visiting it isn't easy. There are a series of tours every year that take in the monastery and the cellars, but they're only in German and book up quickly.

The Open Wine-Tasting includes six wines, while a Musical Strolling Wine-Tasting tour comes complete with atmospheric music at six chosen wine tasting points and a concert in the church – though there are only maybe half-a-dozen or so a year.

Your best bet is to content yourself with a visit to the monastery itself (open all the time) with an audioguide and slugging back Riesling in the Vinothek, hotel or restaurant. That said, if you really want to visit a winery, it has one 500m away on the Steinberg that does do guided tours. Hessische Staatsweingüter is modern and more accessible than the cellars of the monastery.

SCHLOSS JOHANNISBERG, RHEINGAU

If you're a fan of off-dry or sweeter styles of Riesling (and most right-thinking people are), you owe these guys one. In 1720, it was the Benedictine monks of this estate who put in the first big plantation of the grape in the Rheingau – some 300,000 vines – effectively committing themselves heart and soul to a variety that was still something of a curiosity. It was quite a statement of intent. They followed this up 50 or so years later with the other big discovery that would shape the country's wines: that leaving the grapes on the vines after the normal harvest gave juice of intense sweetness.

Like many scientific advances, it owed much to chance. In the 18th century, the monks had to receive permission to start the harvest from the Prince-Abbot of Fulda. But the messenger sent to get the order was delayed by several weeks and, by the time he returned, the grapes appeared to be rotting on the vines. Either through courage or desperation, the cellarmaster picked and vinified the grapes anyway – and Spätlese (late-picked grapes) wine was born.

There's a monument dedicated to the tardy courier next to the winery's excellent Vinothek. Tours are by appointment only, but with a minimum group size of ten, there's no guarantee you'll get in. Nevertheless, try contacting them in advance to see if they can find a space for you. It's worth the effort. Lit by flickering candles and lined with oak casks, the dark original cellars are things of beauty. Even if you can't get underground, a fair bit of the castle is open to the public (including, of course, the shop), while the view from the Schlossberg vineyards down to the Rhine is spectacular.

SCHLOSS VOLLRADS, RHEINGAU

Anything you want, so long as it's Riesling... Yes, this wine estate uses only one grape variety, but it does so beautifully – and has done for most of its 800-year existence. It was good enough for Goethe, anyway, who paid a visit in 1814.

Schloss Vollrads is one of the best-known wineries in Germany, aristocratic of ownership (until the last count died in 1997) and with an unimpeachable vinous pedigree. Around 120 years ago, it was the driving force behind the establishment of the German VDP – an association of the country's top wine producers.

It makes the full gamut of wines, going up through Spätlese to Auslese. It also does a Riesling brandy and a sparkling wine, not to mention an alcohol-free version, Secco. All in all, it produces ten to 15 expressions every year, but it's best known for its Kabinett wines – light, lowish alcohol, elegant Rieslings that are ideal for effort-free sipping. There are other standouts, too, not least the Erstes Gewächs and Grosses Gewächs (premier and grand cru) wines, which come from its A-list vineyard on the Schlossberg. Combine old vines, a premium site and sensitive winemaking, and the results can be magnificent.

The winery runs regular public events and individual tours, but these need to be booked in advance and, with a minimum of 12, you'll probably be looking to tag on to the back of another party. Tastings, however, are free.

REICHSRAT VON BUHL, PFALZ

You probably don't need extra reasons to visit these guys, but here are three anyway: they're a fully paid-up member of the VDP (the association of the country's best wineries); they were a favourite of the composer Mendelssohn, who knew a thing or two about romantic beauty; and they were deemed sufficiently majestic to be the official wine at the opening of the Suez Canal in 1869. Oh, and if bugs' lives are important to you, they're also certified organic.

You might think that a life *sans* pesticides would be hair-shirt difficult in the cooler climes of Germany, but in fact the estate has vineyards scattered across the best – and warmest – sites of Deidesheim and Forst. If those names ring a bell, we spoke about them in relation to Bassermann-Jordan (p144), which is no coincidence since Reichsrat von Buhl came about when the original Bassermann-Jordan estate was split into three.

At its height, it was 200 hectares, but has now shrunk to a high-quality 50. That contraction is a sad reflection on the diminished saleability of the country's wines, but not on their quality – here they're superb.

Around 90 per cent of its output is Riesling and you can taste its entire range of 30 or so wines for free in the Vinothek, though some of the Grosse Gewächs from the likes of Paradiesgarten, Herrgottsacker, Pechstein and Kieselberg tend to sell out early in the year.

If you want to take in the cellar, book a Weinprobe: a tasting of three or six wines in the Vinothek, plus a visit underground to share a glass of sekt surrounded by the big old barrels.

RUPPERTSBERGER WEINKELLER HOHEBURG, PFALZ

Given the number of wonderful small growers in Germany, it might seem odd to suggest a visit to a co-operative. But this is a good one, in a good area, making pretty good wines. It also does reasonably priced tastings and – in a region where cellar tours are not always easy to come by – includes guided tours (*Kellerführungen*), too.

Ruppertsberg was created in the 1960s by the merger of two other co-ops and, with some serious heft behind it – the 86 members cultivate over 400 hectares of vines – it's laudably modern.

Just a cock's stride from the uber-wine village of Deidesheim, this is a nice example of a more commercial winery doing well-priced wines and happy to show you how it does it.

BADEN

WEINGUT WEBER

You can't help but be impressed with this thoroughly modern winery, which takes food and drink and presents them in thoroughly 21st-century fashion. Its floor-to-ceiling glass windows mean that the winemaking and bottling seem to be taking place in the actual vines, while the barrel and bottle cellars are tunnelled deep into the hillside – some 50m or so of dark spaces.

It does a variety of visits that allow you to see all of this – from a bargain mini-tour featuring three wines, to a reasonably priced 'Classic' that gets you all of the above plus a plate of home-made sausage and cheese. If you want to go the whole hog – possibly literally – the culinary wine tasting includes a three-course meal in its restaurant.

Wine-wise, there is a wide range of grape varieties on offer: Grauburgunder (Pinot Gris), Weissburgunder (Pinot Blanc), Sauvignon Blanc, Müller Thurgau and Spätburgunder (Pinot Noir) as well as a Riesling.

It can arrange tours in French and English if you let it know – the only downside is prices are based on a ten-person minimum, so call ahead to see what the uptake has been like. If you're a group of four, you might try the three-hour Segway tour, which includes coffee and cake in Ettenheim, an aperitif in the winery, and great views from the vineyards.

As you drive up to the winery, you'll come through a large plantation of 450 walnut trees, which it's very proud of – the black walnut is apparently known as 'Baden's truffle' round here. So no surprise that a) it offers tours of the garden, and b) it also makes a walnut liqueur. If that's not quite your scene, you can also try its schnapps or gin.

MARKGRAF VON BADEN

The state palace of Schloss Salem has been the seat of the Margrave of Baden since 1802, when it took it over from the Cistercians. This should all be explained in the pretty exceptional value history-based tour that takes in the abbey, plus monks' refectory and cloister and adds three wines into the bargain.

The winery also runs more specifically wine-related tours, encompassing the cellars (and ancient wooden grape press), while those who like to get out and about will enjoy the attractive vineyard walk, starting from the Vinothek in Birnauer Oberhof. It's a two-hour hike up to the pilgrims' church, where you can drink wine in the vineyards looking out over the lake as reward for your exertions.

The history tour is the only one you can just roll up to and pay a guaranteed fee – the others are predicated (and priced) on a minimum number of participants (usually ten). It's a popular tourist area, so if you are visiting at peak times, the chances are the places will be filled. But if they aren't, you might end up paying more than you think. Alternatively, the Markgraf's estate at Schloss Staufenberg to the north-west is an amazing spot to kick back and enjoy a glass of wine – especially if you're heading north-south down Autobahn 5 or heading in or out of Alsace via Strasbourg. Perched high on a crag on the western edge of the Black Forest, there's a decent restaurant and a wine terrace with superb views.

STAATSWEINGUT MEERSBURG

If you fancy mixing wine with wider holiday entertainment, Meersburg is a great place. On the shores of the Bodensee (Lake Constance), it has dreamy views over the yacht-flecked water towards Switzerland, and the advantage of being surrounded by vine-draped slopes.

There's proof of a wine operation here as far back as 1210, but these guys are not sitting on their laurels – this was the first winery in Germany to be classified carbon neutral and has an enviably right-thinking charter covering fair pay, reinvestment levels and social engagement, as well as sustainability.

It offers tastings in the barrel cellar and its airy tasting room, which looks out over the lake. These seem to be more set up for groups, but most wine lovers will be happy with the regular Friday evening two-hour tours that take in cellars, winery and a tutored tasting of six wines. They run from May to October, with a Tuesday option for the high season of June, July and August. They're really good value, but sell out quickly, so book in advance.

There are also themed tours of the town (explaining its wine history) and some of the best vineyards – but these have an eight-person minimum. Whatever you do, this is a great winery to visit, particularly if you're Riesling-ed out after the estates further north. Here there's Pinot Blanc, Pinot Noir and Chardonnay. And, of course, a bit of Riesling as well…

FRANKEN

BÜRGERSPITAL

With its 700-year history and its proud membership of Germany's VDP grouping of top wine estates, Bürgerspital is an influential and high-quality player in the region. It owns 120 hectares of vines and, unsurprisingly, while there is some red wine – mostly Pinot Noir, with some Blaufränkisch and, more surprisingly, Cabernet Sauvignon and Merlot – it's mostly planted to white grapes. Silvaner and Riesling you'd expect, but there are also Pinots Blanc and Gris, Chardonnay, Gewürztraminer, Scheurebe and even Bacchus.

Its best vineyards (around Würzburg) are on eye-wateringly steep south-facing slopes where the grapes can make the most of the sunshine, while the winery itself is in a beautiful old courtyard in the centre of town.

It can arrange tours to order, though these are aimed at larger groups – a minimum of 25 participants. It also holds four or five themed events a month, such as wine and cheese matching. But of more interest to the passing tourist is the fact that from March to October it runs a weekly guided tour of the cellar that lasts an hour and a half and comes with a free 25cl bottle of Silvaner.

If you want to supplement it with something else, you can taste and buy wines as well as nibble on snacks in its Weinhaus. For something more substantial, try the restaurant next door, Bürgerspital Weinstuben.

JULIUSSPITAL

There's a tendency in the world of wine to assume that small estates are inherently better than large ones, but it's not always true, and a visit to this winery in Würzburg (just down the street from Bürgerspital) proves it. It's part of a wider foundation, established in the 16th century as a charity to help look after the poor, the sick and the disadvantaged, and today profits still go to the various hospitals and care homes the trust runs.

With 180 hectares of vines scattered over the region, it's the second-biggest wine estate in the country and, this being Franken, nearly half of it is planted to Silvaner – a popular and somewhat underrated white grape.

Taken together, it all adds up to a fascinating visit. It runs 90-minute public guided tours several days a week (no reservation required) that take in the barrel cellar and concentrate either on the history of the foundation and the grounds or the winery, depending which you select. Both include a tasting of three different wines. The tours are in German, but the guides are happy to repeat the key messages in English.

There are also lengthier (and slightly pricier) book-in-advance tours that last around three hours and include a tasting of six wines, but they have a minimum of 25 per group.

If you're not able to catch a tour, the Vinothek is a fine place to get to know what one of Germany's oldest wine regions is all about, secure in the knowledge that whatever you spend is going to a good cause.

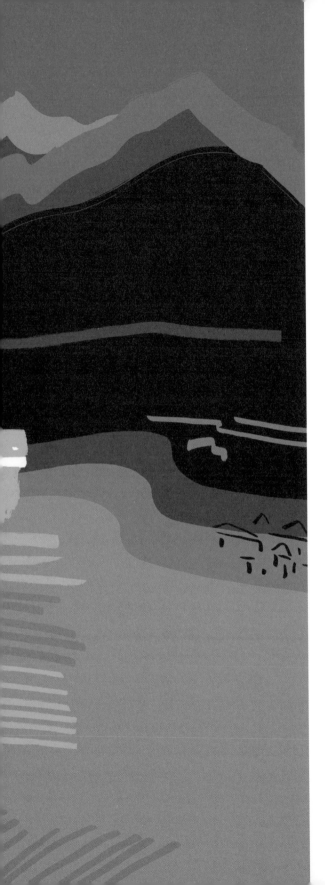

AUSTRIA

What is it they say about things seeming darkest just before the dawn? Back in 1985 a number of Austrian wineries were caught adding diethylene glycol to their wines to beef them up a bit and make them taste sweeter. The antifreeze scandal, as it came to be known, was global news and, like most traumatic events, caused the anguished protagonist – in this case, the Austrian wine industry – to take a long hard look at itself.

Cue much ripping up of long-held beliefs and a wholesale reinvention, transforming itself from a producer of cheaper, inferior versions of German wine to one thoroughly focused on doing its own thing and doing it well.

Austria is now a fantastic place for a wine visit. It has proudly native grape varieties (Grüner Veltliner, Blaufränkisch, Zweigelt), as well as more comfortingly recognisable international grapes such as Sauvignon Blanc and Pinot Noir. It does fantastic things with Riesling that are demonstrably different to what Germany and Alsace produce. Stylistically, its wine styles span everything from bone dry and minerally to super-luscious and sweet. And unlike most of Germany, for instance, it has a good range of red wines to accompany its more typical whites.

Austria's star region is the Wachau – a spectacularly beautiful 36km stretch of the Danube between Melk and Krems. The flatter lands by the river are home to row after row of vineyards, marching purposefully up towards the steeper hills and bluffs further from the water. Even here they don't stop: many of the best vineyard sites are narrow terraces literally carved out of the rock face. UNESCO-protected, the area should be on every wine lover's 'must-do' list.

The secret to the Wachau (and, indeed, all of the vineyards of Niederösterreich) is the conflict between warm summer air drifting in off the Pannonian Plain to the east and chillier air from the Waldviertel near the Czech Republic. It makes for warm days and cold nights – perfect for getting grapes that are ripe, but also fresh.

It also helps to explain why the vineyards of Carnuntum and Burgenland, south-east of Vienna and exposed to the full hairdryer treatment from the Hungarian flatlands, should be gaining an increasing reputation for their reds.

One of the great advantages for the wine tourist is the compact nature of Austria's wine-lands – and the fact that Vienna is pretty much smack in the middle of most of them. It's the only wine-producing country in the world where you can stay in the capital and feasibly see most of the country's wine regions in a series of day trips. All but the farthest reaches of Styria are within 100km of the city – and many are a lot closer.

Not only that, but Vienna is the only capital (indeed, the only large city) in the world with a genuine wine industry within its boundaries. Fly in and you can have a perfectly good few days of vineyard visits without ever venturing more than a half-hour taxi ride from the centre. This is bona fide urban wine tourism – check out the WienWein group to find out more.

There's one other thing worth mentioning. Austria was the birthplace of Rudolf Steiner, the thinker and philosopher who, among many other things, was the pioneer of biodynamic agriculture. Steiner's philosophy was that a healthy ecosystem in which everything was in balance, from bugs to plants to soil, would allow most crops to fight off diseases on their own, without human-made intervention. Its proponents spend a lot of time making natural preparations to spray on the land, and work to a lunar calendar. It requires real commitment, but it has a growing following among Austria's wine growers. So if all things green and beautiful are important to you, this is the place to visit.

NIEDERÖSTERREICH

DOMÄNE WACHAU, WACHAU

If you're looking for a quick way to find the soul of Austria's best-known wine region, a visit here will do it. Based by the railway in Dürnstein, Domäne Wachau is a co-operative, and the 440 hectares farmed by its members make up a third of the region's vineyard area. Once owned by the Catholic Church, its size means it's the only winery in Wachau that has wines from every one of the top vineyard sites.

Like most decent producers, it's a neat combination of modern technology in the winery and tradition in the cellars and vineyards, and it has an amazing array of bottles to try – almost two-dozen single-vineyard wines alone. Here you can really get stuck into exploring the Wachau's various terroirs, from the warmth of the Loibenberg to the hallowed slopes of the Kellerberg.

It offers bookable tours, which give you a chance to poke around the enormous old casks in the cellar, while the four-wine tasting will explain the vagaries of Steinfeder, Federspiel and Smaragd (p156). Be aware that there's a minimum group size for bookings in some months, though.

JURTSCHITSCH, KAMPTAL

The succession of the younger generation of Jurtschitsches has seen a move to organics and a willingness to get rid of lesser vineyards in order to concentrate on the superior ones. It's all about expressing terroir – not unlike the movement among young wine growers in Germany – and it's best experienced by exploring their top estates.

They have six crus, four planted to Grüner Veltliner, one solely to Riesling and one with both. So if you visit, you can compare how the two grapes perform in the same vineyard, as well as how different Grüner can be in different sites.

Think there's no such thing as terroir? Well, they describe their Schenkenbichl Grüner as 'like eating oranges in a hay barn not far from the ocean' while the Dechant version is 'Earl Grey, black pepper and wet stones'. How different is that? Picking out the variations should be fun, especially if the winemaker's in attendance. On the edge of Langenlois, Jurtschitsch is a stone's throw from the extraordinary Loisium WineExperience (p155), so you could easily combine the two in a single morning.

MARKOWITSCH, CARNUNTUM

Carnuntum is, broadly speaking, the wine region south-east of Vienna, between the capital and the Neusiedlersee. It's warmer than the vineyards to the north, and that's reflected in the wines on offer at this exemplary small, modern winery. While there is some Grüner and Riesling (plus a bit of Chardonnay and Sauvignon Blanc), almost three quarters of Gerhard Markowitsch's wines are red.

There's a fascinating selection to immerse yourself in: Blaufränkisch, Pinot Noir, St Laurent and the local hero, Zweigelt, which is sometimes made as a single varietal and sometimes spiced up with Blaufränkisch and Merlot or, in the case of the Carnuntum Cuvée, with Blaufränkisch and Pinot Noir. Markowitsch resolutely refuses to pick a favourite, so you'll just have to try them all!

Phone ahead and the staff will be happy to set up a free tasting, though the number of wines they open might depend on how enthusiastic you are and if you're likely to buy anything. Visit on a cold Thursday in November when no one else is around and they're unlikely to uncork a dozen bottles just for you!

Just a hop and a skip off the main A4 from Vienna, it's open most of the week and is easily doable as a day visit from the capital, or en route to the sweet wine producers of the Neusiedlersee.

SCHLOSS GOBELSBURG, KAMPTAL

Kamptal's wines are centred on the town of Langenlois, and just to the south of it is Schloss Gobelsburg. Like many wineries in this part of the world, it has the Church to thank for its existence: the monks of the Zwettl monastery (who had already been making wine in the area for 600 years) acquired the castle in 1740 and moved their wine production to Gobelsburg when their previous winery burned down. It survived being shot at by the Russians after the Second World War and is now safely in private hands.

The estate has a wide mix of terroir to play with – from the steep, stony terraces of the Heiligenstein to the gravelly pebbles of the Gobelsburg plateau. And as a result, it manages to grow a range of grape varieties well. Riesling, Grüner Veltliner, Zweigelt and St Laurent you might expect, but Merlot and Pinot Noir (the latter brought in by an enthusiastic abbot) are less usual.

One of the highlights of its range are its five Ried (cru) wines. From very different single vineyards – the sites' individual particularities faithfully reflected by the Riesling grape – they offer an interesting spread of styles.

Visits to the winery and cellar (which need to be booked at least two days in advance) include a tasting of five wines, but if you want to try something more rarefied (and expensive), that can also be accommodated – just call in advance to discuss it. The vineyards aren't part of the tour, but the estate is happy to provide directions so you can have a look yourself.

Oeno-experience

If you're anywhere near Langenlois, you should make time to visit the Loisium WineExperience. An aluminium cube set in the middle of the vineyards of Kamptal, it looks like a giant game of Tetris. But head down into the 1km of subterranean galleries and you'll learn an awful lot about wine in general and Austrian wine in particular. There's a well-stocked wine shop and a stimulating range of seminars on offer, too – plus a spa hotel next door.

SEPP MOSER, KREMSTAL

The Mosers can trace their wine history in Austria back almost 900 years, when one of their cassocked ancestors was in charge of the abbey vines at Ebersdorf. Fast forward to 1849 and Anton Moser set up the family winery in Rohrendorf – a 170-year history that makes them one of the grand names of Austrian wine.

Over the last ten years, they've made the shift to biodynamic grape growing. Not for the faint-hearted, the practice aims to imbue vines with strength and energy, then let them get on with the business of growing by themselves. That means not only no herbicides, pesticides and the like, but also the creation of home-made 'teas' and 'extractions' to treat the vines, organic composts to spray on the soil (nettle manure), and a thorough understanding of the lunar calendar.

The winery's home is the Atrium House. Nestling among the vines in Rohrendorf, it was initially built by Lenz Moser in the 1960s in a Romanesque design as a place for him to sit and watch the world go by in his later years. But over time, it has gradually acquired more winemaking equipment and can now process all the fruit from the family's 50 hectares of vineyards in Kremstal and the Neusiedlersee, south of Vienna. Indeed, the advantage of a visit here is that you can try a wide variety of wines, from the classic Kamptal white, Grüner Veltliner, to the Zweigelt red and sweet wines of the south. As a one-stop shop just 70km from the capital, it makes an attractive day trip.

NIKOLAIHOF, WACHAU

The first documented proof of winemaking on this land goes back to the tail end of the Roman era – 470AD – making it the oldest winery in Austria, and almost certainly one of the oldest in the world. And in a way, not much has changed because, like Sepp Moser, Nikolaihof is a committed practitioner of biodynamic wine growing.

While biodynamics is now becoming more fashionable, owners the Saahs family were early adopters, starting the process of converting their vineyards way back in 1971 at a time when most wineries were more interested in looking for jazzier chemicals to pep up their vines or nuke pests.

With such an ancient past, it's no surprise that there's plenty for amateur archaeologists to get stuck into – everything from the remnants of an early-Christian basilica to the cellar, which is constructed in an old Roman crypt.

Steinfeder, Federspiel and Smaragd

No, not a Viennese firm of lawyers, but possibly the most arcane quality classification in the wine world, used only for bottles from the Wachau. Steinfeder wines, named after a reedy grass found near the vineyards, are nearly all drunk in Austria and are the lightest: up to 11.5% alcohol. Federspiel bottles, named after a falcon, are between 11.5% and 12.5% abv, while Smaragd, named after a sun-loving emerald green lizard that lives in the vineyards, are the richest and most concentrated.

To taste and visit at Nikolaihof, you need to book a table at its Weinstube (wine tavern). You can try whatever you like from its range with your meal, and someone will be happy to show you round the cellar and old press house afterwards. There's also a guesthouse (with a natural swimming pond) and since it's in Mautern, at the eastern edges of the Wachau – right by the bridge over the Danube – you could use it as a base to explore Kamptal and Kremstal as well.

FX PICHLER, WACHAU

It may not have the baroque flourishes of a top Bordeaux château, but for true wine connoisseurs, Pichler's modernist stone winery – looking slightly like a classy ski-station with its floor-to-ceiling windows – belongs in the same league. Franz Xavier is one of the best white wine producers in the world, and a stickler for capturing the terroir of his vineyards.

Since production levels are small (he farms only 18 hectares) and demand astronomical, a visit might be the only chance you get to taste them outside of the world's top-end restaurants. Just over half of what he makes is Grüner Veltliner with the rest almost entirely Riesling plus a smidgeon of Sauvignon Blanc.

Much of FX's wine is grown on stony old medieval terraces that back up on to the hills along the Danube and can only be worked by hand. It's a caring, expensive, labour-intensive operation, but it pays off in the crystalline purity of the wines. There aren't cellar or vineyard visits on offer here, but it doesn't matter. Tasting wines this good is reward enough. Every tasting is individual, so what you get to try and what it costs will vary depending on what you're looking for. Just make sure to arrange it in advance.

WIENINGER, VIENNA

Vienna is the only capital in the world with a genuine wine industry, so if you're there, it makes sense to check out at least one of its producers.

Just half an hour's drive from the centre, Fritz Wieninger has been a pioneer in reintroducing Gemischter Satz wines – a traditional method that involves growing up to 15 grape varieties in the same vineyard, then picking and vinifying them together. Fritz rightly describes it as 'a Viennese classic that had been nearly forgotten' and it's clearly something he feels strongly about – he's head of the Gemischter Satz Association.

His 52 hectares are biodynamically farmed, with vines planted on the slopes of the Bisamberg and the Nussberg, two quite different terroirs on opposite sides of the Danube. As well as Gemischter Satz, he makes Grüners, Rieslings and Chardonnays, plus Pinot Noir and a couple of red blends.

BURGENLAND

WILLI OPITZ

The year 1995 saw great vintages recorded all over Europe, including in Austria. So great, in fact, that it also marked the moment that Willi Opitz chose to jack in his job at a pet-food company and commit full-time to his burgeoning wine business.

His winery is situated in Illmitz, on the Neusiedlersee. The broad, freakishly shallow lake (only 2m at its deepest point) generates vast clouds of fog that are perfect for creating noble-rot 'stickies', and Willi produces a good range of white (and, more unusually, red) sweeties for you to try.

Since it has guest rooms and apartments as well, the winery makes a very attractive place to base yourself if you want to check out the area. As well as offering food, a variety of wine tastings and a shop, it will help set up any number of extra activities, from vineyard tours and carriage rides, to cycling in the Neusiedler See-Seewinkel National Park and boat trips on the lake.

This is a great visit if you want to get under the skin of what makes this highly unusual wine region so special. And you can even buy a CD that Willi made of the sound of his wines fermenting.

CLAUS PREISINGER

The Neusiedlersee might be renowned for its sweet wines, but this region is good for reds, too – and the youthful Claus Preisinger is one of those at the forefront of the movement. Based in the town of Gols, he spends winters playing ice hockey on the frozen lake, and the summer tending his vineyards, dedicated to Zweigelt, Blaufränkisch, St Laurent and (less typically for the region) Pinot Noir.

Claus is one of a small group of young growers driving this part of Austria forward with wines that are a winning mix of modern and traditional. His winery, for instance, slices through the vineyards like a Stealth Bomber, and he is also a devout follower of biodynamics.

For a small winery, he has a reasonable range of wines – four whites and nine reds – and they're a fascinating bunch to try, featuring single varietals, Austrian blends and Austrian/international blends.

It's open on weekdays and very accommodating to visitors – just book a couple of days ahead. One of the joys of this visit is that it's a small operation, so you'll be shown round by one of the winemakers or Claus himself. There are vineyards round the winery, so you can see those, as well as the production and barrel areas, depending on what interests you.

Tasting wise, you typically get three wines – a white and two reds – though if you're really interested, they may well bring out a few more. If you're only going to do three, try the 'no sulphur' wines. If you buy, the tasting will probably be free, but if you just want to taste and go, expect a modest charge per person.

STYRIA

HARKAMP

Should you be heading south towards Slovenia, this winery, in southern Styria, which makes a combination of still wine and sekt, might not be a bad place to stop off.

If your experience of the latter is the eminently forgettable stuff knocked out in huge German factories, you might be tempted to keep driving. But think again. This is a boutique operation – barely 100,000 bottles a year – and the fizz is made in the 'méthode traditionelle' style: secondary fermentation in the bottle and three years ageing on lees. Its top wine, made with Chardonnay, Pinot Noir (both used in champagne) and Pinot Blanc, deserves to be taken seriously. You should also take a look at the still whites, too.

You can visit its rather sweet 19th-century house pretty much any time, and someone will be happy to sort out a tasting and tour of the winery for you. As well as five sparklers, there are nine whites and three red wines to explore.

The biodynamically farmed vineyards are 10km from the winery, so visits aren't officially part of any tour, but they're happy to drive you up to the vines if you want a look. The best vineyard is the beautiful Oberburgstall and, happily, it is also where its hotel is located. The attached tavern, part of the Slow Food Styria movement, looks just the job for hungry travellers.

SATTLERHOF

This is about as far south as you can make wine in Austria without being across the border in Slovenia. And these guys are one of the top producers in the region – one of only nine wineries in the STK (the Steirische Terroir- und Klassikweingüter), an agglomeration of producers who take their land and products very seriously.

Their grapes are grown in four different sites and the focus is on whites: mostly Sauvignon Blanc, plus Pinot Blanc, Muscatel and Chardonnay (here called Morillon). It's a very different mix of grape varieties from the rest of Austria – much more Slovenian – and gives an interesting perspective on an often forgotten part of the country's wine map.

Tastings are available throughout the day in the bright, modern shop, where you can sample all of the current releases. If you want to make a longer stay of it, there's a fine-dining restaurant, a tavern, a hotel (complete with pool and sauna with views out over the vines) and apartments.

EASTERN EUROPE/ BALKANS

It's safe to say that the 20th century wasn't especially kind to the vineyards (or, indeed, the people) of Eastern Europe and the Balkans. War, of course, is bad enough, but what came after it was, viticulturally speaking, even worse. After all, the vineyards of Champagne rebuilt successfully after the horrors of the First World War and the front line ran pretty much through the heart of the region. But then Champagne never had to deal with communism.

The system, it's safe to say, was a total disaster for any vineyards unlucky enough to find themselves on the wrong side of the Iron Curtain. Families who had worked land for generations had it appropriated, and rather than grapes being grown in small, individual plots by someone who knew their peculiarities, the state followed a model of vast wine farms that simply harvested as much as they could from the space available.

The nuances that made wine interesting weren't just ignored, they were actively discouraged: grape varieties were selected on how large their yields were, rather than how good the end product; the little hills and wrinkles that make vineyards fascinating were bulldozed just to make life easier for machines; and high-quality, hillside vineyards were left to go to ruin because they required too much effort to cultivate. It's extraordinary to think now, but some of the finest vineyards for tokaji – known with some justification as 'the wine of kings, the king of wines' – were simply abandoned for 40 years. As a symbol of the idiocy of that particular political system, it takes some beating.

Coming back from this has been hard. Communism might have finished, but disentangling the mess of land ownership has proved tortuous, and it's probably fair to say that it's only in the last ten years that places such as Romania and Bulgaria have started to find their feet. There's no shortage of old vines, great sites and proud tradition, but they're rarely rich pickings for the wine tourist.

The countries of the former Yugoslavia, by contrast, are faring rather better. Slovenia and, to a lesser extent, Croatia are now firmly on the radar of wine lovers. Beautiful and tourist-friendly, they have a lot to offer, with quirky production techniques and (often) unusual varieties that still manage to be accessible.

BARTA, HUNGARY

Barta is located in Mád and it's tempting to say you should visit simply to take a selfie with the town sign. But this is a fantastic place to explore in its own right. The vines are planted on the steep slopes of the Old King vineyard (Öreg Király-dűlő), where the terraces were abandoned under communism as too difficult to work. But since the Barta family bought the estate in 2003, they've put lots of effort into repairing them and now farm organically.

Although this region is famous for its ultra-sweet dessert wines, most of Barta's output is dry. Made with the tokaji grape Furmint and the harder-to-pronounce Hárslevelű, its wines are modern, elegant and yet still undeniably local.

A visit includes a trip up into the Old King vineyard to see the restoration work. And if you're appreciative, tastings in the winery may well include some older vintages. There's also accommodation in the form of a guesthouse and a few blingy suites in the old mansion.

DISZNÓKŐ, HUNGARY

Like Barta, Disznókő's vineyards are in an enviable position, on the south-facing slopes of the Zemplén Hills – a site given a 'first growth' classification back in 1732, 123 years before Bordeaux ranked its own top plots. But unlike their near neighbours, these guys *are* sweet-wine specialists. They do make drier versions – and a rather good late harvest – but you really ought to be getting stuck into the 5 and 6 Puttonyos super-sweeties here.

The shop is open every day for six months from May, and if you book ahead, they'll set up a visit where they'll explain exactly how much work – and how many grapes – go into the super-concentrated wine in your glass. The cellars are a celebration of sweetness sufficient to give your dentist conniptions.

KORTA KATARINA, CROATIA

Americans Lee and Penny Anderson first travelled to the Balkans in 2001 with a charity helping people who had been dispossessed and displaced by the civil war. Before long they fell in love with Croatia and, to their surprise, its wine, and started buying small parcels of land on the Pelješac peninsula.

Shortly after, they bought an old hotel on the edge of the Adriatic – the Rivijera in Orebić – giving them a place for a cellar with the kind of views that would distract all but the most dedicated winemaker. A couple of hours north-west of Dubrovnik, it's a pretty drive and an easily doable day trip.

They're open for tastings from April to the end of October, and while you can just roll up, it's probably better to book in advance. All the tours include a visit to the winery, with the differences in price depending on which wines you try and whether or not they're accompanied by food.

The basic tasting is likely to be enough for most visitors, giving you the chance to try a white, rosé and the region's signature Plavac Mali red, a big, gutsy beast not unlike Zinfandel or southern Italian rossos.

MATOŠEVIĆ, CROATIA

With hilltop villages, sleepy farms and sun-glinted coastlines, Istria, the triangular peninsula in Croatia's north-eastern corner, is a beautiful place to visit. And if you can tear yourself away from gawping at its general loveliness, a visit to see Ivica Matošević is highly recommended.

His wines are really well made, and his various treatments of the local white Malvazija grape (also big just over the border in Slovenia) provide an interesting masterclass in different terroirs and ageing techniques. His work with Chardonnay also shows that he's a sensitive, intelligent operator.

You can pop into the winery for a quick taste any time, but given it's a small operation, it's probably courteous to call or email ahead.

MANASTIR TVRDOŠ, BOSNIA AND HERZEGOVINA

Only 30km from Dubrovnik, this thoroughly unusual winery is as good a visit as any in more celebrated wine regions. The Tvrdoš monastery was, like many Christian structures, built on the site of an old Roman temple, meaning that its foundations date from around the fourth century AD. And one thing you can say about the Romans is that they knew how to pick a location.

Situated on steep, wooded slopes, it looks imperiously down over the Trebišnjica river. This is a place of striking images: the dome of the church and the old stone walls; the high, dry plains surrounded by mountains; vineyards tended by black-robed monks and nuns; the contrast between the stone cellars, full of ancient barrels, and the shining stainless steel technology on show in the winery.

The resident brothers and sisters produce wines made from local varieties such as Vranac (red) and Žilavka (white) alongside Cabernet Sauvignon, Merlot and Chardonnay. You can visit the monastery and winery for free and add on a tasting in the cellars.

MARJAN SIMČIČ, SLOVENIA

With his winery barely 50m from the Italian border, Marjan Simčič, a charismatic and funny winemaker, tells wry stories of how, while Italy has stayed the same, his country has changed its name multiple times in barely two generations.

What hasn't changed is the region's enviable climate, the grapes grown there, or the ancestral methods of vinification that Marjan, the fifth generation of his family to make wine here, adheres to tenaciously. The Goriška Brda wine district is, as they nicely put it, 'where the Alps and the Mediterranean shake hands' and that mountain coolness and southern-European warmth makes it easy for grapes to ripen, but still retain their freshness. The family's 18 hectares of vineyards, planted in terraces that wrap sinuously around the contours of the hills, lie on both sides of the border and, too narrow for tractors, are tended and picked by hand.

If you're in Italy's north-east corner, this is an easy and worthwhile hop across the border. For a reasonable fee, a member of the family will take you round the vineyards and winery and lead you in a tasting of six wines, including three of their Cru Selection and two of the Opoka Cru wines. Unless you're a fine wine obsessive, that should be more than enough, though if you want to upgrade, the Lux Tasting includes their Opoka Cru and (very top end) Leonardo wines with a selection of local cheeses.

VILLA MELNIK, BULGARIA

Communism, it's true, did Bulgarian wine no favours – all the sadder since it has a long, proud tradition of grape growing. Places like this, however, might be the future. Privately owned, and opened in 2013, it's a striking winery in a striking landscape, with no expense spared in its creation. Wine-wise, the focus is largely on tried-and-tested French grape varieties – Merlot, Syrah, Cabernet Sauvignon, Viognier, Chardonnay and Sauvignon Blanc (from which it makes an oh-so-on-trend orange wine). But it also has wines made from indigenous Bulgarian grapes, too: Mavrud and the intriguing Shiroka Melnik – supposedly once a favourite of Winston Churchill's.

Tours are comprehensive, taking in vineyards, winery and cellar as well as a tutored tasting. If you visit at the right time, you might even be able to pick a few bunches or do some pruning. While it's two-and-a-half hours from the capital, Sofia, it's an hour less from Thessaloniki in northern Greece, so you could include it as part of a tour of Macedonia.

BESSA VALLEY, BULGARIA

There's been no shortage of western European wineries scenting opportunities in Bulgaria. After all, it has a lot of old vines that only need a bit of investment and expertise to make them sing again. But, still, attracting wine world aristocrat Stephan von Neipperg – whose family have 800 years of wine growing and six châteaux in Bordeaux under their belt – was quite a coup for this valley west of Plovdiv.

Unsurprisingly, given his in-depth knowledge of St-Émilion, the count liked the clay/limestone soils and, as in the Right Bank, planted them largely to the clay-loving Merlot. Syrah, Petit Verdot and Cabernet made up the rest. These are expensively made and packaged wines, unashamedly aimed at export markets.

Nevertheless, visits here are well-priced. They all include a tour of the vineyards, cellar and winery, with the cost varying according to the size of the tasting. The standard three-wines option is eminently affordable, but even the VIP tasting is good value and gets you access to the more expensive creations.

GREECE

France, Spain and Italy might be the big beasts of European wine, but Greece, you could say, is the daddy of them all. Not in terms of production size, obviously – the place only produces about half as much wine as Portugal – but this, in a sense, is where it all began. The ancient Greeks were the first culture to take wine seriously and their influence was profound, particularly in Italy. Sicily was once part of Greater Greece, and a key wine-producing region. Down the centuries, the island's grapes spread up into mainland Italy and became central to ancient-Roman wine growing.

Cynics might say that it's been mostly downhill since and until recently, they might have had a point. For most of the 20th century, there was no shortage of boring grape varieties planted in areas of no wine-growing distinction at all. One winery owner told me that the biggest improvement to the flat vineyards east of Athens came when they built an airport over them.

But the last 30 years have been exciting for Greece's wine industry. At a quarter the size of Chile's, it's still relatively small, but private investors with deep pockets and more widely travelled winemakers have combined to create what is now one of the most interesting wine countries in Europe.

You probably wouldn't realise this by visiting your local wine shop – outside their homeland, the vast majority of Greek wines tend to end up in restaurants rather than shops. But if you make the effort to visit even a small number of wineries, you won't fail to be excited by what's on offer.

Greece's great selling point – and also it's biggest challenge – is its native grape varieties. Go to a tasting at any of the wineries on the following pages, and you'll be confronted with a range of bottles from grapes with names that seem to have been created by randomly picking letters out of a Scrabble bag – and that's even after they've been translated into the Roman alphabet.

But don't be put off, as there's lots to uncover. For instance, you might expect a place as hot as Greece to be better for reds, but the whites here are also star performers and some are among the most exciting in Europe. Having almost disappeared entirely 40 years ago, Malagousia is undergoing a deserved resurgence; Moschofilero – a white grape that turns pink – is a joyous bundle of exotic flavours that's impossible to dislike; while Assyrtiko – particularly on Santorini - is one of the great unique wine styles of the world.

For reds, the two stars are Xinomavro in the north – a perfumed, big-structured wine not unlike Barolo that can last for years – and Agiorgitiko in Nemea on the Peloponnese, which is a kind of Greek combination of Cabernet Sauvignon and Merlot.

A hundred years ago, it would have been all native grapes, but since the 1980s there have been a lot of arrivals from the rest of Europe: Chardonnay and Sauvignon Blanc for whites; Cabernet Sauvignon, Merlot and Syrah for reds. They're made in a wide range of single-varietal wines, international blends and local/international combinations, making a tasting at a Greek winery a sometimes riotously stimulating experience.

Key to mitigating the heat from the Mediterranean sun are the wind – from vineyards near the sea – and height. Greece has no shortage of mountains, and the combination of cool air and altitude ensures lower temperatures at night, allowing vines to recover and grapes to retain some of their natural acidity. It also means that many vineyards are in beautiful locations, either high in the hills or looking over the sea.

For the tourist, Greece is a dream. Yes, it can be a little scruffy round the edges, but it has heart in abundance, spectacular geography, and an apparently endless supply of ancient history to uncover. None of this makes it quick to get around, however – Santorini, for instance, is an eight-hour ferry from Piraeus. So, just relax, go with the flow and be realistic about how much you can squeeze in.

GAIA, SANTORINI

Santorini is a special place. Lying 200km east of the mainland, it's not the easiest to get to, but it's worth the effort – and not just for the whitewashed towns clinging by their fingernails to the cliff edges. Wine-wise, it's also fascinating.

The whole series of surrounding islands is, essentially, a volcanic block. In fact, they once made up a much bigger island before a mammoth eruption over 3,000 years ago blasted it apart, with the sea rushing in to the erupted heart.

At the same time, the vineyards are some of the most exposed in Europe, and, to counteract the intense light and non-stop wind, the industry has created a unique viticulture. Rather than trained up on wires or grown in bush vine form, the ancient vines are wound round into a kind of basket shape, with the grapes hanging down inside to protect them from the elements. Grown here surrounded by sea, in volcanic soil, the Assyrtiko grape takes on a unique and prized mineral quality.

Yields in such difficult conditions are exceptionally low, so the wines are not cheap. But they are unique and magnificent – and Gaia is acknowledged as their best proponent. The winery is located on the eastern edge of Santorini, handily close to the airport, and is open for visits from May to October.

You'll need to book ahead for a tour, which includes a look round the winery and the amazing vineyards. You can also taste all of the wines from both Santorini and its sister winery in Nemea (see below) for a pittance. Don't even think about skimping...

GAIA, PELOPONNESE

It might seem a bit of a cop-out recommending the same producer twice, but Gaia only makes wine in two places and is a master in both. Plus, unless you're on a wine tour of Greece, it's unlikely you'll see both Santorini and Nemea on the same visit, so the special treatment seems justified.

Gaia set up in Nemea just over 20 years ago, eschewing the simple option of pumping out big volume easy-drinking wines from the valley floor, and struggling away with rocky soils and terracing up on the slopes at altitudes of up to 850m to create wines of ambition.

The range on offer here is fascinating. The most obvious stars are the Agiorgitiko (reds), but there are some interesting multi-varietal blends, as well as the chance to try the peachily aromatic Moschofilero white. And since you can also try wines from its Santorini winery, you get a chance to compare an interloping Assyrtiko from here with one from its homeland. And, again, all for a steal of a price.

KTIMA GEROVASSILIOU, CHALKIDIKI

If you like sea views, you'll enjoy Epanomi, home to Gerovassiliou. It has vistas over the Gulf of Salonika to the north and west and over the Aegean to the south. On a clear day, you'll also get a fine view of Mount Olympus.

Vangelis Gerovassiliou was one of a group of Greek winemakers who studied abroad in the 1970s and returned with a high-quality winemaking education and bursting with ideas. After a while working for the influential Porto Carras winery, he returned to the region of his birth, Epanomi, and bought some vineyards.

He's known as the godfather of Malagousia because he almost single-handedly saved the variety from extinction. And for this we should all be eternally grateful, because it's a wonderful grape – succulent and refreshing in an Albariño-like spectrum of flavours from peach to lime and citrus. 'I believed in it from the start,' he says. 'It was so expressive.' Amen to that.

Come to this modern, elegant winery and it's the one variety that you absolutely must try, though he also does some very good Chardonnay and Viognier as well. There's a nicely curated wine museum full of ancient bottles and amphorae (some over 2,500 years old), winemaking equipment and a vast array of (often bizarre-looking) corkscrews. There's a particularly good restaurant, and even if you're not eating, it's a restful place to spend half an hour sitting on the veranda with a coffee looking out over the vines.

Thirty minutes south of Greece's second city, Thessaloniki, Gerovassiliou is easily doable from there as a half-day trip, and afterwards you could continue on to the beach, which is just a few kilometres away.

DOMAINE HATZIMICHALIS, CENTRAL GREECE

About 150km north-west of Athens, in Atalanti, the Hatzimichalis wine estate is, with 200 hectares of vineyard, one of the biggest and one of the most impressive in Greece. To the east is the Gulf of Evia, while the vineyards are surrounded on three sides by mountains – including, to the south-west, the brooding 2,500m Mount Parnassus. The vineyards themselves aren't particularly high, but the cooling factor here is not altitude, but wind, which swirls everywhere, blowing down from the mountains and in from the sea.

There used to be a lot of vineyards round here, but they were wiped out by phylloxera in the 1960s and Dimitris Hatzimichalis was the first to try replanting. At the time he was a turkey farmer and wisely used the animal business to subsidise the early years of his wines while he found his feet, which explains the winery's flamboyantly tail-feathered turkey logo.

Hatzimichalis has an amazing patchwork of different grape varieties on offer – both Greek and international – which makes for a riotously interesting tasting that includes a lot of local/international mixes you won't find anywhere else, as well as some high-quality single-vineyard wines.

GENTILINI, KEFALONIA

Kefalonia is rather better known than it used to be, thanks in no small part to the smash-hit book *Captain Corelli's Mandolin*, but few tourists come here for the wine – and probably with good reason. Most of what is produced on the island is garbage.

Gentilini, however, is worth a look. Their basic red might come from Nemea, but they also have plenty of locally-grown wines, too. For reds, they've hung their hat on Syrah, sometimes adding in the local Mavrodaphne. For whites, their best wines are all about the Robola grape. The Venetians used to call the latter 'Vino di Sasso' – stone wine – and when it's grown in high, rocky soils it can give wines of crunch and zip – a kind of Greek take on Riesling.

You can do tastings-only at their rather cute wooden cellar door or add in winery tours if you want. On the coast road between Argostoli and the airport, it's a convenient stop-off, while their six-room 'retreat' (complete with pool) could make for a relaxing place to stay while you're on the island.

MONEMVASIA, PELOPONNESE

Monemvasia: it's a winery named after a grape variety named after a town... Let me explain, grapes first: Monemvasia is what you probably know better as Malvasia – now something of a star performer in Slovenia, northern Italy and Madeira. They were making wine here with it in the Middle Ages and trading it around the Mediterranean as Monemvasia, after the place it was shipped from, but it was subsequently resold as Malvasia by Venetian traders.

That was the heyday. The Turkish occupation in the 15th century saw the destruction of the vineyards on the mainland and the end of the wine trade. But then in the late 1990s an enterprising group decided to resurrect the industry.

The winery is in Laconia, not far from the town of Monemvasia itself and one of the most famous castles in Europe. The two lie on a natural chunk of almost uninvadable rock jutting out into the Med, and connected by a narrow bridge to the mainland. The winery-plus-rock combo makes for a fantastic double visit.

The new winery opened in 2018, and has an enhanced tourist offering with videos, audio-guides and the like. A visit features wines that are not just Greek, but local to this part of the Peloponnese, providing a unique opportunity to try something genuinely different, such as the Monemvasia-Malvasia. A sweet wine made with grapes that are picked, then dried on mats for ten days to shrivel and concentrate, it has real succulence and complexity and has justifiably picked up a lot of gold medals in wine competitions.

NEMEION ESTATE, PELOPONNESE

Nemeion is George Vassiliou's boutique wine project in Nemea. He bought his land in 1999 and set to work building this super-modern winery, which was finished in 2006.

Nemea is famous for its work with the Agiorgitiko grape (it means St George, and is pronounced Ay-or-git-iko, if that helps). It's Greece's most-planted red grape and can make everything from 'soft and easy-drinking' to 'tannic, ambitious and age-worthy'. In Nemea, serious producers such as Nemeion go for the latter.

Key to its success is altitude. Vines need to get away from the heat of the valley floor and up into the hills. And if you visit, so should you, because it's beautiful: creamy limestone soils, cypress trees standing like toothpicks and the heavy scent of herbs, grasses and olive trees. Carpets of vines stretch over the somnolent hillsides, and bare rock breaks through, like the exposed backbone of a giant dinosaur skeleton.

SANTO WINES, SANTORINI

Gaia might be the acknowledged master of Assyrtiko on Santorini (p170), but it's not the only show in town when it comes to visits. If you're on the island for a while and fancy doing more than one winery tour, you'd do well to check out this co-operative. It's on the western edge of the island, with spectacular views out over the collapsed, sea-filled caldera of the volcano, and is probably one of the most inspiring places to sit and drink wine on the planet. If you don't like a tangy glass of Assyrtiko here, then face it – you just don't like Assyrtiko. As well as winery visits, it does flights of four, six, 12 or, for the palate-hardened pro, 18 wines, accompanied by food. Go in the evening – the sunsets from the tasting terrace are magnificent.

SEMELI, PELOPONNESE

These guys have around 100 hectares of vines in Nemea, plus long-term partnerships with a lot of other growers across the appellation, making them one of the most influential players in the area. They're in the Koutsi region, and quite high, at 600m above sea level, where it's not uncommon to get snow in the winter.

Their winery was ground-breaking in Greece when it opened in 2003, and remains one of the country's best. This perhaps explains why their range of whites is so good, extracting maximum flavour from some of the elegantly flavoured varieties they work with. They're not averse to using Chardonnay and Sauvignon Blanc, but their work with the local Moschofilero grape is what sets them apart. It's a wonderful grape variety and they really know how to get the most out of it, blending it with other varieties and also using it to make several expressions on its own.

As well as tours and tastings, there's also the chance to do pruning or harvesting at certain times of year. Just under an hour from both Corinth and Mycenae, this is a good place to pop in on your cultural history tour.

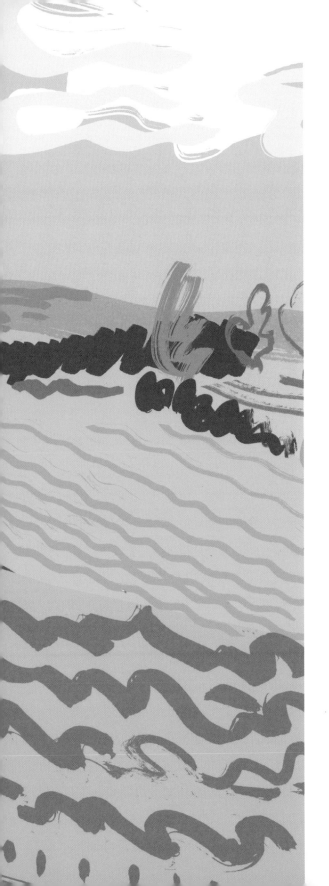

UK

Certain sections of this book simply wouldn't have existed 20 years ago – and this is one of them. While grapes have been grown in the UK on and off since Roman times, it was mostly the preserve of keen amateurs, optimists and the occasionally deluded. Three Choirs – set up in 1973 – is one of the few to be approaching its 50th anniversary.

The modern industry – as opposed to back-garden hobbyists – began largely around the turn of the millennium, when a few far-sighted visionaries decided the future might lie not in still, but sparkling wines, and began to plant 'champagne grapes' – Chardonnay, Pinot Noir and Pinot Meunier.

Logically, it makes sense. The climate in the UK is not that dissimilar to northern France (a little milder in winter and a little cooler in summer) and in large areas the soils are practically the same. Drop a grower from the Côtes des Blancs on the South Downs and they'd find the lumps of chalk very familiar.

The only downside of this area is the price of land. The south-east of England, in particular, is a hugely expensive place to buy vineyards, but as demand for English sparklers has grown, so an increasing number of farmers have turned over parts of their land to vine growing.

And demand *has* grown. English fizz is now a staple on retailers' shelves and wine lists around the country, often filling the price category that once belonged to non-vintage champagne. In a final ironic twist, the Champenois have even begun buying land in south-east England – in 2015, Taittinger purchased a majority stake in Evremond, a new vineyard in Kent.

Most UK vineyards are still very small and while they're usually happy to show people round, if you're used to Napa Valley-style facilities, you might be disappointed. Those picked out on the following pages are probably the best set up for visitors.

CAMEL VALLEY, CORNWALL

As Bob Lindo floated to earth under a parachute, the jet from which he'd just ejected soaring away above him, he figured there must be an easier way to earn a living than as an RAF test pilot.

And while his next career move of setting up a vineyard in Cornwall could hardly be described as stress- or indeed risk-free, it's incontrovertibly less likely to lead to him plummeting earthwards in several tonnes of out-of-control metal.

Camel Valley began in 1989 when Bob and his wife Annie planted 8,000 vines on the Cornish slopes of their recently acquired farm. While the vines found their feet, they packed themselves off to Germany on winemaking courses. It was an expensive leap into the unknown – without a parachute – but it's safe to say their gamble paid off. They now own the largest vineyard in Cornwall, with their wines picking up medals in top competitions.

They make still wines, including a decent Bacchus, but for most observers the stars are the sparklers. As you'd expect, there are examples made from Pinot Noir (a rosé and a blanc de noirs) and Chardonnay, but the flagship remains the 'Cornwall' Brut. A blend of Chardonnay, Pinot Noir and Seyval Blanc, it is more 'English' than many of the country's champagne-inspired sparklers.

Their regular guided tours, which run daily on weekdays, are good, but the weekly Grand Tours are significantly better: led by a winemaker, they include vineyards as well as winery, and a very well-informed tasting.

CHAPEL DOWN, KENT

Chapel Down is comfortably the largest winery in the UK and has been an influential player in driving the stupendous growth in English sparkling wine – all the more impressive given that it only started in 2001.

Its winery and visitor centre are on the Kent/Sussex border, 100km south-east of London, on the edge of the High Weald. But with increasingly serious volume commitments, it also takes grapes from growers across the whole of the south of England.

There's plenty of nice 'unstructured' stuff to do here: pottering round the shop, ambling round the gardens, or striding through the vineyards – you are, after all, in an Area of Outstanding Natural Beauty, so there are worse ways to spend an afternoon. But if you want to get to know English wine, it makes sense to do a tour, which covers the vines, production process and, of course, a tasting. If you want to go as a larger group (15 or more), the staff can also arrange a bespoke itinerary for you.

The restaurant serves up locally sourced, seasonal food and has a Bib Gourmand and two AA Rosettes. The winery also leases vines, and if you've taken out a share of a vineyard (or had one bought for you as a gift), you get a free visit once a year, a case of Bacchus Reserve white, and the chance to take part in the harvest.

RIDGEVIEW, SUSSEX

The South Downs is one of the best areas to go looking for quality English vineyards. The same chalk seam that works so well for grape growers in Champagne dips under the English Channel and resurfaces in the 200m-high ridge that sits like a raised eyebrow across Sussex and Hampshire.

Ridgeview, in the village of Ditchling Common, just north of Brighton, lies right in its shadow. It has 5 hectares of vines of its own situated around the winery, but also takes fruit from selected growers across the south of England.

The place owes a lot to the vision of one man. When the late Mike Roberts first put in his tanks and barrels with the intention of making great (not just OK) sparkling wine, there was no shortage of sceptics. But having sought advice from consultants in Champagne and been assured that the site was perfect, he totally proved them wrong. Ridgeview's taut, poised, complex wines made from champagne grapes attracted attention almost as soon as they were released in 2000 (possibly to the chagrin of the Champenois).

The tours include a look round the vineyards and the winery, plus a tasting of four or five wines in the big-windowed tasting room, which provides a panoramic view across the top of the vines towards the Downs. You get a similar vista, albeit 5m lower down, from its wine garden. With benches practically in the vines, it's a lovely place to laze in the sun on a summer's afternoon. And you also have to love any winery based on the wonderfully named Fragbarrow Lane.

RATHFINNY ESTATE, SUSSEX

Just three miles from the sea between Brighton and Eastbourne, on south-facing chalky slopes, Rathfinny Estate is an almost ridiculously perfect site on which to grow sparkling wine grapes. Former financier Mark Driver and his wife Sarah certainly saw the potential.

In 2010, when they bought it, it was an arable farm with no vines. Within a decade it had become one of the most talked-about projects in the UK's wine industry, its upward rise emblematic of the growth in English fizz.

From the start, Mark and Sarah wanted the estate to be not just a producer of great sparkling wines, but also a hotspot for tourists, and they had a tasting room, tours and vineyard visits set up from the moment the first bottles hit the market in 2018. If you want to do a tasting, you can just drop in, though tours, which take about two hours and include winery and vineyards as well as tasting, need to be booked ahead.

With ten ensuite rooms, the estate's Flint Barns offer a good base for exploring the Downs, and a rather louche night's accommodation if you're walking the Cuckmere Haven stretch of the South Downs Way, which is just a couple of hundred metres to the north.

THREE CHOIRS, GLOUCESTERSHIRE

One of England's oldest, and biggest, wineries – it owns 30 hectares and its first vintage was the scorcher of 1976 – Three Choirs stands out from the other UK vineyards mentioned here because its main focus is still, rather than sparkling, wine.

And while it does have some Pinot Noir, much of what it grows is, if you like, traditional (ie rain-resistant) English varieties. Give yourself a mark for every one of these you recognise: Siegerrebe, Madeleine Angevine, Schönburger, Seyval Blanc, Huxelrebe, Müller-Thurgau, Reichensteiner, Bacchus and Rondo. If you scored over three, you're either an English winemaker or you need to get out more.

Tours are in a relaxed 'self-guided' format: you get a map for a trail through the vineyards, a video to explain the whole Three Choirs story and an open invitation to the cellar door for a tasting of five wines. The only timetabled element is the tour of the winery – other than that, you can play it by ear.

If you're thinking of staying in the area, you might want to take one of the winery's lodges. They're not badly priced, and the tour and tasting is included as part of the package.

DENBIES, SURREY

If you've already ticked off one (or all) of the South Downs wineries mentioned here, a trip to Denbies gives you a chance to do a North Downs counterpart. Denbies is in the beautiful Surrey Hills and it's hugely accessible. Only just outside the M25, and half an hour by train from London, it is one of the closest wineries to the capital – easily doable in a day, though there are plans for the country's first Vineyard Hotel.

Established in the mid-1980s, Denbies is one of the country's biggest vineyard-owners: its 250 hectare estate on the slopes outside Dorking is the home to over 100 hectares of vines. In a good year, it can knock out 400,000 bottles – a lot for a UK winery.

Denbies used to belong to Queen Victoria's master builder, Thomas Cubitt, and though nothing (sadly) remains of the 100-room, three-storey mansion that he built, it's still a beautiful place to visit. As you'd expect from such a slick operation, it offers a wide range of tours and tastings that are well worth exploring – the Vineyard Train comes complete with commentary and camera-friendly views over Box Hill. But it's also a great place to spend an unstructured couple of hours gently wandering round the estate and vineyards.

If you want to justify that third glass of fizz, they host a marathon every autumn. Don't expect a PB – the slopes make this one for views, rather than speed, which perhaps explains why most participants do it in fancy dress.

NORTH
AMERICA

CALIFORNIA

California is all about the feel-good factor. Whether it's the glitz of Hollywood, the toned bodies on the beaches or the apparently endless sunshine, there are not many negative things associated with the aptly named Golden State. And you get the same feel with the wine industry, too. This is a place that has tradition, but is never in hock to it; that cares deeply about what it does, but also has fun doing it; and, crucially for the wine tourist, is desperate to share its enthusiasm.

California is amazingly good at providing engaging visits. Wine and golf? Wine and Gold Rush? Wine and cinema? It does them all, and if you like matching wine and food, it's pretty much everywhere you look. If much of Europe puts the 'wine' before the 'tourism', in California, the two meet at least on an equal footing. For the winery visitor – particularly the first-time winery visitor – it's a refreshingly friendly and open place to come.

With all the sun-drenched, open-top sports-car imagery, it's tempting to think of California's climate as super-hot. But it isn't. At least not always. Indeed, the key to understanding the region is not so much sun, but fog. Hot air rises off the land during the day, sucking in colder air off the Pacific, and creating big banks of mist that drop the temperature significantly at night.

How much fog a valley gets often dictates what is planted there. And it explains why high hillsides above the fog line might grow plush Zinfandels, while the fog-filled valley bottom just a few kilometres away is growing chilly, acidity-high grapes for sparkling wine. Getting your head around such nuances is part of what makes winery visits here so interesting.

NAPA VALLEY

The Napa Valley is the poster-boy for Californian (some might say New World) wine – the region with the perfect hair, big teeth and lucrative Vegas residency. But it's worked hard to get there, and it came the hard way. Understandably, its wine industry practically shut down during Prohibition, and struggled mightily for almost 30 years after the Second World War. The key moment in the turnaround came when Robert Mondavi opened his winery in 1966 – the first new venture in Napa since the 1920s alcohol ban. It marked the start of the modern Californian industry, with ambitious wines and higher prices.

Mondavi knew decent land when he saw it, and how to make the most out of it – and wasn't happy to settle for cheap and cheerful. Others followed his lead, and this strip of terrain between the Mayacamas and Vaca Mountain ranges is now an almost unbroken sea of vines. And those vines have made Napa rich. The beautifully built wineries have visitor centres, restaurants, theatres, art installations – they're celebrations of the good life, and tourists flock to them all year round. At weekends, the cars and coaches start to arrive at 10am and by midday the place is heaving, staying that way until 5pm. Most wineries offer walk-up tastings, but it's usually best to book visits if you can.

Napa does have a range of grape varieties, but it's not really the place to come if you don't like Cabernet Sauvignon. The stereotypical Napa style is big, fruit-forward and oaky – wines that make a statement. But there are also growers who deliberately avoid that in favour of a more restrained approach – visits here needn't be all about power.

There are many attractive aspects to Napa – the plethora of interesting things to do and top places to eat chief among them. But for the tourist the big advantage is how easy it is to get a handle on and, only 50km long and 8km across at its widest point, how easy it is to see most of it relatively quickly.

You can feasibly fit in two or three visits on a day trip from San Francisco (and plenty of people do), but you'll get more out of it if you stay a couple of nights and savour the valley when it's cooler and quieter – when the greasepaint comes off and it's just a country boy with a guitar again.

CONN CREEK

Set up in 1973, this was one of the early starters in the rebirth of Napa. A smaller winery on the Silverado Trail, overlooking Lake Hennessey, it's in a lovely spot, and though it isn't averse to dabbling with other grape varieties, its focus has always been on that most noble of Bordeaux varieties, Cabernet Sauvignon.

The AVA series showcases Cabernets from vineyards across Napa Valley, and it makes for an interesting tasting opportunity at its cellar door. You can explore the single varietal wines and a range of regional Cabernets, allowing you to discern how a Calistoga Cabernet (from the north of the valley) differs from one from the granitic slopes of Mount Veeder or the famous Rutherford Bench. Upgrading to the Anthology tasting puts the focus on the AVAs and its flagship Anthology wine.

The latter is a blend of the various Napa vineyards in the AVA series, and if you want to have a go at creating your own top-end wine, sign up for the Barrel Blending Experience. It's not cheap, but it's a fantastic package that gives you the chance to play winemaker.

CORISON

There is absolutely nothing gimmicky about a visit to Corison. Like owner Cathy Corison herself – one of the true *grandes dames* of American wine – it's honest, straightforward, somewhat understated, heartfelt, and totally worth seeking out.

Corison has been making wines from central Napa's 'benches' – the alluvial beds between Rutherford and St Helena long recognised as harbouring the valley's best Cabernet vineyards – for over 30 years.

While it's easy to make big, ripe wines with big, ripe price-tags, Corison does none of this. Her wines are powerful, yes – this is California, after all – but even in hot years they're balanced and elegant. There is nothing overblown or showy about them, which means they often don't attract the scores they should in blind tastings. This is a good thing. People who know wine, know Corison – and she has been laudably good about keeping her prices affordable – at least by the elevated standards of A-list Napa.

Tours and tastings (including a visit to her excellent Kronos vineyard) are available throughout the day, though you'll need to book. The Library Tasting will get you all the current releases, while the Collector's Vertical Experience provides the chance to try older vintages of some of Napa's most elegant wines. It's pricey, but these are the kind of wines that benefit from a bit of age on them, so if you're a fine wine lover, it's pretty good value.

THE HESS COLLECTION

Love wine? Love art? Then it's hard to think of a better visit than this one anywhere in the world. Up on Mount Veeder, the Hess Collection is the kind of gem that materialises when an extremely wealthy man indulges his twin passions.

Swiss millionaire Donald Hess also has wine estates in Argentina and South Africa, and set up his Napa winery in 1978. To his immense credit, when he bought his 220-hectare site, he left two-thirds of it unplanted to create a 'wildlife corridor' and in 2015 the estate was classified as sustainable.

Up in the Mayacamas Mountains on the western edge of Napa, Mount Veeder is a very particular place. High, rugged and with steep volcanic slopes, its Cabernet Sauvignons are big of structure, taut of mouthfeel and full of flavour.

Getting to try them is part of the joy of a visit here. You can roll up to the stand-up bar any time and try four wines from the tasting menu for a middling fee. It's not a bad deal, particularly if you add in the chance to view the second great reason to come here: the artworks from Hess's large private collection, including paintings by Francis Bacon, Franz Gertsch, and others.

There's a wide range of visit options, from wine and food pairings, to vineyard tours that explain the sustainability angle, and – should you fancy making a day of it – a tour and luncheon. The latter isn't remotely cheap, but does include a guided tour of the visitor centre, art museum and gardens, before a wine-matched lunch looking out over the vines.

If you're not in for a three-figure outlay, the Elevated Tasting might be a better bet, giving you the chance to try wines that aren't on the normal list.

INGLENOOK

Inglenook is one of Napa Valley's grand old estates. The farm itself dates back to the 19th century, and began to grow grapes and make wine in the 1880s when it was bought by former Finnish sailor and fur trader Gustave Niebaum. He wasn't someone who did things by halves: he also put up a grand château and dug cellars directly into the hillside.

Despite the ambitious start, it hasn't always been plain sailing. Production stopped for a few years when Niebaum died in 1908, then again for over a decade during Prohibition, and despite its legendary 1941 Cabernet Sauvignon picking up a perfect 100 points in *Wine Spectator* (it's widely regarded as one of the best Napa Cabs ever made), the estate fell on hard times. The family sold up, and the winery was passed to and from big companies who didn't seem to know what to do with it.

Then in 1975, director Francis Ford Coppola used his profits from the first two *Godfather* films to buy the estate. Robert Mondavi himself (see below) congratulated him on snapping up one of Napa's finest properties. Over time, Coppola has gradually bought back all the old land, and, finally, the rights to the original name. It's been a turbulent 50 years, but one of Rutherford's iconic properties is finally back.

This is a different visit to Coppola's estate in Sonoma (p189). As you would expect, it's a refined, respectful experience – more like a trip to a European wine estate. There's a just-about-fairly priced tutored Heritage Tasting, though for a bit extra you can get the same with a tour of the grand old château and caves also thrown in. It's understandably popular, so book well in advance.

ROBERT MONDAVI WINERY

Robert Mondavi is an icon in the world of Californian wine – and justifiably so. When he built his first winery here in 1966 nobody was making wines of any real distinction and the industry was on its knees. Indeed, his winery – nicknamed 'Bob's Folly' by sceptical locals – was the first built in Napa since Prohibition had ended over three decades earlier.

Mondavi was the person who truly believed in the potential of Napa wine before anyone else. He was the first who saw what it could be, who got around to making it, and who understood the importance of welcoming visitors, too. The string of wealthy wineries and purple-lipped tourists who fill the valley every weekend are, in no small measure, there because of him.

So there's an element of pilgrimage to a visit to the Robert Mondavi Winery – though that doesn't make the giant sculpted head of the late 'Mister', as he was always known by staff, any less eerie when you arrive. But enter in through the Mexican hacienda-style archway and you're in something of a wine wonderland.

The Signature tour involves a walk through the To Kalon vineyard (one of the best in Napa – it's like getting to stroll through the vines of Lafite), the beautiful gravity-fed winery, the cellars and a tutored tasting of three wines.

Spaces are limited, so you'll need to book in advance, but if you miss out on the tour, it's possible to do a walk-up tasting of various wine flights. For newbies, the Wine Tasting Basics is a nice touch: 45 minutes of what to do and what to look for when tasting. There's also a whole raft of wine-and-food-related options, as well as a Five Decades Dinner. The latter is rather pricey, but gives you the rare chance to taste Napa wines with some serious age on them.

SPOTTSWOODE

If you'd like to imagine what it would be like to live in a charming old house surrounded by vineyards, take a look round here. Spottswoode is open for tourist visits, but it does relatively few a day, and they are only for small groups. The downside of this is that you'll need to book your spot well in advance; the upside is that visits are wonderfully informative and relaxed.

If you've been put off by some of the more Disneyland-esque wineries in California (and they're not for everyone), this will feel like a cool drink of water on a hot day. The house is a delightful Victorian oddity, as are the gardens stuffed full of tropical plants.

A visit takes in the house and grounds, as well as the cellars that it acquired off a neighbour in 1884 and the vineyards. At the end, you can try its Sauvignon Blanc, plus a couple of Cabernet Sauvignons, including the Estate Cab.

Even though there's no hint of snobbery about Spottswoode, there's something rather regal and European about this visit – perhaps because, like so many famous French wineries, it made its name under the leadership of a woman. Mary Novak was a key figure in Napa and her daughter Beth has taken over the reins in a similarly quiet-yet-assured fashion.

SPRING MOUNTAIN VINEYARD

It's easy to spend your whole visit to Napa trundling along the valley floor. That, after all, is where many of the famous wineries are located, and it's tempting just to follow the herd down Route 29. But make an effort to come to this place. Just outside St Helena at the northern end of Napa, Spring Mountain Vineyard is located on Spring Mountain, on Spring Mountain Road, so could hardly be more straightforward to find.

Once three separate properties, it is now a single 300-hectare estate that winds over and around the slopes and folds of the Mayacamas range, stretching up to 600m above sea level. As well as providing luscious views, the altitude has an effect on the wines, too, so if you've mostly been tasting Cabernets from the warmer, lower vineyards, you ought to see a difference with these.

The walk-up tastings are good but pricey, though for a property as beautiful as this, you're probably better off sucking up the extra expense and going for the full-on visit to the vines, gardens, house and winery. It's an atmospheric two hours at one of the most beautiful estates in the valley.

STAG'S LEAP
WINE CELLARS

If Robert Mondavi is the man who kick-started the Californian wine renaissance, Stag's Leap is the winery that applied the accelerator. In 1976 a young British wine merchant organised a tasting in Paris that pitted a line-up of Californian Cabernets against the celebrated First and Second Growth wines of Bordeaux. Tasted blind, the Californians did far better than expected and one of them, Stag's Leap, came out top overall.

The so-called Judgment of Paris bore out what Robert Mondavi had been saying – that Californian wines were just as good as the aristocrats of Europe – and thrust Stag's Leap into the global spotlight. It's stayed there ever since, but has never seemed quite at ease with its fame – certainly, it's one of the least showy of five-star producers.

The winery is pretty, but unobtrusive, a few arty sculptures scattered around the grounds the only sop to celebrity. Otherwise, this is a place as classy as the wines it turns out.

At the bottom end of the Silverado Trail, the Stag's Leap AVA is a touch colder than some of the areas further north, and, combined with its volcanic soils, gives wines with a cool-hearted elegance. Like Corison (p184), this is a good place to come if you like European styles of Cabernet, but aren't so sure about the full-throated Californian versions.

The visitor centre has a gorgeous view over its celebrated Fay Vineyard (which produced the wine that won in Paris all those years ago), butting up towards the Vaca Mountains. If you're happy just gazing at the vineyards with a glass of something rather good then go for the four-wine tasting flight. Cellar-nuts might want to pay the extra for the winery tour, but frankly I'd be tempted to put that money towards buying a bottle of the Fay Cabernet.

By the way, be sure not to confuse Stag's Leap Wine Cellars with Stags' Leap Winery up the road – they're separate operations.

The wine line

One of the oddities of the Napa Valley is that it has a private railroad running up and down it. The Napa Valley Wine Train was built in 1864 to take visitors to the spa town of Calistoga, but its usefulness was somewhat negated when Highway 29 was constructed parallel to the tracks. It's a nice half-day out, though. The three-hour, 58km round trip is a fun way to see the valley, while the 100-year-old train carriages still have a certain mahogany and velvet glamour.

NORTH COAST

For a long time, Sonoma was 'the other region' – Napa's less wealthy neighbour that did good work behind the scenes without always getting the credit it deserved. Well, no more. Napa might be the undisputed king of Cabernet, but for wineries that want to expand their horizons and explore different microclimates, Sonoma has far more to offer.

It's the fog, you see. In some places it arrives earlier and leaves later than in Napa, making it so cool you can make decent fizz (no coincidence that most of California's best sparklers come from out this way). In other areas, above the fog line, there's the day-long sun you need to grow powerful Cabernet and Zinfandel.

For the visitor, exploring Sonoma, Mendocino and so on is less straightforward than Napa. They're larger for a start – the Sonoma Coast AVA alone is 2,000km² – and where Napa is basically two roads running north-south, here there are myriad sub-valleys and off-shoots that make it harder to get your bearings and easy to get distracted.

But that's also what makes it interesting. Hilly, verdant and more remote, it's a place to explore at leisure rather than in a hurry.

BENZIGER, SONOMA

Biodynamic grape growing is becoming ever more commonplace, but these guys got into it earlier than most. Mike Benziger and his new bride came out to California in the early 1970s, and began the transition to biodynamic farming 20 years later. By 2000 their whole farm had been certified biodynamic.

That makes a visit here more 'farm-like' than most wine estates, with Highland cattle (handy producers of manure) and sheep on 'weed-removing' duty in the vines. They also have an 'insectory' – useful for producing 'good bugs' to get rid of 'bad bugs' and an organic fruit and veg garden. It's all rather bucolic and lovely.

The best way to experience it – particularly if you're in a hurry – is to join their Biodynamic Vineyard Tram Tour, which trundles its way into the vines and round the estate, with a tour of the cellars and a tasting. It's not bad value, and as well as getting you properly out into the vineyards, older/younger visitors might appreciate the lack of walking. The Tribute Estate Tour is twice the length, at an hour and a half, and not that much more expensive, so worth going for if you're after the full story. They do walk-ups in their tasting room, too.

FRANCIS FORD COPPOLA WINERY, SONOMA

How can you not love a winery whose slogan is 'Cinema, Wine, Food, Hideaways and Adventure'? You could spend a long time at this Geyserville operation even if you weren't that committed to trying the wines or visiting the winery – gaming tables for chess and backgammon plus *bocce* courts (an Italian version of *pétanque*) all provide perfect ways of idling away a warm Sonoma afternoon.

But be strong, be dedicated, and try out one of the tours. I wouldn't bother with the bottling line visit, but the Private Tour and Tasting should provide you with enough stories to dine out on for a while. If you're less committed, or in a hurry, the straight tutored tasting isn't bad, though is perhaps a little pricey for what you get.

This being filmmaker Coppola's winery, there's also lots of movie memorabilia scattered throughout the property (Don Corleone's desk, anyone?), so you can gawp and taste as you go, possibly mumbling in your best Brando imitation.

And if you're going to make a day of it, there's also the kind of H-shaped pool that you would only find in the grounds of a film director's estate as well as a hearty restaurant. Part park, part cinematic museum, part winery, this is not by any stretch your average visit. But it's the kind of place that a family can come secure in the knowledge that the kids (or less interested adults) won't be sulking inside after half an hour.

GOLDENEYE, ANDERSON VALLEY

There are a string of great wineries scattered along the far end of Highway 128, particularly as it starts to near the coast. Vines here have to share the rugged countryside with pines and firs, giving it a wilder feel than Napa. As the foliage suggests, this is a significantly cooler area. So cool, in fact, that it's home to some of California's best sparkling wine grapes. And while one or two old-time Zinfandels are grown up high above the fog line, essentially when it comes to reds, Pinot Noir is king.

Dan and Margaret Duckhorn already had a winery in Napa that was – and still is – famed for its Merlot when they came here in search of somewhere to make great Pinot. And while they do make a fizz, a Gewürztraminer and a Pinot Gris, Noir is their main focus.

The wines are not cheap, but that isn't their intention. Rather than make a couple of 'Anderson Valley' Pinots, they have, instead, created a series of single vineyard wines that explore the area's different terroirs.

So, though their Essentials Tasting is beguilingly well priced – and includes a couple of wines from the Duckhorns' Russian River winery as well – the Estate Tasting, complete with a tour alongside one of their educators, is more likely to unlock the secrets of Anderson Valley for you.

J VINEYARDS, SONOMA

The Russian River Valley is one of the coolest spots in the north coast. How cool? Well, cool enough to be able to make properly good sparkling wine – not something that's easily found in sun-filled California.

Founded by Judy Jordan, J Vineyards began as a sparkling wine producer back in 1986, and remains one of the best-known quality winemakers in California. It uses the same grape varieties as champagne – mostly Pinot Noir and Chardonnay, with a little Pinot Meunier thrown in – and has a range of styles that any Reims grower would be pleased with, from non-vintage and bruts to vintage, demi-sec and rosé. There's even a blanc de noirs (white fizz made with red grapes) and a brut available in magnum.

In case you're not interested in sparklers, there's also a sizable selection of both Pinot Noir and Chardonnay still wines. It all makes a visit here practically a Pinot and Chardonnay workshop, enabling you to try the varieties in almost every style of which they're capable.

The Standard tasting is a decent introduction, though pay a bit extra and the wine flights in the Legacy Tasting are more interesting, with still and sparkling line-ups available. With vineyard and cellar tours and an understandably popular five-course food and wine pairing experience in the restaurant, there's a lot here to suit every budget or level of interest.

LITTORAI, SONOMA

Ted Lemon, who set up Littorai in 1993, learned his craft from some of the greatest names in French wine, such as Aubert de Villaine of Domaine de la Romanée-Conti. He was one of the first in California to head towards a natural, vineyard-centred philosophy at a time when the focus was much more on shiny winery equipment.

The Littorai farm is modelled on the 'closed circle' philosophy of Rudolf Steiner, the father of biodynamics. A strong opponent of modern, chemical-centred farming methods, Ted only takes grapes from vineyards that are farmed alternatively. The winery, too, is totally ecological.

The tastings are all tutored, but what you really ought to do here is get out into the vineyards and understand what Ted's eco vision is all about. The tour is not that much more expensive than the straight tasting, and well worth the extra. The wines are excellent, too. Groups are limited to six people, so book ahead.

RAVENSWOOD, SONOMA

There aren't many wineries that have inspired their devotees to get tattoos of their logo. In fact, Ravenswood is probably in a minority of one in that area. Of course, it helps that the image of three interlocking ravens looks cool, but it's also because there's something proudly, defiantly American about the place.

Ravenswood was set up by the wry, intelligent Joel Peterson in the 1970s, who began by trawling the region to buy fruit from growers and making wine at weekends, while also continuing his day job as a scientist, before finally taking the plunge and going it alone. Ravenswood's speciality has always been Zinfandel – the variety that California has made its own. Big and unashamedly powerful, it fits well with the winery's slogan of 'No Wimpy Wines'.

A walk-in tasting lets you try six wines on the terrace, though it's probably better to call ahead and shell out the extra for a look round the vineyards and winery – including the chance to try straight from the barrel. True devotees might want to have a go at blending their own olde style California field blend of Zin, Petite Sirah and Carignan.

SONOMA-CUTRER, SONOMA

Sonoma-Cutrer only does two things – Chardonnay and Pinot Noir. But, boy, does it do them well. Its Chardonnay, in particular, has a fine reputation. While the winery is located just to the north-west of Santa Rosa, it has vineyards on different soils and exposures scattered around the area. This gives it myriad fruit styles to play with and it blends them expertly to create its various Sonoma Coast and Russian River Valley ranges.

But it also uses some to make single-vineyard wines. The Les Pierres vineyard has the kind of huge stones that would make a Châteauneuf-du-Pape grower sigh with pleasure, and its wines are distinctively taut, mineral and age-worthy. The Cutrer vineyard, in the heart of the Russian River, is its biggest and makes wines that are still elegant, but more approachable at an early age.

These guys don't make any bad wine, so while their standard Heritage tasting might not let you try any of the single vineyard bottles, it's still a good deal for four high-class wines. But if you are into tasting terroir, the also well-priced Grand Cru Reserve tasting provides access to the single vineyard Pinots and Chardonnays. A bit extra gets you a tour of the vineyards and cellar as well. On top of that, they also offer croquet, bookable in paid-for two-hour slots.

CENTRAL COAST

Most wine tourists head north out of San Francisco for the vineyards of Napa and Sonoma, but increasingly those in the know are taking Highway 101 in the other direction. You don't even have to head that far. The Santa Cruz Mountains are only just south of San José, while the Santa Lucia Highlands, another wine hot-spot, are just past Monterey.

If you're a wine lover rather than, say, an experience lover, this stretch of coastline between San Fran and LA is a fantastic place to come exploring. The *enfants terribles* who set up here 30 years ago are now established old stagers with a twinkle in their eye, while the next generation coming up are taking advantage of the cheaper land and grape prices to push the boundaries.

Cool, dry and wind-blown, the vineyards here can grow a wide range of grape varieties, but particularly as you head further south, cool-climate grapes seem to do best. No coincidence that Santa Barbara is becoming the US equivalent of Beaune – a home for great Chardonnay and, particularly, Pinot Noir.

AU BON CLIMAT, SANTA BARBARA

Downtown Santa Barbara is a fine place to go wine tasting, as befits the town's status as the heartland of the cooler climate southern valleys. There are half-a-dozen tasting rooms in the El Paseo area and you could spend an entire day wandering from one to the other with a big smile on your face.

But if you just do one, I'd suggest Au Bon Climat. Winemaker Jim Clendenen is a self-confessed Burgundy nut, and it comes through in his wines, which are a winning combination of west coast sun and minerally elegance.

It might seem disappointing not to be able to visit his winery in Santa Maria, but the tasting room in El Paseo has an amazing range of over 100 wines. So if you want to try a vertical of your favourites, give Au Bon Climat a call and it'll let you know if it's possible. If you're a lover of Chardonnay and Pinot Noir, this is one of the best visits in California.

ANCIENT PEAKS, SAN LUIS OBISPO

Ancient Peaks is a good stop to get a handle on the Central Coast areas – particularly if you're driving between Monterey and Santa Barbara, where it pops up just around the time you might be starting to feel thirsty.

It runs vineyard and ranch tours, there's a café if you're just stopping, and it also has walk-up tastings for not very much. But the standout here is the unique opportunity to check out the vineyards from the air and at speed, by taking a zipline canopy tour.

Run by Margarita Adventures next door, the Pinot Express is a 500m descent that whizzes you over the vines and into a replica mining camp. Take part and you get a tasting for free, plus a GoPro video to download onto your social media platform of choice.

BONNY DOON VINEYARD, SANTA CRUZ

There's a long line of enormously entertaining eccentrics in the wine world, but Randall Grahm is most definitely in the premier league. His initial intention in setting up this place in 1983 was to create Pinot Noir, at a time when almost everyone else was heading full-throttle towards Cabernet Sauvignon.

Deeming his attempts a failure, he then started experimenting with Rhône varieties, releasing Le Cigare Volant, a homage to the Grenache/Syrah/Mourvèdre-based wines of Châteauneuf-du-Pape in 1986. A restless innovator, he's always up to something, and his tasting room in Davenport, on Highway 1 and a stone's throw from the Pacific, is a quirky, welcoming place. Officially, there are no vineyard/winery visits, but give enough notice and talk nicely and he and his staff might just be able to accommodate you.

RIDGE VINEYARDS, SANTA CRUZ

Ridge also has a winery in Sonoma (Lytton Springs in Healdsburg) but its Monte Bello home, near Cupertino (shrine of all things Apple), is the better known of the two. It specialises in Cabernet Sauvignon and Zinfandel, with its recently retired winemaker, Paul Draper, acquiring the kind of semi-mythological status that Steve Jobs has among techies.

At 800m above sea level, the Cabernet vineyards are some of the highest in California, which keeps the vines out of the fog, but also makes them decidedly cool. They often don't pick the grapes until the end of October, and the wines have a much more European structure to them – firm of tannin, mineral and lifted in character rather than sweet-fruited.

Ridge was first built in 1886, and had potential rather than proven pedigree when Draper took over as chief winemaker in 1969. In the 48 years until his retirement, he turned it into one of the most critically acclaimed wineries in the States. Along with Joel Peterson of Ravenswood (p191), he was a key influence in making Zinfandel not just respectable but desirable.

Given the calibre on display here, the tastings and visits are absurdly well priced, though note that some require a reservation. Two other tips: get proper directions before you set off, as sat navs sometimes struggle to direct you to the property. And if you want to picnic on the grounds, keep an eye on any dogs or small children, as there are sometimes rattlesnakes lurking about.

Ghetto heaven

Forget beautiful châteaux and romantic vineyards, the Lompoc Wine Ghetto is a series of around a dozen super-boutique tasting rooms on an industrial estate. They all belong to small producers with young owners who are often pushing the boundaries of style. Their opening hours might vary, and there's no guarantee how many of them will still be around in ten years' time, but they're a great place to get a taste of cutting-edge California and the cult wines of the future.

SANFORD, SANTA RITA HILLS

Richard Sanford and his botanist friend Michael Benedict were the first to see the potential of these more southerly valleys, planting their Pinot Noir vines here in 1971. Like so many star partnerships, they went their separate ways less than ten years later, but their Sanford & Benedict vineyard continued to make a stir and in 2011 was bought back by the team behind Sanford Winery.

These are some of the oldest Pinot Noir vines in California. And some of the most famous, too, after Sanford's appearance in the film *Sideways*, something of a cinematic hymn to the variety. But there's no doubting how good a location this is for the grape, with the vines getting just the right amount of sunshine and fog. Don't overlook the Chardonnay, either. Silky and elegant, it blends finesse and ripeness in equal measure.

Prices are more expensive than at other wineries in the region (the *Sideways* effect). But if you want to tick this one off your bucket list, you should pay the extra and get a tour of the vineyard and attractive winery as well. If you're a total Pinot fiend, it offers tastings of older vintages and (serious nerd territory) of different clones of Pinot Noir and Chardonnay.

SANDHI, SANTA RITA HILLS

Raj Parr, co-founder of Sandhi, is one of the new names making a big impression on California's wine scene. A poster boy to sommeliers (and lovers of terroirism) everywhere, he was born in Calcutta and began his wine career working as a wine steward at Rubicon in San Francisco. Over the years, as he became more expert at assessing and appreciating wine, he began to toy with the idea of creating his own. And in 2011 he teamed up with winemaker Sashi Moorman to launch Sandhi, making Pinot Noir and Chardonnay from specific vineyard sites in the Santa Rita Hills.

These are some of the most stylistically 'European' wines in California. Parr and Moorman have no time for big fruit, big oak or big alcohol – their wines are elegant, lifted and, they would argue, more site-specific as a result. Their Chardonnay from the Bentrock vineyard – north-facing and battered all day by cool sea breezes – is the perfect wine to disprove the ABC (Anything But Chardonnay) naysayers. There are those who think this style – and these cooler central valleys – might be the future of top-quality US wine and purists argue that Sandhi's Domaine de la Côte Pinot Noir is one of the best in the US. Call ahead for an appointment.

TABLAS CREEK, PASO ROBLES

A tie-up between the Rhône Valley's Perrin family and US wine importer Robert Haas, Tablas Creek is aimed at proving the potential of southern French grapes on California's Central Coast. They set up their own plant nursery back in the 1990s, and have been assiduously propagating vines there ever since in a celebration of increasingly obscure Mediterranean varieties.

Of course, you'll no doubt have heard of the early plantings: Grenache, Syrah, Mourvèdre, Viognier, Roussanne and Marsanne. But since the millennium, Tablas Creek has been branching out to ever more arcane varieties that make up the 'also-rans' in Châteauneuf-du-Pape – a prize if you've ever heard of Bourboulenc, Picardan and Terret Noir.

The vineyards have been organically farmed since 2003 and were finally certified biodynamic in 2017, with teams of sheep, alpacas and even two 'guard donkeys' on staff. Tablas offers tours of the estate twice a day, so you can get out to see the plant nursery, the biodynamic vineyards and, no doubt, the odd quadruped or two.

Tablas makes a wide range of single-varietal wines, but also many blends. So you can taste the constituents, then decide whether the whole is greater than the sum of its parts (as European winemakers often contend) or whether a pure expression of one grape is better (a more New World philosophy).

WENTE VINEYARDS, LIVERMORE VALLEY

Wente is in the Livermore Valley, more or less in the middle of the triangle formed between San Francisco, Stockton and Modesto. So if you're heading from the west coast vineyards to the Sierra foothills, it's easy enough to swing by here en route.

You may not have heard of this area, but 50 years ago the Livermore Valley had as much area under vine as Napa. Wente, founded in 1883, was one of the few wineries not to shut down during Prohibition, making it the oldest continuously run family winery in the States.

Because of its location (neither near the coast nor fully inland), Livermore is essentially a warm valley with cool breezes, and as a result Wente is able to make a bit of everything: Syrah, Pinot Noir, Merlot, Cabernet Sauvignon, Riesling, Sauvignon Blanc, Petite Sirah, Zinfandel. It even does a fortified wine.

A tasting is thus a nice chance to work through lots of varieties. But it's particularly well-known for its Chardonnay, and produces it in a wide range of prices and styles, from the cheerfully fruited Morning Fog to the richer, oakier Nth Degree.

There is an awful lot here: tours, half-a-dozen tasting options, the chance to blend your own wine from different plots, a totally blind tasting out of black glasses (can you tell red from white? It's harder than it sounds!), and a class on how to pick out the typical wine aromas.

It also does a riding and walking tour of the vines, where you can learn and taste among the foliage. And if you decide to take on the Greg Norman-designed 6,500m-long golf course, you might also spend some time in the vines as you hunt for your ball. Some of the holes run right alongside the vineyards.

SIERRA FOOTHILLS

Head east towards the Sierra Nevada, and you get wineries with a different feel – and different wines, too. Zinfandel is the king round here – sometimes from super-old vineyards and mixed with very different, often Italian, varieties.

This is unequivocally red-wine country, with whites often more of an afterthought. And as it's smaller, more homespun and significantly cheaper, it offers a great – and often overlooked – counter to the bling of Napa.

BOKISCH VINEYARDS

Markus Bokisch spent his childhood holidays in Spain and fell in love with the country and its wines. He and his wife Liz worked for Raimat in Penedès (p105) before returning home and planting their vineyard with the grapes they knew.

The result is a little bit of Spain in California. So if you want to see what Tempranillo, Albariño, Garnacha, Verdelho, Verdejo and even Graciano taste like across the Atlantic, this is your chance. They also have a couple of single-vineyard old-vine Zinfandels plus their Rasteau Row wine, which is made from a row of vines they brought over on a whim from the southern Rhône village of that name.

They're only open for visits at weekends, but typically have seven of their wines available to taste at any time. There's a small charge but it gets reclaimed against any purchases, and since you're highly likely to run into Markus or Liz Bokisch, they can give you chapter and verse on just how you go about growing Albariño in the dry hills of Lodi, rather than in the Atlantic-lashed north-west corner of Spain.

Set on a high hillside, the winery offers a stunning vista over the Terra Alta vineyard and oaks down into the valley. Handily, there are several delis nearby where you can pick up provisions and stretch out in the grounds for a relaxed, but high-class picnic.

DRIVEN CELLARS

Chris Chinco only set this winery up in 2005 – his intention to make decent, well-priced wines for family and friends rather than show-off bottles for collectors. Such a down-to-earth philosophy fits with its peaceful location, on a hilltop looking out over the Shenandoah Valley. There are worse places to spend a couple of hours, it must be said.

Chris's varietal mix is unusual – Syrah, Petite Sirah, Tempranillo and Zinfandel – but while it's interesting to see how Spain's finest fares in California, the Zin is the wine I'd head for. From 115-year-old vines in the Shenandoah Valley, it's picked up some top awards in the past and looks like a steal at the price.

The tasting room is open several days a week and you can also check out the vintage cars and tractors collected by Chris's dad, which are scattered around the property. Just down the road from Renwood Winery (p198).

IRONSTONE VINEYARDS

If you've got kids in tow and want a winery experience that offers more than just grapes and vineyards, Ironstone Vineyards, more or less due east of San Francisco, is just the ticket.

Of course, it does have wines – plenty of them. And, coming from the central vineyards around Lodi, they're an awful lot cheaper than their equivalents in California's A-list areas. The tasting room offer is a steal with its six samples, and there's also a free tour most afternoons. While this isn't a top-end winery, the cellars – hewn out of pure limestone – wouldn't look out of place in Champagne and once you've cooed over the knobbly white ceilings, there's plenty of other stuff to do.

The Heritage Museum surveys the history of the area's Native Americans and also has memorabilia from the Gold Rush era, including old mining maps, photos and letters written by 49ers to family and sweethearts. It also claims to have the biggest gold leaf specimen in the world. There's nothing quite as impressive in the on-site jewellery shop, but there's no shortage of diamonds, emeralds and the like. A lively visit if you're en route to Yosemite National Park or spending some time in the Sierra Foothills and Gold Rush country.

MICHAEL DAVID WINERY

A third of the way from Stockton to Sacramento, Michael David Winery is something of an institution. The family have been farming here for 150 years, and growing grapes for most of that time.

A visit is a really immersive experience, with a bakery, deli and café on site. There are certainly worse ways of spending an afternoon than eating wood-fired pizza, glugging Zinfandel and playing *bocce* – Italian boules. You could no doubt also work in their Elevated Tasting Experience, where the wines are personally presented to you by a server at the side of their lake.

The winery is best known for its Seven Deadly Zins wine – a cheerfully uncomplicated glugger, though their Freakshow range – complete with OTT Victorian circus imagery that seems to have come straight from the overwrought imagination of Terry Gilliam – is worth a look for the labels alone.

This makes a fun family visit, and since the café is a favourite of local winemakers, you might run into some of the owners of other places you're planning to see.

RENWOOD WINERY

If you're fed up with Cabernet Sauvignon and want something a bit different, it pays to head slightly off the beaten track. Renwood is in Amador County, east of Sacramento, just off Highway 49. It was only set up in the early 1990s, but this place isn't about ancient cellars or grand manor houses, it's about Zinfandel.

Zin is reckoned to be closely related to the southern Italian variety, Primitivo, but the Californians have made it their own. Renwood's King of Zins walk-up tasting option is a steal for Zin-fiends, though the Special Reserve flight would be my pick. It's still cheap and lets you try some pretty serious old-vine Zins that have a fairly hefty price tag, plus a Petite Sirah – one of an interesting range of less-common grapes also grown here. There's also a dessert wine flight. If you want to add in a winery/vineyard tour, they're exceptionally well-priced, too.

TURLEY

You might have heard of the Turleys. Helen Turley is a famous winemaker in her own right who has made wine at some of the biggest names in California over the last 20 years. This is her brother Larry's place, and he's no slouch either. Larry started Frog's Leap in Napa (while still working as a doctor at night) but as it grew, he quickly realised two things: that he preferred smaller projects to large ones and that his interest lay in Zinfandel. And, boy, has he indulged the latter here.

Turley makes a frankly extraordinary 47 wines from over 50 vineyards, the vast majority of them single-vineyard Zinfandels and Petite Sirahs. Many of the vines they come from are old – over 50 years – and some are positively ancient, dating back to the 19th century.

Well-priced walk-in tasting flights are available throughout the day.

WASHINGTON & OREGON

I'm going to open this section with an apology. There's a tendency in the wine world to put Washington and Oregon into the same 'Pacific Northwest' pigeonhole – as I've done here. Rest assured, it's for reasons of space and convenience, because the two areas have about as much in common as Burgundy and the Rhône. And neither is remotely like California.

If Napa is about Cabernet Sauvignon and the Sierra Foothills are about Zinfandel, Oregon is about Pinot Noir. Pinot Gris and Riesling too, perhaps, but definitely Pinot Noir. It's a place of cooler, cloudier summers and lower temperatures, of smaller estates and smaller ranges. A visit to the Willamette Valley isn't about trying ten different grape varieties, it's usually about trying several different vineyard expressions of the same one.

The French have a word for these differences of expression – terroir – and it is probably fair to say that this is the place in the New World that makes the most Burgundy-like of Pinots. Most of the wineries are clustered in a pretty small area, too, so you don't need to spend hours in a car. Tasting flights are largely cheaper than in California, though the really good, interesting bottles usually start at around $60.

You'd think Washington's wine industry would be at least a bit similar to its neighbour's. But in fact it is almost the exact opposite. With the towering Cascade mountains absorbing all the rain off the Pacific, it's a place of endless sunshine and drought in summer and bone-chilling cold in winter.

The Yakima Valley, about a three-hour drive south-east of Seattle, is where most of the grapes are grown and it's home to a kaleidoscope of varieties: French, Spanish, Italian, German... you name it. The experimental rush will likely start to consolidate over the next 20 years, but right now it's an exciting time to visit. If you don't fancy the drive over the mountains, a number of wineries have tasting rooms in Woodinville, just to the north-east of Seattle.

ADELSHEIM, OREGON

David Adelsheim admits that his decision nearly 50 years ago to plant 'a grape that nobody knew in a place that nobody had heard of' was a 'leap of faith', not to mention 'naïve', but there's no doubting it has paid off.

The grape in question was Pinot Noir (this was decades before the *Sideways*-inspired Pinot-mania) and the place was Oregon's Willamette Valley. That the two are well-suited can be seen in the degree to which Adelsheim has grown. It now has over 70 hectares of vines – all certified sustainable – and takes fruit from other growers in the area, too.

It does make white wines (Pinot Gris, Pinot Blanc and a decent range of Chardonnays) and there's also a Syrah. But essentially this is all about Pinot – 14 different iterations are produced here – and a visit is a wonderful opportunity to get a handle on the Oregon style.

The shop offers a range of flights but none are expensive, and the costs are, in any case, rescinded with a minimum purchase. Some wine and food options are available, but the stars here are the Pinots – you're better off saving on the upgrade and buying a couple of bottles of its top stuff.

BERGSTRÖM, OREGON

It's amazing how many new wineries are set up by doctors – but then again, given the costs involved, maybe it isn't! Either way, Bergström joins a proud tradition of sawbones and tonsil-botherers creating their own alternative form of medicine.

John Bergström left Sweden as a teenager in search of a better life, and after years running a medical practice, bought and planted a five-hectare estate in the Willamette Valley. In the 20 years since, it's grown to now cover over 30 hectares of sustainably farmed vineyard.

That said, it's still a small operation – and that lends a visit here real heart. The tasting room is located in the winery, so even if you don't do a tour of the facilities, you'll probably see some of the actual winery team actually doing actual winemaking stuff while you taste.

The tasting flight might look expensive for this part of the world, but it focuses on its limited production single-vineyard Pinot Noirs (which retail for three times the flight price a bottle) and its Sigrid Chardonnay (getting on for $100 a pop). There's also a nice synergy about sampling wines in the winery that made them, looking out over two of the vineyards (Winery Block and Silice) that grew them.

Provided the weather is reasonable, someone will be happy to take you out into the garden and vines to talk about how the grapes are grown and 'show you the compost pile'.

DOMAINE DROUHIN, OREGON

The Drouhin family have some serious chops when it comes to wine in general – but to Pinot Noir and Chardonnay in particular. They began making wine in Burgundy in the 1880s (p19), and branched out to buy vineyards in the Dundee Hills just over 100 years later. Robert Drouhin first came across Oregon and its wines in the 1960s, and the tastings he set up with the region's bottles competing against big-name peers from Burgundy in 1980 first brought home to the world just how good this part of the US could be for Pinot Noir. Eight years later, the family heard of some promising-looking land up for sale, and Domaine Drouhin was born.

You can rock up to the tasting room and sample, but this is a winery where it pays to have the tour and get the full story. There aren't many producers in the world who are acknowledged experts with the same two varieties made thousands of kilometres apart, so there's plenty to learn.

Not only is the tour of the four-storey, gravity-flow winery interesting in its own right, but you also get to do a comparative tasting of five wines from Burgundy and Oregon afterwards. A must-visit.

THE EYRIE VINEYARDS, OREGON

If you come to Oregon, you have to come to Eyrie. Because this is the winery that started it all. When David Lett began looking to grow grapes here there were literally no other vineyards. None. Zip. Nada. And with thousands of hectares of virgin territory to go at (and no one else's mistakes to learn from), the choice was daunting.

Eventually, after years of looking at soils and climate, he decided the south-facing slopes and volcanic soils in the upper third of the Willamette Valley were the sweet spot for the varieties he wanted to grow, which were Pinot Noir, Chardonnay and Pinot Gris. He and his young bride bought an eight-hectare estate and took name inspiration from some hawks that nested in nearby fir trees.

Here the grape growing is organic, the winemaking gentle and the pedigree incontestable. Plus the tastings, at their winery in McMinnville, are really well-priced. The most expensive and best is the Exploration Flight, which comprises seven wines, two of which are limited production and one of which is a library release. It's still only half what you'd pay in Napa.

SOKOL BLOSSER, OREGON

It was youthful idealism that drove the recently married Susan Sokol and Bill Blosser to buy up what was then an old plum orchard 50km south-west of Portland. When their VW camper van pulled up in the Dundee Hills in 1970 the Stanford graduates had little knowledge of farming – and even less of winemaking. But like true '60s kids they didn't let life's supposed harsh realities get in the way, and within three years they had vineyards, a home and, by 1977, their first winery. They were some of Oregon's earliest adopters, and their success is a fitting symbol for the region's potential and its coming of age as a Pinot Noir region, in particular.

With 50 hectares of vineyard, it's mid-sized, though remains family run, and its success over the last 40-plus years has allowed the couple to create a fabulous winery and visitor centre. The main room is all stripped wooden floors and floor-to-ceiling windows with vineyard views, while the 'wine library' is a calmer space for contemplation and considered tasting.

You can choose from standard flights, reserve flights and the chance to add a plate of cheese or charcuterie to your range. If the weather's good, it makes sense to take them out onto the picnic tables, which are practically in among the vines. If you fancy something more active, they also do occasional vineyard hikes in the summer, where you can saunter through the foliage, learning about the geology, climate and organic farming practices.

DESERT WIND WINERY, WASHINGTON

There's something quintessentially American about the accelerated timescale of this place. The Fries family only harvested the first grapes from their Desert Wind Winery in 1994. By 2001 they had created their own wine label and six years later had a fancy south-west style winery, with tasting room, shop and accommodation.

In those early days, there were just three grape varieties: Sémillon(!), which admittedly was a bit left-field, and the rather less imaginative Cabernet Sauvignon and Merlot. Since then they've branched out enormously with an array that includes, among others, Malbec, Barbera, Tempranillo, Cabernet Franc and the port wine star, Touriga Nacional, here used to make a table wine.

There's a rotating list of wines available to taste for not very much at all, though that fee gets waived if you buy anything, and they do tours of the winery and barrel room, too. Allow 60 to 90 minutes for the whole thing.

MILBRANDT VINEYARDS, WASHINGTON

Three hours from Seattle, Prosser is the birthplace of Washington's wine industry. Most of the wineries here are small, and while they will sell bottles from their shop, not all of them are that well set up for visitors. Milbrandt, however, is an exception and offers standard and reserve tastings at its cellar door.

Butch Milbrandt used to farm a large area of potatoes and apples, but took a punt on planting grapes back in the late 1990s. He's not been shy about experimenting in the meantime, either. His large estate is planted to Merlot,

Grenache, Petit Sirah, Mourvèdre, Tempranillo, Primitivo, Syrah, Cabernet, Malbec, Viognier, Chardonnay, Riesling and Pinot Gris.

You can make your own mind up about your favourites, but the chance to try so many classic varieties in one visit is fascinating.

CHATEAU STE MICHELLE, WASHINGTON

An astonishing 300,000 people rock up to this place every year. It helps that it's only half an hour from Seattle, but there's more to it than that. Chateau Ste Michelle realised early on that the more you offer people, the more likely they are to come, and there's plenty going on here besides cellar door tastings.

Most obvious is the summer programme of concerts that attracts an impressive array of names and pulls in large numbers of visitors.

But the wine offering also manages to be lively and innovative without ever straying into the realms of theme-park kitsch. There's still, amazingly, a free tour and tasting, just as there has been for the last 50 years. But there's also a wide range of ways of upgrading that. The Single Vineyard and Limited Release tasting is the most expensive, but hardly extortionate. And if you want to do more than try a few glasses, there's a pricey Cabernet-themed food and wine pairing experience; a Sensory Sojourn that teaches you how to recognise the flavours in grape varieties and, right at the top of the tree, the chance to blend your own wine.

PARADISOS DEL SOL, WASHINGTON

There are fewer than 20 wineries in the magnificently/scarily named Rattlesnake Hills area. High and dry, it balances desert sunshine with seriously cool nights. This combination suits lots of grapes, and Paradisos del Sol has made the most of the possibility.

Near the town of Zillah, it's a small, homely, quirky winery that's short on facilities, but long on charm. It's more like a homestead that happens to make wine than a full-blown 'winery experience'.

It doesn't make a large number of wines, and those it produces are only made in small batches (barely more than 300 cases). But that's an added reason to explore what's going on. It's heartening to see someone making Chenin Blanc outside South Africa and the Loire, or Sémillon outside Bordeaux and Australia, while its red blends are oddball mixes that combine varieties from across Europe with gay abandon.

Officially, there's a small fee for tasting, though it's often not collected, and, with a plethora of animals hanging around, this is just a fun place to spend a couple of hours – especially if you're on a road trip with kids in tow.

NEW YORK

The US wine scene is dominated by the Pacific seaboard. Even serious oenophiles know relatively little about what goes on towards the Atlantic and all but the most one-eyed east-coaster would admit that, in the grand scheme of things, this side of the country is a minority interest.

Though vines were planted here back in the 17th century, there was a lengthy fallow period. Long Island, for instance, grew no grapes for almost 200 years and the modern industry didn't really get going until Louisa and Alex Hargrave stuck vines in the ground on the North Fork in 1973.

But the place has made up for lost time, and the last 40 years have been inspiring. There are over 1,200 hectares of vineyard and more than 60 wineries now on Long Island alone. Unsurprisingly, given that this is the summer/weekend stamping ground of the New York elite, many are open for visits. And just an hour or two on the Long Island Expressway from the city, it's as accessible as Napa is from San Francisco, and totally doable as a day trip.

The other main area for visitors is the Finger Lakes – and it makes for a fascinating contrast. If Long Island is Bordeaux-like – maritime, low-lying, moderately temperated, genteel and planted with Cabernet Sauvignon, Merlot and Cabernet Franc – there's a more 'frontier' feel to the Finger Lakes, and not just because they're near the Canadian border.

This is very much on the margins of where you can grow grapes at all. An extreme maritime climate with brutally long, cold winters meant that, until recently, most of the vineyards were home to hardy grape varieties that could withstand the frost risk – the only downside was they didn't make particularly good wine.

The region owes its rebirth to Dr Konstantin Frank. Fittingly, perhaps, given the length and severity of the winters, he was a Ukrainian viticulturalist, and he found a way of getting Chardonnay and Riesling to ripen reliably in the Finger Lakes. These are never going to be big, powerful wines, but the Rieslings, in particular, have a rare finesse and lift to them – and are great for baffling experts in a blind tasting!

LONG ISLAND

BEDELL CELLARS

Kip Bedell planted his first vines here in 1980, and though he's since sold up to film exec Michael Lynne, the small-batch philosophy of the early days remains. One of the Long Island producers with serious pedigree, Bedell Cellars' wines were served at Obama's inauguration in 2013.

Its Musée wine might be the (pricey) flagship but there are good pickings to be had throughout the range, particularly if you like art. All its labels are created by artists, and the original designs are on view at the winery.

The hundred-year-old tasting room is airy and elegant – safe to say it's come a long way since the days when it looked out over rows of potatoes – and it's always open for walk-ins, though since it's not a big place, it's not a bad idea to book ahead if you can. Tasting flights include a cider and a white as well as three reds and are fairly priced. Tours are available but, with a three-figure price tag, you'd have to be pretty desperate to look at some barrels to consider them.

CHANNING DAUGHTERS

This is a highly unusual winery. The fact that its ten hectares of vineyard are home to over two dozen grape varieties gives you an indication of its idiosyncratic nature and incredible attention to detail.

The winery describes its wines as 'hand-grown' and certainly there's a strong artisanal element here. The entire crop is picked by hand and everything is vinified separately. In a throwback not normally seen outside of the Douro, the reds are all foot-trodden.

It is continually experimenting with varieties, vineyards, yeasts, barrels and fermenting techniques. For a place so small (just 14,000 cases a year), there's an extraordinary amount going on. There are six wines open to taste every day, which should provide a decent snapshot of some of what they're up to. No vineyard or winery tours are available, but frankly, with such a stimulating range, it doesn't matter.

PAUMANOK

Actual tours of wineries on Long Island tend to be pricey, so should you be the only person in a 50km radius watching the greenbacks, a visit to Paumanok could be the answer. Its tours are among the most fairly priced in the area – though there's usually a minimum charge, so you'll need five or six others on board to benefit from the lower rates. That said, it does also offer a free self-guided option that allows you to wander round the vineyards.

The money you save on the tour may well give you more to spend in the tasting room, and thus better get into a range of wines that merits some exploration. Though only a small winery (12,000 cases), Paumanok makes an extraordinary 25 different wines. As you'd expect, there's no shortage of the big three Bordeaux reds – Cab Sauv, Merlot and Cab Franc – though they're also joined by the far less widely planted Petit Verdot. Unlike in Bordeaux, the varieties are all made into separate single-varietal wines; perhaps you could get a glass of each and try a bit of unofficial blending of your own.

The white range is interesting here, too, taking in a couple of Chardonnays (with and without oak) and a Sauvignon Blanc, as well as two versions of Chenin Blanc and Rieslings from dry through medium to a full-on late harvest sweetie.

SANNINO VINEYARD

If you're looking for a one-stop visit that will tell you much of what you need to know about grape growing and winemaking in this part of the world, this place should be high on your list.

Though it's only been going since 2006, Sannino is well set up for tourists with a good, focused range of visitor options that allows you to concentrate on the stuff that interests you. There are tours specialising in the vineyard, tours that take in the winery and tours that look at the intricacies of barrel ageing and blending (complete with tasting straight from the cask).

There's also the chance to play winemaker for the day. Owner Anthony Sannino first explains the characters of the different grape varieties he grows and his winemaking process, before letting you loose to blend your own cuvée. Bookings are made per couple rather than individually, so you'll have to hope your partner's vinous vision doesn't differ wildly from your own. In the event of a dispute, you could always patch things up with a romantic stay at the winery's B&B.

WÖLFFER ESTATE

Once the weekend getaway of its founder, the wine side of Wölffer Estate has grown in both size (it now has around 20 hectares of vineyards) and reputation since it started 30 years ago. Though there's a bit of Pinot Noir planted here, it concentrates on Bordeaux varieties, making a range of single-varietal and blended reds.

Quality is high and – as you would expect – the style is distinctly different from Californian versions. It all lends credence to the boast of locals about Long Island's potential, and explains why the wine industry on this last spit of land before Europe has grown so fast over the last four decades.

Renovated in 2017, the winery is a thoroughly attractive wooden-floored, high-raftered space with squashy leather sofas, armchairs, tasting tables and views directly out into the vineyards. It's the kind of place you could easily lose an afternoon with plates of cheese, charcuterie, Cabernet blends and a good book. If you want a look around, it does hourly tours that take in vineyard, lab, tank room and barrel cellar.

Its Winestand, a kind of outdoors wine bar, open from May to late autumn on the main Montauk highway, has a fun atmosphere at weekends, with live music and a large range of Wölffer wines and ciders available by the glass. It's a fun place to stop off on your way to or from the beach. There are also some amazing stables, which run a summertime pony camp for kids.

FINGER LAKES

ANTHONY ROAD WINE COMPANY

The Martini family describe their winery as a 'labour of love', which is about as good a description as you'll get of grape growing in this part of the world. Their story is symbolic of the region as a whole, beginning with wide-eyed newbies arriving here in the 1970s, planting climate-resistant grapes that fell out of fashion in the 1980s and having to replant the vineyards with noble varieties.

They now have a fine range of Rieslings (including a sparkler!); Chardonnays that are probably the closest you'll get to chablis-style in the US; and wines made from Pinot Gris (always worth a look, wherever it's planted) and the non-noble Vignoles, which has to be worth trying for curiosity value alone.

The bottles are well priced, and the tasting room is super-cheap – not least because the cost includes a voucher off any purchases. With local artists' work on the walls and views out over Seneca Lake, it's a lovely place to stop, and they're happy to accommodate picnickers.

FOX RUN VINEYARDS

Like many New York State wineries, Fox Run was something else before it became a winery, in this case a dairy farm. But since the vines went in in the 1980s, it has been all about making wine fun and accessible.

In this, it does a brilliant job, with free tours every day of the year bar holidays, and a café and market open from April to December that sell local deli food and come complete with wine-matches suggested by winemaker Peter Bell.

Every so often, it goes one stage further and offers evening masterclasses in food and wine matching. Run by Bell and the restaurant's chef, these unpick the elements in the food and wine and explain how they work together (or not) to give you a fantastic grounding in the art of pairing. If you happen to be in the area when one's on, try to book a place. Otherwise, you'll just have to visit its restaurant and do an impromptu version yourself.

There is a mix of typical Finger Lakes wines (Riesling, Chardonnay, Cabernet Franc, some non-noble varieties) and less typical ones. Lemberger – called Blaufränkisch in Austria where it does great things – is an interesting addition.

If there's one time you should visit, it's during the Garlic Festival – a giant food, drink and music summer party that takes place in the middle of August.

GLENORA WINE CELLARS

If you're planning on spending a bit of time touring the Finger Lakes area, Glenora could make an attractive base. It has a 30-room inn and a restaurant that look out over its vineyards, which stretch down towards Seneca Lake.

The winery was one of the first to open here, in 1977, and has had plenty of time to refine its offerings for visitors. Tours are well priced, but more experienced wine tourists should pay a couple of dollars more for the Staves and Steel tour. An unusual concept, it looks at how the vessel a wine is fermented in – whether it be an oak or stainless steel barrel, or a (currently trendy) concrete egg – affects its flavour.

If you fancy something less 'winey' and more indulgent, the six-course wine-and-chocolate-pairing flight looks a legitimate way of mainlining sugar in the name of research.

DR KONSTANTIN FRANK

If you come to the Finger Lakes, you have to come here – it's the law. Konstantin Frank was the Ukrainian who arrived in the US in the 1950s and just ten years later pioneered the work that would transform this region's wine-growing fortunes.

A plant biologist, his work with rootstocks made it possible to grow 'noble' grape varieties, not just hybrids, in the Finger Lakes's cold climate.

The range of wines includes plenty of Riesling, Cabernet Franc and Pinot Noir, as you'd expect, but also some interesting interlopers that you're unlikely to find anywhere else in the US. While there might be a little Lemberger (Blaufränkisch) scattered around the Finger Lakes, there's not a lot of Grüner Veltliner (Austria's great white variety) and hardly any Rkatsiteli or Saperavi.

These two Georgian grapes seem a logical fit in this climate, so you might see more of them in the future. In any case, the chance to compare them with more familiar varieties such as Sauvignon Blanc or Merlot is not to be missed.

The history here makes this a special tasting room to visit, not least because it's Dr Frank's old house. You'd need a heart of stone not to be moved by the chance to taste wines in the place where the modern Finger Lakes story began. The views out over Keuka Lake are just an added bonus.

RED NEWT CELLARS

The Finger Lakes, as I'm sure you're realising by now, is big on Riesling. But while most places have three or four versions, the guys at Red Newt elevate it to a whole other level. They have expressions that range from dry through medium to sweet, but also six single-vineyard versions and some older vintages as well. Since Riesling is one of the best white grapes for ageing, it's worth trying to get hold of a couple of these if you drop by.

Founded by a Finger Lakes winemaker and his caterer wife, it's no surprise that the winery's bistro is one of the area's gastro high spots, serving superior comfort food all year round, 99 per cent of it from the region.

Walk-up tastings are available, but if you're there over a weekend, book a VIP tasting, where you'll be guided through a range of wines in depth. Particularly for such a terroir-expressive grape as Riesling, having someone explain the particularities of the vineyard and the ideas of the winemaker adds an extra dimension and will help you get your head around the Finger Lakes.

CANADA

The Vikings are generally better known for pillaging than making rosé, so it's one of the more jaw-dropping facts about Canada's vinous history that its first wines were apparently made by Leif Erikson when he landed in Newfoundland in 1001AD.

It's safe to say it didn't kick off a thriving culture. Though various French and German immigrants attempted to repeat the flavours of the Rhine and Burgundy with varying degrees of success down the years, even heading into the 20th century, Canadian wine remained very much a cottage industry.

The problem – fairly obviously – is the climate. While summers are plenty warm enough for grapes, they don't last long; winters, on the other hand, are brutal and extended, and many of the best wine grapes simply can't handle the conditions. What's needed are mitigating factors, which explains why, although grapes are grown from British Columbia on the Pacific to Nova Scotia in the east, the two main centres for fine wine production are the Okanagan Valley and the Niagara Peninsula.

The former is enjoying something of a boom at the moment. From barely 40 wineries around the turn of the millennium, there are now over 170 registered. At 250km long, it's known as Canada's 'pocket desert', combining a relatively low-lying, hot valley floor and alpine peaks soaring to 2,000m. This offers a wide range of microclimates for wine depending on height, lake proximity and exposure. Five hours inland from Vancouver, it's a stunningly beautiful place to visit and, because, like Washington State, it's protected by the Cascades, it's a dry one, too – its 300mm of rain a year is the same as Tucson, Arizona.

Canada's biggest wine region, however, remains Ontario, where the majority of the country's fine wine is grown. The industry is at its most concentrated west of Niagara Falls on the Niagara Peninsula. The presence of a large body of water (Lake Ontario) keeps things cool in spring, making vines less likely to be caught out by late spring frosts, and also stores up heat over the summer to delay the onset of autumn.

No surprise that Canada has perfect conditions for making icewines (from grapes that stay out on the vine and shrivel in the winter freeze) and its stickies are some of the best in the world – whether made with noble grape varieties or hybrids such as Vidal.

You'd have to be exceptionally dedicated to want to cover both these regions on the same trip – they're 3,000km apart. But the Okanagan could easily be the end (or beginning) of a trip up and down the Pacific coast, and is only a hop from Vancouver. Meanwhile, Niagara Peninsula has one fairly obvious tourist attraction of its own, and since the wineries lie between the falls and Toronto, just an hour and a bit away, it would be perverse not to take in at least a few.

OKANAGAN VALLEY

HESTER CREEK

When Italian immigrant Joe Busnardo was looking for somewhere to plant the cuttings he had brought over from his mother country, there were only a few other vineyards in the Okanagan Valley. But he liked the look of the warm, sun-filled lands south of the town of Oliver, and with good reason. Not only is the Golden Mile Bench warm and dry, but the alluvial soils are free-draining (think Médoc) and the nights cool. The result: ripe grapes, with natural freshness.

Now over 50 years old, Hester Creek has been making wine in the Okanagan longer than most, and has developed into an all-encompassing destination that includes a 45-seater restaurant, classes and accommodation, as well as wine-themed activities.

Private tastings of four to five wines are reasonably priced, though need to be booked in advance. I'd suggest upgrading to the Tutored Tasting, which gets you more time, better wines and a tour thrown in. Other attractions include music on the patio every Saturday, and regular barbecues and cooking classes, too.

MISSION HILL

Mission Hill certainly makes a statement. On the shores of Okanagan Lake, it's a classic wealthy man's investment, but don't let that put you off. With its imposing architecture – which includes a 12-storey modern belltower – it's the kind of winery that looks like it belongs in Napa Valley. Indeed, it's now hard to believe that when owner Anthony von Mandl took it on it was a tired, neglected property with dirt floors.

Mission Hill has vineyards on both sides of the lake, as well as down in the warmer lands near Osoyoos, which means it can grow everything from Riesling and Pinot Noir to Cabernet Sauvignon and Shiraz.

The wine bar takes walk-in visits all year round, and if that's all you're doing, it's worth asking if any of its older or more expensive wines are on offer.

But if you're happy to spend more time, book the Elements Experience. It's not expensive (certainly not by Napa standards) and involves a sommelier taking you through a vineyard and explaining the microclimates of the valley before heading to the winery for a tour of the barrel cellar and a short film.

NK'MIP

Overlooking the town of Osoyoos at the southern end of the Okanagan Valley, Nk'Mip (pronounced ink-a-meep) is the first aboriginal cellar in North America. Part of the 12,000-hectare Osoyoos Indian Reserve, it's owned by 500 members of the Osoyoos Band.

You can try a certain amount of wines for free at the Tasting Bar, though there are a couple of upgrades available. The top one gets you access to the reserve wines – called Qwam Qwmt, they're grown on 40-year-old vineyards, though you might need a hand with the pronunciation.

If you want to delve deeper into its story, there's a 90-minute tour that includes vineyards and winery. Stay for a bite at the restaurant, as well – it's modern, but with a nod to traditional aboriginal techniques. There's plenty of aboriginal gear on sale in the shop, as well as food and wine. With a great back story, and some fun wines, this is unlike any other winery visit you'll ever make.

OKANAGAN CRUSH PAD

If you like funky, natural and modern, this is the place for you. Christine Coletta and Steve Lornie built their open, inclusive, glass and concrete winery in Summerland back in 2011, and it's acquired an impressive reputation in a short time.

The vineyards are farmed organically, while winemaking is almost totally natural – certainly minimum intervention. Its use of natural yeasts and concrete eggs (rather than steel tanks) are both bang on trend.

The guest centre is right in the heart of the winery, meaning you can see whatever winemaker Matt Dumayne is up to at any given moment. He's easy to spot: he's the one with the ZZ Top beard and tattoos. They do offer private tastings, and if for some reason you've had enough of wine, they also make a gin.

NIAGARA PENINSULA

CHÂTEAU DES CHARMES

The Bosc family have, to put it mildly, a decent background in wine. They began by making wine in Alsace, seven generations ago, before they were given land by the French government to set up vineyards in Algeria. Things were going well until the small matter of the country's independence revolution saw them leave in something of a hurry.

Paul Bosc moved his young family to Canada in the 1960s and began working in the wine industry. Before long he was convinced of two things: that Canada needed to lose its hybrid grapes and work with noble varieties, and that the estate model – where wineries grow their own fruit on their own land – was the way to go. To realise this aim, he set up Château des Charmes in 1978.

Located on the warmth of the St David's Bench, between St Catharines and Niagara Falls, the sustainable vineyards are part of the tour – they're keen to show you how they look after the land, as well as explain the terroir of the eastern edge of the wine region. Winery and tasting come after.

If you're as interested in putting your palate to the test as you are in taking selfies in cellars, for a few dollars more they'll change the 'tasting element' of the tour to allow you to try four wines with four 'gourmet snacks'. If you get a chance, try to compare the Chardonnays from the St David's Bench and nearby Paul Bosc Estate vineyards.

FROGPOND FARM

Plenty of karma points for a visit to Frogpond Farm. Niagara's first organically certified winery, it's been powered by a combination of wind and solar power since 2006 and is fully sustainable.

It has a combination of mid-weight reds (Merlot, Cabernet Franc) and medium- (Riesling) to fuller-bodied whites such as Chardonnay. But this is also the place to get to grips with some rarer varieties or styles. The hybrids Vidal and Chambourcin are interesting, and you should check out the Gamay too – the grape isn't much seen outside Beaujolais, and even less so in the New World.

The highest-class oddity, however, is the Cabernet Franc icewine. Lush and plush, it will have you scrambling to find a hunk of chocolate or blue cheese to pair with it.

HENRY OF PELHAM ESTATE WINERY

The trio of brothers who run this wine estate are the sixth generation of their family to farm this spot of land, just outside St Catharines. Of course, if you go back to the 18th century, it was more about sheep than vines – it was in 1984 that, having looked carefully at heat and climate maps, they decided to put in Chardonnay and Riesling.

Unsurprisingly, there was a fair bit of scepticism from the locals, many of whom maintained that *Vitis vinifera* couldn't survive, let alone flourish, here, but the Speck family were not to be denied.

It's safe to say their confidence has paid off, and they now have a wide range of wine styles in their portfolio, from sparkling wines to icewine.

The Short Hills Bench appellation, on Niagara's eastern edges, is one of the warmest regions on the peninsula, and allows them to grow not just Chardonnay, Sauvignon Blanc, Riesling and Pinot Noir, but also Merlot and Cabernet Sauvignon. You should definitely check out the Baco Noir, too. It might be a hybrid variety initially only bred because it could withstand the brutal winters, but they clearly like it. They even do an old-vine version.

Drop-ins allow you to taste all manner of exclusive and back-vintage bottles as well as current ranges, while tours take in vineyards, winery and what they maintain is Canada's largest underground barrel cellar.

INNISKILLIN ESTATE

When Donald Ziraldo and Karl Kaiser received their winery licence in 1975 it was the first to be granted by the Liquor Control Board of Ontario since 1929. Over time, the pair added to their first vineyards (planted with Chardonnay, Riesling and Gamay), experimenting with other varieties as they went, and becoming pioneers not just of Canadian wine in general, but of one style in particular.

Inspired by cold European wine regions, they tried to make their first icewine in 1983, leaving the grapes out on the vines into winter to shrivel and concentrate into super-sweet juice. It worked brilliantly – the only problem was the berries were gobbled up by hungry birds who knew a good thing when they saw it.

The next year was more successful. Having bought nets to protect the vines from the feathered marauders, the subsequent icewine (made from Vidal) raised the eyebrows of everyone who tried it – an award at a big wine festival in Bordeaux a few years later merely sealed the deal.

You can pay by the glass at their tasting bar, and they have a wide range of all the usual Canadian wine styles to try, from Bordeaux blends and Pinot Noir to Chardonnay, Riesling and Pinot Grigio.

But as the place that started the whole Canadian icewine movement, you really ought to get to grips with the stickies here. There's both a tasting bar and a tour exclusively dedicated to the style, so try to do at least one. They only do one public icewine tour a day, however, so book ahead to be on the safe side.

PELLER

Canada's biggest publicly listed winery, Peller was the dream of a Hungarian immigrant who arrived in Canada in the 1920s with a string of successful businesses under his belt back home. Andrew Peller's plan was, not unambitiously, to create a wine culture in his adoptive country. As the current generation wryly admit, he was right in his vision, but probably 40 years too early!

Peller began in the Okanagan Valley, but bought himself some land in Niagara on the lake in 1969. It's one of the more expensive visits in the region, but it's also probably the best put together, featuring a complimentary glass of the estate's signature icewine on arrival, a vineyard visit, winery/cellar tour and then, if you're feeling brave (or just over-heated) a spell in the ice lounge.

Made from 13,000kg of ice, it's kept at the perfect temperature for harvesting icewine grapes. Since this happens to be -10°C you also get a parka before you enter, to keep hypothermia at bay. The restaurant is one of the more ambitious in the wine country, and as well as lunches, brunches and formal evening meals, also offers interesting food and wine pairings.

RIVERBEND INN & VINEYARD

A Georgian mansion with around eight hectares of vineyards, this is more a hotel with vines than a full-on winery. But if you're looking for somewhere upmarket to stay in Niagara, why not lay your head somewhere that does its own?

Riverbend makes Vidal, Sauvignon Blanc, Chardonnay, Merlot and Cabernet Sauvignon, and all of them are available for tasting in paid-for flights at the bar. They're not especially cheap, but it's a beautiful spot, and would make a handy 'basic tasting' if you're struggling to fit in too many other winery visits en route to the falls – or simply want to carry on sampling once your day's travelling is done.

REIF ESTATE WINERY

Ewald Reif arrived in Canada from Germany in 1977. Within a year, he'd bought a farm and planted his first vineyards, making him one of the earliest of the new wave of Niagara wine producers. In the early days, he sold his grapes to other wineries, but by the mid-1980s he had a working winery of his own, complete with some large wooden vats for ageing the wines, shipped all the way from Germany.

There are nods to the 'old country' in Reif's wine range, too – Gewürztraminer, Riesling and, more unusually, Kerner, for instance – but the Bordeaux reds and hybrid Baco Noir are pure Niagara.

The Sensory Wine Bar has a range of interesting themed flights for you to get stuck into, from a blind tasting and (older) back vintages to a selection of chocolate, cheese and charcuterie matchings. You don't necessarily have to reserve a slot, but since tastings can take half an hour, it might help you avoid having to hang around should you hit a busy patch. If you're more interested in the sights on offer, its Public Wine Tours run three times a day and give you a good look at the estate, plus a Riesling, a Cab/Merlot and a Vidal icewine to try for next to nothing.

TAWSE WINERY

How do you make a small fortune in wine? You start with a large one. It's a hoary old joke, usually told by chastened romantics who've seen their impassioned investment dwindle to nothing. But Moray Tawse, the wealthy co-founder of a Canadian financial corporation, is doing his best to buck the trend.

True, no expense has been spared at this state-of-the-art six-storey winery west of St Catharines, but Tawse has been making waves since shortly after it opened in 2006. While many Niagara producers have a 'fruit salad'-like approach to winemaking – throwing in a bit of everything – this place is a lot more focused. Most of what it does is white, and almost all of that is Chardonnay or Riesling. The founder, perhaps unsurprisingly, is a big lover of Burgundy.

With 80 hectares, Tawse has put together an interesting range of single vineyard wines, fully organic and biodynamic. There are tours and drop-in tastings, though the former can be popular, particularly at weekends, so it's advisable to book ahead.

The shop sells lots of rare edition wines and back vintages, as well as Riedel tasting glasses, decanters, wine books and even furniture made out of barrels.

VINELAND ESTATES WINERY

As a base for exploring the Niagara Peninsula, Vineland Estates is tough to beat. It has been big on food for over 30 years, and its restaurant – complete with views over the vines to Lake Ontario – is one of the better in the region. If the weather's good, there's a shaded terrace; if it's not, you'll just have to settle for the 19th-century farmhouse. First-World problems...

It offers a string of unusual tour options (including a snowshoe tour in winter, and a Girls Day Out), but the most interesting looks to be its A Black Glass Affair, where you taste without seeing the wine's colour. Telling red from white is not as easy as you think... There's also a standard tour and tasting that takes in vineyard, winery and tasting room.

There's a large portfolio to choose from that covers all the typical Canadian styles (Riesling, Chardonnay, Bordeaux reds). So if this is part of a wider tour of the region, make the effort to home in on wines that you don't get everywhere else. For me, that would be the Cabernet Franc icewine, the orange, skin-fermented Chardonnay, and the 100 per cent Pinot Meunier sparkler.

CHILE

A wine friend of mine once called Chile 'God's own vineyard' and I've yet to come across a better description. The country's climate is enviable.

Warm and dry, but rarely actively hot, with cooling influences from the Andes on one side and the Pacific on the other, it's about as perfect a place to grow grapes as you'll find anywhere on the planet.

Though Catholic missionaries were making Communion wine here hundreds of years ago, it wasn't something you'd have wanted to drink without a religious incentive. The country's wine industry started in the 19th century, when industrialists built themselves elegant summer estates to escape the heat of Santiago.

Admittedly, this isn't quite the romantic story of horny-handed peasants struggling to wring a living out of a patch of blessed dirt; but it shows the industry has a lot more heritage than many realise. And given that these men of means tended not to skimp when it came to building their country piles (complete with vineyard), visits to their grandiose haciendas can be inspiring.

Many of these estates were set up in the Maipo Valley next to the capital. When first conceived they would have been a few hours (or a day's) buggy ride from Santiago. But the city has expanded to such an extent that some are now reachable on the metro. It remains a good place for Cabernet Sauvignon, particularly in the higher, cooler vineyards of the Alto Maipo.

If the Maipo (still home to most of Chile's best Cabernet Sauvignon) has the heritage, the Casablanca Valley is the new kid on the block. More or less halfway between Santiago and the fleshpot of Viña del Mar and the joyous boho chaos of Valparaíso, it's a hugely popular destination for families heading to and from the coast.

Until recently, it was home to the country's best white wines. Here the Pacific fog acts as a cold compress first thing in the morning and late in the afternoon, counteracting the heat of the sun. While the Leyda Valley has probably taken over the 'best whites' mantle, Casablanca remains the better tourist option.

Colchagua, a couple of hundred kilometres south of Santiago, is one of the most dynamic wine regions in the country. It's also one of the best for tourists: base yourself in Santa Cruz and you have access to a large number of visits. The place itself has come a long way in the last 20 years – what used to be a no-horse, let alone one-horse, town now has plenty of good bars and restaurants. Since the region runs from close to the coastal range (with a definite maritime influence) up to the foothills of the Andes, there's a wide spread of wine styles made here, too.

Talking of horses, it's striking how many of Chile's wineries offer features beyond simple tours and tastings. Trekking, cycling and, yes, horse rides in the vineyards are a wonderful way of getting to know a country that seems to have been blessed with a quite indecent amount of natural beauty.

There are, of course, many more wine regions in Chile, but the country's extraordinary geography (over 4,000km long and never more than 350km wide, it's shaped more or less like, well, a chilli) means that unless you're happy to take repeated flights or spend a lot of time driving up and down Ruta 5, it's probably best to stick to the wineries within a couple of hundred clicks of the capital.

If you must explore, the Maule Valley to the south is home to a renaissance of seriously old vines and unusual grape varieties, though wine tourism has yet to properly take off there. The Elqui Valley in the north is home to a handful of wineries and has an extraordinary clarity of light and breathtaking night-time skies.

Is it worth a 500km drive? In absolute terms, yes (and make the effort to get to the Mamalluca Observatory as well). But probably not if you're only on a two-week holiday...

SANTIAGO/MAIPO

CASILLERO DEL DIABLO/ CONCHA Y TORO

With respect to the wonderful chalk efforts in Champagne, this is perhaps the most famous cellar in the wine world.

The Devil's Cellar (*El Casillero del Diablo*) was a myth created by the winery's aristocratic owner, Don Melchor Concha y Toro, to protect the wines that he stored there. Fed up with light-fingered workers half-inching his best bottles, he spread the story that the devil had been seen lurking within its walls. The workers stayed away, Don M got to drink his best bottles, a memorable brand was created, and now, over 100 years later, it has become one of the best-known wines in the world.

A tour here takes in not just the diabolical cellar and a tasting, but also the beautiful house and grounds of the family's one-time summer residence. For a 50 per cent premium, you can upgrade in order to taste the fancier Marques de Casa Concha bottles, though Casillero is pretty solidly good in itself.

You can get a taxi here from the city centre, though it's far cheaper to get the metro to Las Mercedes (blue line) and take one of the winery's minibuses or a cab from there.

COUSIÑO-MACUL

Set up in 1856, Cousiño-Macul is one of the oldest wineries in Chile. Even more remarkably, it's still in the hands of the same family – now on its seventh generation.

It's best known for its Antiguas Reservas Cabernet Sauvignon – a classic, slightly old-style expression of what the Maipo Valley can do with Chile's signature grape. Not quite as fruit-charged as some versions, it has no shortage of devotees and is particularly food-friendly.

When Luis Cousiño first set up his estate, it was in the countryside. Now the capital has expanded to surround it. On the plus side, it's one of the most accessible wineries in Chile, just a short hop in a taxi (or a half-hour walk) from the Quilín metro stop (blue line).

It offers two guided tours of the cellar, which has plenty of old-world charm. The Regular option looks better value than the Premium, which gives you six rather than four wines, plus a plate of cheese, to taste afterwards – hardly inspiring. If you are looking to upgrade your experience, your best bet is to head out with bikes and a guide for a pedal round the vines. That option also includes a visit to the family's old house.

SANTA RITA, ALTO MAIPO

When Domingo Fernández Concha set up his winery in 1880, he didn't spare any expense. A top German architect was employed to design his country home, and a top French landscape gardener was taken on to design the gardens. The result, over a century later, is a magnificent country estate that has been turned into a multi-faceted visit.

An hour or so's drive from the capital, in the Alto Maipo (towards the Andes), this is the kind of place where you could easily spend a whole day or, if your wallet will take it, a night as well. A stay at its gorgeous 19th-century neoclassical Casa Real hotel – refurbished in 2017 – feels rather like stepping into a genteel Agatha Christie novel, all wooden floors and soft breezes. There's even a billiard room that would be perfect for unmasking suitably indignant murderers.

The food's decent, too (though you'll need to book in advance unless you're staying at the hotel) and if you go full board, you get a private tour of the winery, themed tasting and a trot round the on-site Andean Museum thrown in.

There are myriad wine visits available, though the chance to cycle through the vineyards of the Maipo and do a tasting at three of the group's different wineries looks a real standout. They will even pick you up from your hotel. If that sounds a bit energetic, you can opt for the Winemaker Experience and have a go at blending your own wine, using real winery equipment.

COASTAL

CASAS DEL BOSQUE, CASABLANCA VALLEY

Juan Cúneo Solari was one of the first to set up a winery in the Casablanca Valley. The son of an Italian immigrant, he built Casas del Bosque (Houses of the Forest) in 1993, and it's grown into a well-respected and much-visited producer in the intervening years.

All of its tours take in vineyards, barrel room and winery, so you just need to decide how many wines you feel like tasting afterwards. The Mirador option – where you get to taste at a viewpoint among the vines – is the most scenic, and there's definitely something to be said for drinking wine among the vineyards where the fruit is grown.

At the weekends, you can eat at the Mirador restaurant, too, while the winery's Tanino eatery also comes highly rated. If you're outside, be sure you have a coat or jumper with you. If the fog comes in down the valley – as it's likely to do any time outside January and February – you'll suddenly understand just why this is Chile's premier site for growing Sauvignon Blanc!

MATETIC, SAN ANTONIO VALLEY

The Matetic family migrated to Chile from Croatia in 1892. Over 100 years later, they bought their first vineyard. Because they didn't rush in during the early days of the country's modern wine boom, by the time they were ready to buy land (and they bought plenty), new areas such as San Antonio were starting to be considered suitable for vines.

The appellation is to the south of Casablanca and is the closest to the Pacific, just 4km away. Surrounded by forests and folded hills, it's a beautiful region – wild, pretty and wind-blown. Even at the height of summer, the temperature rarely gets much above the low-20s centigrade. This makes it ideal for heat-sensitive grapes such as Sauvignon Blanc and, especially, Pinot Noir. Matetic does wonderful versions of both these varieties, though it's the fragrant, perfumed, complex Syrah that has become its flagship. It's hugely worth a look.

Organic and biodynamic, the family is understandably keen to get you out into the vineyards to see what they're up to. A look at the vines constitutes part of any tour, and if you're lucky, you might run into the flocks of geese on daily pest control duty.

As well as straight vineyard visits, there also more wide-ranging activities for exploring the valley, either on foot, bicycle or horseback – a superb opportunity to get a feel for this beautiful, and still underdeveloped, part of the wine world.

VERAMONTE, CASABLANCA VALLEY

When Agustín Huneeus planted 40 hectares of Sauvignon Blanc and built the Casablanca Valley's first winery in 1998, his model was Napa. His vision was to create a destination where people would come and stay for a while – eating, visiting and hanging out. This was winery as attraction, social hub and celebration of the good life.

Unsurprisingly, Veramonte has a range of well-priced tours to suit both the first-timer and more ambitious wine lovers who fancy a bit of food and wine pairing. Since it also own vineyards in Colchagua, you can do tasting flights that cover both the latter and Casablanca. But I'd be tempted to go for a Casablanca-only line-up. Taking in Sauvignon Blanc, Chardonnay, Merlot and Pinot Noir, it covers all the region's key wine styles and gives you a better sense of the place where you're tasting.

Given it's about halfway between Santiago , the fleshpots of Viña del Mar and the coast, and a lot of Santiaguinos get up early to beat the traffic, it's also well set up for brunch.

Living in a (wine) box

Made out of a jumble of old shipping containers halfway up a hill, the WineBox Valparaíso is a quirky, bohemian and undeniably different hotel. Very Valpo in fact. The brainchild of Grant Phelps, a Kiwi who's made wine in Chile for 20 years, it's stacked with decent wine – much of it created by him.

COLCHAGUA

CLOS APALTA

If you measure the ambition of a winery by how many floors it has, Clos Apalta has to be right up there. This futuristic six-storey creation, built in 2005 by Alexandra Marnier Lapostolle (of Grand Marnier family fame) and her husband, seems to have been put together with a joyous disregard for the final cost.

Set into the hillside, its vast windows, contained by curved wooden struts, stare blankly out over the vineyards like a bristled creature of the deep.

Clos Apalta's mission was to make one of the best (and most expensive) wines in Chile from the 150 hectares surrounding the estate. Recognised as some of the country's top sites, its vineyards face south and east, meaning they're slightly cooler, getting the sun in the morning and early afternoon, then shaded by the horsehoe-shape of the mountain later in the day. The reds are concentrated and pure, but elegant as well as powerful. They're not unlike good Napa examples and are understandably popular in the US.

To visit, you can reserve through the Colchagua Wine Tours or online through the Lapostolle Wines website – but get in early because slots book up fast. Once there, you get to see the vineyards, before walking the sparkly, granite-floored halls to a tasting in the depths of the circular barrel hall.

The neighbouring 'Casitas' are tranquil places to stay, but also book up fast, as does the restaurant. If you miss out, Lapostolle has a more prosaic winery and tasting room in Cunaco, near Santa Cruz, where you can try the full range, including some exclusives.

CASA SILVA

There aren't many wineries that have their own polo pitch. In fact, I can think of just one: this one. Making wine might be the family's day job, but horses are clearly where their heart is. Come here and you could be treated to a polo match or a rodeo demonstration from the local *huasos* (Chilean cowboys), herding sulky cows around a pen.

With its hippophilia, open spaces and colonial architecture, a visit to Casa Silva is rather like stepping back to the era of the grand aristocratic country estates – a feeling that extends to the old cellar. And if you're stiff from a few hours in the saddle, you can rest your legs at the boutique hotel next door to the winery.

MONTGRAS

Ten kilometres north-west of Colchagua's wine town, Santa Cruz, is MontGras. Set up in the early 1990s, it was certified fully sustainable in 2015 and is beguilingly good.

With estates in Leyda and Maipo as well as Colchagua, the company has a wide style of wines to go at, from classic silky Chilean Cabernets and gluggable Chardonnays to more ethereal examples from cooler climates.

There are some unusual varieties, too. Cabernet/Syrah blends might be common in Australia, but are unusual here, and it maintains that its multi-varietal Rhône blend (Grenache, Syrah, Carignan) could be the way forward as the country's winemakers move on from straight mono-varietal wines.

There's also a fantastic range of activities on offer beyond the usual tours and tastings. Mountain-biking or trekking through the vineyards will help you justify a slap-up meal in the restaurant afterwards, though pure wine nuts might prefer the four-hour Wine Master Class that takes you through how to taste, spot different varieties, and match with food.

If you visit at harvest time, you can even spend a couple of hours picking and foot-treading grapes. Since kids are encouraged to take part, it looks like a fun (and probably highly competitive) family activity.

VIK

Like most successful businessmen, Norwegian billionaire Alexander Vik is no stranger to controversy. But you can safely describe his venture in the Millahue Valley as one of the most stunning wineries in Chile without fear of provoking an argument.

Millahue means 'place of gold' in Mapuche and it's certainly a 24-carat spot – and one that Vik and his team have thoroughly made the most of, in a way that only those with immensely deep pockets can. There aren't many wineries, for instance, where you can walk through a 'mirror of water'.

Built in 2006, the winery also has a clear roof (so all natural light), walkways for visitors and a 'running water plaza' with sculptures. Something of a paean to the architect's art, it seems fitting that the tastings take place on what looks rather like an altar. This is a place of wine worship as much as production.

With spectacular views out over the hills and vineyards, the Vik winery manages to be both thoroughly modern and in sync with its surroundings. The swirly titanium-topped hotel might owe something to Frank Gehry's design for Marqués de Riscal (p98) but its couple of dozen suites all have dreamy vineyard views, and with a wine spa and a couple of restaurants, this is the kind of place to stay for a special occasion.

Vik makes only one wine: an ambitious (and expensive) blend of Cabernet Sauvignon, Carménère, Cabernet Franc, Merlot and Syrah. There's also any number of activities on offer (horses, trekking, cycling, tasting, winery visits), but in a sense, the amazing place and its undeniable ambition are enough.

EMILIANA

There's a lot of talk about organic and biodynamic viticulture nowadays, and many vineyards have converted over the last few years. Emiliana, however, has been fully organic since way back in 2000 (it used to be called Viñedos Organicos Emiliana, which is something of a giveaway) and is, in fact, increasingly moving towards the biodynamic philosophies of Rudolf Steiner.

Six hundred chickens keep the vines bug-free; alpacas nibble grass and keep foxes away from the chickens; while a vibrant herb garden is used to make the preparations crucial to maintaining healthy vines. Its 'laboratory' is nothing more than a trestle table, pestle and mortar, and sacks of home-made powder.

The basic tour takes in all of this – gardens, vineyards, cellars, and four-wine tasting (including its very good Coyam) – and can be upgraded to add a cheese or chocolate accompaniment.

If you want to try its top wine, Gê, that has its own separate tour. But if you're happy to spend that kind of cash, you're better off trying one of the Emiliana Experiences, whether it's having a go at blending your own version of Coyam out of Cabernet, Merlot and Carménère, or kicking back with a picnic in the scenic vineyards. Just keep the alpacas away from your empanadas...

ARGENTINA

If the dominant factor in Chile's vineyards is the Pacific – how its breezes and fog impact on the non-stop sunshine – Argentina's is height. Mendoza has been described as 'an oasis in a desert' and there's no arguing with the aridity, for sure. Here it's so dry that visitors often succumb to 'Mendoza nose' for the first few days of their trip – a drying out of the sinuses caused by the total lack of moisture in the air. Don't be alarmed if you get nosebleeds.

With the constant sun and almost non-existent rain, it would be impossible to grow grapes in this climate at all were it not for two things: the snow that gets dumped on the Andes every winter and forms the meltwater used as irrigation, and the altitude.

The city of Mendoza is high up (750m) but many of the vineyards lie further west towards the Andes, at around the 1,000m mark. At this height, the temperature drops rapidly at night, allowing vines time off from the sun to rest, recover and retain the acidity in their fruit. The altitude also delivers incredibly intense UV exposure, which gives wines of deeper colour. If you want to know why Argentinian Malbec is such a deep, swirling shade of garnet, there's your reason right there.

Malbec, of course, is Argentina's key grape. It's what it does better than anywhere else on the planet. But rather like a famous actor who's known (and loved) for one part, many of the country's winemakers are increasingly wondering how to branch out and be taken seriously for other work. If Tuesday-night Malbec is a primetime sitcom, they want to do Shakespeare.

Now, at least, any developments are coming from a position of strength. It's a far cry from the 1960s when the economy was so wrecked that it made more economic sense for wine growers to leave grapes on the vines than pick and try to sell them…

While visiting Mendoza can be a great way of getting a total immersion into all things Malbec, it's also important to branch out and try some other wine styles. Cabernet Sauvignons from here can be wonderful, and a growing number of wineries are looking at Cabernet Franc, too. While the latter can be leafy and spindly in cooler climates, this amount of sunshine adds a good-natured mid-palate plumpness to its natural perfume – like a slightly over-serious, over-thin New York socialite who's just discovered a penchant for karaoke and take-away pizza.

Given the Argentinian diet seems to centre largely on steak, it's perhaps unsurprising that most wineries pay relatively little attention to their whites. But the move towards higher and higher vineyards has led to some excellent examples of Chardonnay – more so than Sauvignon Blanc – while the floral waft of Torrontés is all-but unique to the country.

One of the oddities of Mendoza is that it's closer to the Chilean capital than to Buenos Aires. At 180km away, Santiago is just a half-hour plane hop over the mountains. Straight up and straight down, it's more an extended lift ride than a flight – and if you're nervous about mountain roads, definitely preferable to the (admittedly spectacular) drive through the Andes. Buenos Aires, by contrast, is a brain-numbingly dull 1,000km drive in the other direction.

It's true that the majority of Argentina's best wine comes out of Mendoza, but it's worth considering some of the other regions. Salta, 1,000km to the north, and Neuquén, 700km to the south (handy if you're en route to Patagonia), are both very different. If the former is extreme high-altitude grape growing (kind of Mendoza on steroids), the latter is more about wind-driven cool-climate viticulture – the place to go for a Pinot Noir fix.

There are three main regions in Mendoza: Maipú (south-east of the city), Luján de Cuyo (to the south-west) and the Uco Valley, an hour or so's drive further on. If you're staying in Mendoza, you can hit the Maipú and some of the Luján de Cuyo wineries in a day and return to the city at night. But given there are plenty of good wineries, and good wine, to explore around the Uco, you're better off staying overnight.

MAIPÚ + LUJÁN DE CUYO

TRAPICHE

One of the grand names of Argentinian wine, Trapiche is a sizable player with a wide selection of bottles and an embracing visitor experience. Having started in 1883 making wine from one small vineyard (called 'El Trapiche'), it now owns a whopping 1,200 hectares, and works with over 300 growers across Mendoza.

Among its single varietals, keep an eye out for the Torrontés, Bonarda and Cabernet Franc, but particularly the range of three Malbecs in its Terroir series. From different areas (and altitudes) of the Valle de Uco, they're a fascinating trio with very different personalities.

The winery is housed in a striking early 20th-century building and there are several guided tours throughout the day that include everything from a video show to the usual barrels and tasting room. You can try from three to five wines at the end, though you need to decide which package you want before you set off.

It also has grand plans for its Espacio Trapiche restaurant, which opened in 2017, and which it hopes to make one of the 50 best in Latin America.

Just south-east of Mendoza, Trapiche is easily reachable from the city, so ought to be a must-visit.

ACHAVAL FERRER

Achaval Ferrer is a small winery that's managed to make a big noise in a short amount of time. Established in 1995, it took over ten years to get to the stage where it was producing 200,000 bottles a year, but by then its Altamira vineyard Malbec had become the first Argentinian wine to pick up five stars in UK magazine *Decanter*. A few years later, the wine from the same site earned 96 points in *Wine Spectator*.

The great thing for wine-curious tourists is not just that Achaval Ferrer's products are excellent, but also that it is all about vineyard expressions. Here you can taste a trio of single vineyard wines from sites across the region at altitudes ranging from 700m to 1,100m and with different soils.

Work through the different expressions of Malbec from its Mirador (Maipú), Bella Vista (Luján de Cuyo) and Altamira (Valle de Uco) sites and you'll learn a lot about how the grape performs in Mendoza's three main areas from a team who really know what they're doing.

This is still not a big firm, and historically visits have only been available by appointment. The good news is they have plans for an all-singing, all-dancing visitor centre, complete with giant-windowed reception, tasting room and terrace that's perfect for basking, lizard-like, with a glass of vino.

CATENA ZAPATA

It is, indeed, an ill wind that blows nobody any good. The desperate poverty in late 19th-century Italy wasn't, for sure, a lot of fun for those unfortunate enough to have to live through it. But it did drive an exodus of people with energy and ideas to pastures new.

Thousands of Italians emigrated to Argentina at this time, among them the Catena family who finally pitched up in Mendoza. They planted grapes, realised they were on to something, and slowly but steadily their wine business grew. But their seminal moment came in the 1980s, when Nicolás Catena, the third generation of the family, went on a year's sabbatical at a university in California. He spent weekends visiting wineries across the Golden State and returned inspired. Going completely against the conventional wisdom of the time, he sold off all the (cheap, big-volume) bulk-wine-producing vineyards and instead concentrated on making the best stuff. To do this, he planted at higher and higher altitudes, while all around his friends and colleagues scratched their heads and reasoned that the Californian water must have sent him nuts.

But the results spoke for themselves. From cooler climates, these were wines of elegance and concentration, silkiness and finesse. They remain some of the best in Argentina, but in the way Catena blazed a trail for others to follow, their influence is even greater than their taste. It's not inaccurate to describe Nicolás Catena as doing for Argentina what Mondavi did for California – dragging it upmarket into the world of fine wine.

The family's winery in Luján de Cuyo should be at the top of any serious wine lover's to-visit list. A butterscotch-coloured ziggurat, it's as distinctive as Opus One's UFO or the pointed towers of Lafite. The basic tour includes a video and tasting, though you can upgrade to also taste out of the barrel or do a Malbec masterclass that includes cheese and charcuterie. Whatever you go for, make sure to phone ahead and book – they aren't keen on non-arranged visits.

NORTON

Because the history of winemaking in Argentina has largely been written by Italian immigrants, Bodega Norton stands out. If the name doesn't look particularly Latin to you, it isn't. The estate was started by an English engineer, James Norton, who was the first person to plant vines south of the Mendoza River in 1895.

It was also the first winery in Mendoza to be built as a château, surrounded by the vineyards, and these now have some nicely mature vines – a fair proportion are 80 years old.

It's in Luján de Cuyo, but not too far from Mendoza, making it doable in a day trip from the city, and there's plenty to explore. As well as tours and tastings, there are picnics in the gardens and the chance to blend your own wine. Visit during harvest time and you (and your kids, if they fancy it) can even have a go at picking your own grapes.

Tasting wise, its Winemaker's Reserve line showcases some of the older vineyards nicely (all from vines over 30 years old) and the single-vineyard Malbecs are worth a look too. Both are available in the various Iconic and 'premium' tasting options, but you can also always try the top-end wines with food at its La Vid restaurant.

VISTALBA

It's a fairly common narrative in the wine world. Family makes wine, family becomes successful selling lots of cheap wine, family sells business to larger company, family invests windfall in boutique project aimed at making top-end bottles, family lives happily ever after.

Such, in a nutshell, is the story of Vistalba. Carlos Pulenta is the third generation of an Italian wine-growing family and this relatively new investment is clearly a highly personal project for him.

Visits start in the Luján de Cuyo vineyards, then move through winery and cellar into the tasting room. You get to try three wines, but you pick the level depending on your interest and depth of wallet. The Tomero wines are single varietals; the Vistalbas an interesting blend of Malbec, Cabernet Sauvignon and Bonarda; while the Progenie are Chardonnay/Pinot Noir sparklers, mostly made using the champagne technique.

I wouldn't bother with the Classic tasting, which essentially gives you the lower-end wines from each range. The Vintage offering gets you into the good stuff, and for a three-wine tasting, it's a stimulating effort. The chance to try a classic Argentinian single-varietal, an unusual Franco-Italian blend, and an ambitious fizz makes this very different from most Mendoza tastings. Each option includes a try of its estate olive oil, too.

The wine bar is open for lunch every day, so you can always try a glass of anything not covered in the tasting there afterwards. If you're thinking of staying over in wine country, this is as attractive a place as any. It has a couple of decent-sized rooms, and a tour and tasting are thrown in.

UCO VALLEY

O FOURNIER

The Valle de Uco, 120km or so south of Mendoza, is rapidly acquiring a reputation for itself as the premium grape-growing region in the area. It's even being sub-divided into further regions – a sure sign it has something a bit special.

O Fournier is in La Consulta, with super-pebbly, sandy alluvial soils that are brilliantly well-suited to grapes: think the Médoc at 1,200m of altitude with almost year-round sunshine. Vines crop at a very low level, giving expressive fruit of real concentration.

It conducts tours in English and Spanish that include a look round its 9m-deep cellars, from which you emerge blinking out on to a lake that reflects the snow-capped mountains in the near distance. It also has a restaurant.

But the big reason to come here is the wines themselves. Not only are they decent, they're also a bit different. O Fournier makes wine in Ribera del Duero and Rioja as well, and those European roots have had an impact on its work.

As well as the usual Argentinian stalwarts, it has Tempranillo and Syrah, and along with the usual single-varietal wines, it also makes some interesting blends. Its Alfa Crux and Beta Crux Tempranillo/Malbec-based combinations (named after the stars of the Southern Cross) are particularly good, while the Urban Blend does a similar, if less-polished, job at a lower price.

SALENTEIN

Salentein was the first bodega to set itself up in the Uco and is clearly pleased with its prescience. 'We founded a winery, we transformed a region', as its website puts it without a hint of modesty.

But there's no denying it has a point: this is one of the most striking wineries in the whole of Mendoza. Situated 1,200m up, the four arms of its low-level cruciform shape point out towards the Uco vineyards that surround it on all sides.

As well as a Merlot and a Pinot Noir – as rare here as vegetarians – it has a top-end wine that's a blend of Cabernet and Malbec, while its Numina takes these two and adds Cabernet Franc, Petit Verdot and Merlot into the mix for the full Bordeaux-blend experience.

Salentein's three plantations in the Uco Valley range from 1,050m up to its San Pablo ranch at an astonishing 1,700m. They're some of the highest vineyards in the world and give it some interesting fruit to play with for its white wines and new sparkler.

With an art gallery showing work by local as well as international artists, a restaurant, wine tours and a quirky 'gratitude chapel', there's no shortage of fare for the vinivorous tourist to get stuck into.

The tours take in vineyards, winery and cellar (containing 5,000 barrels) and all three options allow you to try a couple of the wine ranges. Art gallery visits are thrown in gratis. There's a lot to do here, and at around an hour and a half from Mendoza, it would be a stretch to fit in much more than this on a day trip.

FAMILIA ZUCCARDI

The restless mind is a wonderful thing. And it's a combo of energy and creativity that has driven Zuccardi for more than 50 years. It started in the early 1960s, when engineer Alberto Zuccardi planted vines in Maipú and began playing with irrigation systems that he'd seen in California. It was a taste of what was to come: a constant willingness to try new, or reintroduce old, ideas rather than following everyone else.

Before long, he had developed a special system for growing vines south of Mendoza where there's more sunshine: the 'Zuccardi parral', with vines trained high and grapes hanging down at head height in the shade.

To get an idea of the creativity that drives these guys, just take a look at the wines on offer in their shop: there's a range called Aluvional (from alluvial soils across the region); a white wine called Fósil (fossil) in homage to Mendoza's sea-bed origins; a Malbec that's vinified and aged in concrete; wines made from Bonarda and Tempranillo; and also the far less-well-known European varieties Caladoc and Ancellotta. Oh and a fortified Malbec... Well, why not?

This is a place for trying something different. And Zuccardi's new winery in the Uco – made up of giant pale blocks that seem to rise haphazardly out of the stony soil – is certainly that. Even if you've visited dozens of wineries around the world, you're unlikely to have seen anything quite like this.

Inside, there are no stainless steel vats or towering fermentation tanks, just solemn lines of giant concrete amphorae like a kind of high-tech Roman Brobdingnag. It's just a shape they believe works better and they've put their head down and gone for it...

Not all of Zuccardi's ideas will work, but some may well go on to set the future of the region. The family certainly deserves three hearty cheers for daring to question the norms and turn sacred cows into hamburgers for the *parrilla*.

The tours are all about helping you appreciate the differences in soil and climate across Mendoza, and the restaurant (opened in 2016) has decent food and the kind of floor-to-ceiling windows you'd demand if you were lucky enough to have views like this over the Andes from your dining room.

REST OF ARGENTINA

EL ESTECO

You need to be committed to get this far north. El Esteco is in the Calchaquí Valleys, way up in the Salta region. To reach it, it's best to fly to Salta, from where it's a further 180km drive.

That's the bad news. The good news is that the journey is through truly spectacular scenery that will supply you with lock-screen photos for the next 20 years. If you're committed to the idea of a road trip, you could also fly to Salta and drive back down to Mendoza. It's a long way – 1,100km – but with the Andes for company to the west, what's not to like?

Somewhat astonishingly, El Esteco was founded by two French immigrants back in the 1890s and just as its history (and location) are out of the ordinary, so is its wine offering. Of course, it has the usual Cabernet, Malbec and Chardonnay trio. But there's also a fragrantly beautiful Torrontés (lighter and more delicate here at 1,600m above sea level) and a rather good Tannat, too.

It's a long way to come, but it's also easy to stay. The 32-room hotel is fantastic – and a handy base for exploring other wineries in the area, as well as the nearby wine and vine museum.

You can visit the winery, vineyards – on a horse if you want – and do tastings, wrapping up a hard day's educational work with a leisurely spa treatment.

FAMILIA SCHROEDER

One of the most ambitious of the Patagonian wineries, Schroeder is a new arrival, having appeared on the scene around the turn of the millennium.

Some 800km south of Mendoza, Neuquén is, like the whole of Patagonia, pummelled by winds – to such an extent that wineries plant trees around the vineyards to reduce their effects. The gales also make this region far cooler than Argentina's wine capital, allowing producers to make a better fist of the likes of Pinot Noir. It also means 'classic' Argentinian varieties such as Malbec take longer to ripen. And since the wind-battering also tends to create smaller grapes, the Malbecs from down here are quite different from their Mendoza brothers to the north.

Schroeder's super-modern winery is gravity fed – meaning grapes come in at the top for crushing and work their way downwards through the vinification area without the need for pumps. Their destination is the Dinosaur's Cellar – not a fable to rival Concha y Toro's Devil's Cellar (p220) with the best wines guarded by a scaly leviathan, but so-called because workers unearthed the remains of an Aeolosaurus while excavating the foundations of the new winery.

Available in English or Spanish, tours run hourly every day and take in everything from vineyards to winery and tasting, before ending up in the restaurant, Saurus.

REST OF SOUTH AMERICA

South America's wine scene is heavily dominated by Argentina and Chile, but there are other places you can pop into. Brazil makes a fairly hefty amount of wine – though the standard is patchy; Uruguay makes less (it's the smallest country in South America), but probably has overall higher quality and a less challenging grape-growing climate.

BODEGA GARZÓN, URUGUAY

If you're setting up a winery, there are worse places to do so than within striking distance of two of South America's trendiest beaches at José Ignacio (Playa Brava is for surfers, Playa Mansa for ray-seekers in case you fit either of those categories).

The majority of Uruguay's wineries are clustered round the capital, Montevideo, but there's been a growing school of thought that further east might be even better. The Maldonado region, where Garzón is based, certainly has all the ingredients: poor soils, good drainage, and rather attractive rolling hillside that allows vines to max out on the Atlantic breezes.

The latter work to counter the tourist-bronzing sun, to such an extent that the place is proving well suited to grapes other than Uruguay's usual varieties. Garzón, for instance, has an interesting Sangiovese, a promising Cabernet Franc and a very, very good Albariño. It's different from the versions in north-west Spain, but still recognisable. There's also a rather tasty Tannat.

The strikingly beautiful winery (finished in 2014) is certified sustainable – the first to be built outside North America, apparently – and with its open spaces, views over the vines and creamy stone vaults, is well worth a visit on every level.

Tours and activities feature everything from carriage rides in the vines to drifting around in a hot-air balloon. Some of the prices are clearly aimed at the super-rich sunning themselves in the fleshpots of Punta del Este, but the basic tour is pretty well priced, and since the stars here are the winery and scenery, you don't need to spend big to get a memorable visit.

Keep an eye out for the fermentation vessels in the winery – there's no stainless steel tanks, just wooden or concrete vats.

JUANICÓ, URUGUAY

Canelones, just 40km or so north of the capital, is the traditional heartland of Uruguayan wine, and Juanicó is one of its oldest players.

The estate's history began back in 1830, when the eponymous Don Francisco Juanicó built a cellar in which to age his wines. Fast forward 150 years and the estate's new owners had big plans for the place. They carried out a study into the region's climate and, on discovering that it wasn't a million miles away from that of Bordeaux, decided to concentrate on French grape varieties.

No surprise, then, that it does Cabernets Sauvignon and Franc, plus Merlot, Syrah and Chardonnay. But it's probably best known for its work with the palindromic Tannat grape – tough and tannic in its French homeland, but more succulent in these climes. There are also some other unusual varieties, such as the main port red grape, Touriga Nacional, Cabernet/Grenache cross, Marselan, and the underrated white, Sauvignon Gris.

You probably won't get offered these as part of your tasting (though it might be worth asking), but I'd suggest buying a couple in the shop afterwards. I mean, how many of your friends will have drunk a Uruguayan Shiraz/Tannat or a Petit Verdot?

Juanicó is well set up for tourists, with comprehensive tours of vineyard and winery, complete with tasting and a glimpse of the original cellar. At just over half an hour from the centre of Montevideo, it's eminently doable if you find yourself in the capital and fancy sneaking in a half-day visit.

MIOLO, BRAZIL

Wine in Brazil? You'd better believe it. The country makes more wine than Austria and in 2017 these guys welcomed around 200,000 visitors to their facility in the aptly named Vale dos Vinhedos (valley of the vineyards). Near Bento Gonçalves in the south of the country, it's an attractive region of rolling hills and camera-friendly views that became Brazil's first denomination of origin in 2007.

Miolo's first vineyards went in in 1897, the winery following along 100 or so years later. Like most wineries in Brazil, its speciality is sparkling wines, though it has Chardonnay, Merlot and a couple of Bordeaux blends, too. If you visit, make sure you ask about the challenges of growing healthy grapes in a humid climate.

Miolo does hourly tours pretty much all week, taking in vineyard, winery and cellars, as well as tasting courses – lasting either three hours or a full day. The grounds are lovely – and the perfect place to lie in the sun with a picnic and a bottle of fizz. Unsurprisingly, though, given the numbers mentioned above, it does get busy in the height of the tourist season, from December to March.

SOUTH
AFRICA

Is South Africa New World or Old World? When it comes to wine, the answer, somewhat unhelpfully, is 'both and neither'. While it may not have the thousand-year-plus traditions of Europe, they have been making wine here for almost 350 years, since the governor of the Cape, Simon van der Stel, planted his first vines in Constantia back in 1685 – that's a couple of hundred years before private (as opposed to religious) wine production got going in North and South America and Australia.

Having said that, there's a very non-European attitude to planting – a willingness to experiment, and a revulsion at being tied down by rules and regulations that's far more New World than Bordelais in outlook.

Key to the Cape are the Atlantic and Indian Oceans, which provide regular onshore breezes and help to counter the non-stop African sunshine. Throw in plenty of mountains and you start to get some very interesting microclimates indeed. The epicentre of South Africa's fine wine scene is Stellenbosch. It's a happy example of the first settlers plonking themselves a couple of days' ox-cart ride from where they landed and happening across simply magnificent farming country.

The region is right at the crossroads where 'heat' and 'cool' intersect; it's easy to get grapes ripe in the sunshine, but there's enough breeze off the sea to give the vines some respite. The best vineyards are usually up on slopes where the cooling effect is more pronounced.

Home to most of the country's best-known wineries, Stellenbosch's reputation is based mostly on its Bordeaux blends, and there's no shortage of great Cabernets around. Often with a slight leafy edge, they're quite distinctive. The last decade has seen an increase in show-off icon wines as well, but few are worth the money, and I'd be sceptical about paying extra to try them in tasting rooms. The best value is at mid-price level, where there are some seriously good bottles to be had.

For the modern traveller with hire car rather than ox-cart, the beauty of the Cape is how accessible it all is. Constantia, where the first vines were planted, is barely 20km south of Cape Town, while Stellenbosch and Paarl are both around 50km east of the city.

Moreover, you don't have to travel far to get a very different experience. Elgin, for instance, is basically an undulating series of hills 400m above sea level, surrounded by high mountains. Close to the ocean, it's distinctly chillier – so much, in fact, that its main crop is apples. It makes excellent cool-climate whites, particularly Sauvignon Blanc and Chardonnay, and good Pinot Noir.

You could make it part of a cool-climate loop that swings back up to Franschhoek, taking in Bot River and Walker Bay en route. The latter is home to the Hemel-en-Aarde Valley, which is justifiably acquiring a reputation for its Burgundy varieties. The best wines are moving well beyond simple varietal expression and into proper terroir-based expressiveness. It's also a beautiful spot. Hemel-en-Aarde means 'heaven on earth' and they weren't overselling it. There's great surfing here, too.

Yet if you go 100km north of Stellenbosch, to the Swartland, it's a different dynamic. Further from the sea, it's significantly hotter and home to some of the oldest vines and most dynamic young winemakers in the country. Come here for full-bodied reds, old-vine Chenin Blanc, and often-quirky blends using a smorgasbord of Mediterranean grape varieties.

In the relatively condensed world of South African wine, it's quite possible to take in Swartland to the north and Walker Bay to the east on a two-week trip and not even feel as though you're spending much time in the car.

There's so much happening in South Africa at the moment that it seems invidious to pick out particular styles, but there is real excitement building around Syrah in the Cape, and it makes an interesting counterpoint to the Bordeaux varieties. Incredibly, Pinotage (long the butt of wine-trade jokes) is another variety that's totally worth exploring, while the old vine Chenin Blancs represent one of the great bargains of the wine world.

But wherever you go in the Cape, one thing remains constant: the beauty of the countryside. This is unarguably one of the world's most stunning landscapes – a place of big skies, wide horizons and relentless natural bounty. Add in a wine industry that's a) going places, b) well set up for visitors and c) cheap, and you have probably the best single two-week wine destination on the planet.

THE CAPE

GROOT CONSTANTIA

Groot Constantia is one of the world's great wine estates. For starters, it has serious history, established in 1685 by Simon van der Stel. The then-commander of the Cape was well versed in the nuances of the area, so he knew what he was doing when he selected this 700-hectare site behind Table Mountain as the location for his farm. The land itself is beautiful, the view out over False Bay spectacular.

It's also good for grapes. The vineyards spread out up the slopes of the Constantiaberg, soaking up a winning combination of sun and sea breezes, and by 1709, there were 70,000 vines planted on the farm.

It's best known for its sweet wines. Vin de Constance is a luscious, golden dessert wine that was something of a must-drink around the royal courts of Europe in the 18th and 19th centuries. Napoleon was even allowed to drink it while in exile on St Helena. If you're not a fan of sweeties, don't pass this place by. It also has a range of reds and whites, as well as a fortified red and a brandy.

There's a self-guided tour (download the app on your phone) that takes you round the estate, complete with the vineyards, the old Cape Dutch manor house, winery and a couple of restaurants. There are two cellars set up for tastings and the option of a wine and chocolate pairing – spot on with its imperious stickies. And, if that's not enough, you also get two museums (wine and culture) plus South African art.

STEENBERG

Steenberg is somewhere that's much easier to get to than to leave. As well as a five-star hotel, spa and two restaurants, there's an 18-hole golf course and, of course, the wine estate.

It's best known for its sparkling wines (Methode Cap Classique, or MCC in the local vernacular), which regularly pick up four to five stars in *Platter's Wine Guide*, the South African wine bible. Cellar tours are available – though not during harvest – and there are a variety of tasting options in the bar, lounge and terrace. Plus there's no need to book.

Whatever you do, make sure you ask about Catharina Ustings Ras. The one time doyenne of the estate has an extraordinary story. She dressed as a man to emigrate to the Cape in her twenties and acquired husbands at an impressive rate – many of whom met colourful ends. It's a story of lions, tribesmen, elephants and knife fights – though not necessarily in that order.

This is a good Sunday visit from Cape Town – a place to come for a bit of gentle wine tasting, lunch, and perhaps a few holes once the heat has gone out of the day.

STELLENBOSCH

BOSCHENDAL

Gifted to a French Huguenot by Simon van der Stel (yes, him again) in 1685, Boschendal is one of the oldest wine estates in the Cape and a beautiful example of classic Cape Dutch architecture.

You can do vineyard tours, cellar tours and a variety of themed tastings (Angus beef and Shiraz, perhaps), but this really is a place to linger a while. There is a huge range of activities for visitors, from the gently active – hiking trails through the vineyards or swimming by one of the dams – to pottering in the gardens and having a picnic.

It's particularly well set up for mountain biking. You can rent bikes at the estate and there are five routes, ranging from tough and demanding to gentle and suitable for children. They're a great way to see the estate. And if you want to stay over in the wine lands, its five-star Werf Cottages are a comfortable option.

FAIRVIEW

Every wine region has its mavericks, and Charles Back is the Cape's. He started working with his father in 1978, taking over responsibility for production in the 1990s and immediately began to make his mark.

The Cape might be best known for its Bordeaux varieties, but Charles introduced lots of other Mediterranean grapes: Tempranillo, Viognier, Sangiovese and Petite Sirah, to name just a few. He became famous for his Rhône blends and his punning wine labels.

Goats Do Roam is a joyous blend of French and Italian grape varieties, mischievously designed to reference (and doubtless annoy) the growers of the Côtes du Rhône. The Goatfather is (unsurprisingly) an equally tongue-in-cheek blend of mostly Italian grapes.

If this makes the whole place sound like one big joke, don't be fooled. There's some serious winemaking going on here, as you'll discover if you taste any of its single vineyard wines. And after the typical Cab/Merlot diet of Stellenbosch, it's undeniably interesting to try the likes of Shiraz, Carignan and Grenache.

The tasting room is one of the most popular in the Cape for good reason. For starters, it's excellent value; the tastings take place in horseshoe-shaped 'pods' with super-enthusiastic helpers holding court in the middle; and there's a lot of cheese-related matching and tasting as well.

This must also be the only winery in the world whose most famous structure is an animal pen. The goat tower was built by Charles in the early 1980s and is probably the most-photographed piece of architecture in the Cape's wine lands. As well as providing entertainment for small children – not to mention inspiration for the wine range – the caprine inhabitants also supply cheese for the restaurant and tastings.

This is a delightfully relaxed estate with quality wines and a delightful attitude to life – somewhere to come if you want fun with your wine samples. How much fun? It even (and I can't believe this is even a sentence) offers goat yoga. That's yoga. But with goats. Really.

JORDAN

Gary and Kathy Jordan are South African wine's glamour couple, the Liz Taylor and Richard Burton of the Stellenbosch wine lands, who have been making great bottles for several decades. The estate was bought by Gary's parents in the early 1980s, and carefully replanted over a period of ten years to ensure that the right grape varieties were in places that suited them.

With vineyards that face to all four points of the compass, and a variety of altitudes to play with, they can grow everything from sun-hungry Cabernet Sauvignon to high-quality white wines. They're unashamedly New World in style – there's no hint of under-ripe fruit or stringy tannin here – but well balanced, too. Their Nine Yards Chardonnay and Cobblers Hill Bordeaux blend, in particular, deliver year after year.

The impressive restaurant is a bucolically relaxing place to spend a few hours, sitting on the terrace with a glass of wine and savouring the views out over Table Mountain. But they also have a wide range of tastings and tours available. The basic tasting of six wines is decent value in itself, but if you want to upgrade, I'd suggest going all-in for the vineyard and cellar experience.

With an open-Land Rover trip into the vineyards (complete with amazing vistas of False and Table Bays), you'll get a flavour of the estate and the Stellenbosch terroir. You need six people for it, though, so try and coerce some fellow travellers into joining you.

KANONKOP

In the days before text alerts, they used to fire a cannon when a ship was docking in Table Bay, so people could get down to the port and trade with it. That 'signalling cannon' was on a small hill – the Kanonkop – at the base of the Simonsberg, and today gives its name to the winery of the same area.

One of the big beasts of South African wine, Kanonkop's 100 hectares are planted entirely to red grapes – mostly Cabernet Sauvignon. In a part of the world where most wineries hedge their bets a bit with grape varieties, this is unusual enough, but it has its own idiosyncratic approach to winemaking, too.

In an homage to the past, the estate carries out fermentation not in stainless steel tanks, but in old-style open-topped concrete fermenters. It just thinks that having people punching down the grape skins in the vats with big poles during fermentation makes better wine. Labour intensive it might be, but the results suggest it might be on to something.

This, clearly, isn't a place to come if you're only into light spritzy whites. But if you're serious about reds and want to taste some high-quality examples, it's a fine visit. The top wine, Paul Sauer, is one of the country's best Bordeaux blends.

Kanonkop also does good things with Pinotage. Its Black Label wine is made in tiny quantities and available to try in a special tasting. It's likely to be significantly better (and more expensive) than any expression of the variety you've ever had before. If you don't like it, you really don't like Pinotage.

KEN FORRESTER

Ken Forrester's Scottish relatives were, in his words, 'typically tight and stubborn'. The latter trait, at least, seems to have rubbed off. He's spent most of his working life talking animatedly about the potential of Chenin Blanc to anyone who will listen – and, frankly, even people who won't.

He could hardly be accused of bandwagon jumping. When he bought his vineyard 25 years ago and started his one-man crusade, the variety (known as Steen in South Africa) was being regularly pulled up in favour of Chardonnay – Chenin was still seen as the grape for making brandy. It meant a lot of fine old vineyards went south. But not on Ken's watch.

His use (and trumpeting) of the wines from decades-old bush vines has helped reset people's attitude to the grape – and promoted a style that's distinctively different from the French versions, yet still serious and ambitious. 'We don't make Chenin like the Loire Valley,' he says. 'And I hope we never do.'

In the tasting room there's a lot of flexibility. You can either choose wines from a set-priced tasting menu, or pick and mix as you go. He does great things with Rhône reds, which you can match with wagyu beef – his The Gypsy Grenache-based blend is especially good. But I'd use this visit primarily as a way of sampling three or four different styles and prices of Chenin. Check out some of the cellar-exclusives, too.

If you visit his winery on the slopes of the Helderberg, you should also pop in for lunch at the restaurant he co-owns with his brother, 96 Winery Road. One kilometre from the winery, the food is delicious, and I don't care how hot it is, you have to try the truffle chips.

MORGENSTER

One of the favourite ways in which European winemakers attempt to denigrate their New World counterparts is to say their wines don't age. Although they might be fine to drink as simple early-release wines, they don't improve with time. The insult is clear: you guys can make cheap, mass-market wines, but leave the ambitious stuff to us.

Well, Morgenster takes that ludicrous theory and blows it apart. It's a specialist in Bordeaux blends and releases its Estate Reserve wines in tranches over time. The result amounts to a vertical tasting of current vintages, often covering five or six years, and many with serious age. The youngest wine is rarely less than five years old.

You're unlikely to get to try a string of old wines as part of the Bordeaux-based tasting, but you will get a range of styles and ages, and if you fancy something different, you can sample its five olive oils, too.

Less than an hour from Cape Town, this is a particularly good visit if you're heading east towards Elgin and Walker Bay.

WARWICK

Like many wineries in the Cape, Warwick has a long history – though wine didn't feature in its make-up until the 1960s when it was bought by the Ratcliffe family. Norma went on to become one of the first (and probably best-known) female winemakers in the country, and even though she has since hung up her lab equipment, the winery retains her signature deftness.

Wine-wise, there are two or three strong reasons to visit Warwick. It was among the first to start wrestling with Cabernet Franc, and does a decent single-varietal version, though it's probably at its best alongside Cabernet Sauvignon and Merlot in its Bordeaux blend: Trilogy is one of the most reliable examples in the Cape. Its work with Chardonnay is also impressive, with its naturally fermented The White Lady a frequent high-scorer in *Platter's Guide*.

You can enjoy a picnic either on the lawn or in one of the purpose-built shaded 'picnic pods', and with three play parks for the kids, grassy areas for general charging around and a fountain to splash about in, it's one of the best winery visits for families in the Cape. Cellar tours need to be booked in advance, but aren't expensive, while the tasting room offers two six-wine flights plus the chance to buy older vintages of the Trilogy and Cabernet Franc.

Assuming the weather is OK, there's also the Big Five Vineyard Safari, where you head out in an open-top Land Rover to hunt for the 'big five' grape varieties.

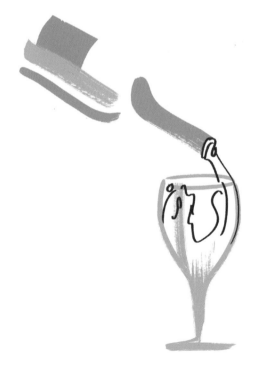

EAST

BEAUMONT, BOT RIVER

Some wineries are big and grand, others are small and quirky and some, like this estate, simply ooze charm. Head over the hills at Elgin and when you drop down on the eastern side, you're in Bot River, the entry point to Walker Bay, and home to the Beaumont family's whitewashed, slightly ramshackle old winery.

The Beaumonts bought the farm in the 1970s, and after a period selling their fruit to other producers, decided to go for broke with their own estate wine 20 years later. It's still a small operation – 10,000 cases – but it's an interesting one. As surfer-dude third-generation winemaker Sebastian puts it, 'Life's too short to satisfy everyone, so we cut out the Chardonnay and Sauvignon Blanc and concentrated on Chenin.'

The latter are, indeed, excellent – particularly the A-list Hope Marguerite, named after his grandmother. But it also has some unusual white blends, an elegant, lighter style of Pinotage and a decent Mourvèdre. The flagship red blend, the always fascinating Vitruvian (a mix of Syrah, Pinotage and, it sometimes seems, whatever else looked good that year), gets its name from the old water mill, which is still operating.

Beaumont runs tours and tastings, sometimes involving the odd sample from the barrel if you're lucky, and encourages visitors to hang out and enjoy the atmosphere. You should. It's a special place.

PAUL CLUVER, ELGIN

Paul Cluver was the first winery to be set up in Elgin in the late 1980s. It's a beautiful region, cooler and more forested than Stellenbosch – rather like Scotland with sun. There's probably no better way of getting a feel for the geography than doing one of the Cluvers' mountain bike trails, which range from 46km routes with 1,000m elevation gains to shorter, gentler rides that can be done with children.

But should you be more interested in barrel-fermented Chardonnay than berms, a visit to the tasting room is a fine way to explore the character of the region. Although it is possible (depending on height and aspect) to ripen even Merlot in Elgin, it's best-known for its cool, fresh whites and Pinot Noir. The latter's reputation is less well established than the former's, but devotees maintain it could be South Africa's top region for the grape.

The Cluver portfolio covers most of what Elgin is capable of, from zesty Rieslings through aromatic Sauvignon Blancs and richer Chardonnays to damp-earth, red-fruited Pinot Noirs. They're a reliably high-quality range, so you ought to find something you like.

If you want to have a go at matching wine to music (yes, that is a thing), you can try some wines while watching a concert in the open-air amphitheatre. Sipping Riesling among the eucalyptus trees as the cool evening air drifts in off the ocean is a unique experience. Just take some extra layers to wear – after all, there's a reason Elgin's able to make such crystalline whites...

HAMILTON RUSSELL VINEYARDS, HEMEL-EN-AARDE

Head east along the coast towards the surfer town of Hermanus (home, unsurprisingly, to some high-class seafood) and hang a left up the Hemel-en-Aarde Valley and you are in a very special place. It's not especially big but it's home to a fine collection of high-quality wine estates, with Hamilton Russell right at the top of the tree.

It's one of the most southerly wineries in Africa and, close to Walker Bay, subject to significant cooling influences from the ocean. In the height of summer, the mercury rarely gets past 25°C. This, as owner Anthony Hamilton Russell points out, is almost exactly the same as in Burgundy, as are the stony, clay-rich soils, so it's no surprise that it only makes two wines, Pinot Noir and Chardonnay.

They're exceptionally good, too – regularly lauded for their elegance, complexity and tension. There's a nominal fee to try (well worth it for stuff of this quality), but it's waived if you buy anything, which, if you've any sense, you will. If you're super-keen, make contact in advance to arrange a vertical tasting in the barrel cellar. If you're lucky, this will be conducted by Anthony himself. An interesting commentator on the Cape wine scene, half an hour in his company is a treat.

NEWTON JOHNSON, HEMEL-EN-AARDE

A relative newcomer to the Walker Bay wine scene, Newton Johnson was set up in the mid-1990s by Dave Johnson and his wife Felicity Newton. A Cape Wine Master, Dave was sufficiently committed to Pinot Noir to write a thesis on it, so it's no great surprise that this was the grape variety that they decided to concentrate on.

They've got six different expressions, varying in soil type, elevation and exposure. Unpicking the differences is rewarding – especially the variations in flavour between the richer, rounder clay-soil expressions and the perfumed mineral punch of the (rarer) granite soils.

It's also interesting to compare them stylistically with those produced by Hamilton Russell, which are solely from clay soils, and from vineyards both lower down the valley and closer to the sea. Its tasting room has become so popular that it's now its single biggest sales outlet.

One other effect of being located further up the Hemel-en-Aarde Valley is that its restaurant has to-die-for views across the vineyards down towards the rolling breakers of the Atlantic. Unsurprisingly, Dave's two sons, Gordon and Bevan, who run the winemaking and commercial sides of the business respectively, spend most of their spare time with wetsuit and board.

It's open for lunch half of the week and for dinner, too, at weekends in summer, when there are also event evenings and wine-themed dinners. After a week's wine tasting, there's nothing more attractive than a cold wet one, so the restaurant's regular wagyu burger and beer night could be just the ticket. Whatever you fancy, book in advance because it fills up quickly.

NORTH

FRYER'S COVE, ATLANTIC COAST

You have to hand it to Wynand Hamman. He's not a man to let obstacles get in the way of a project. He first had the idea of growing grapes up on the Atlantic coast in the 1980s while holidaying in the area as a winemaking student.

The fact that the coast was battered by wind pretty much all year round, that there was a ludicrously low 50mm of rainfall a year, and no access to irrigation to get the young vines started didn't matter. It was going to happen, even if it took a while. Eventually, after running a water pipe from Vredendal 30km away across three other farms, he managed to plant his first vines in 1999.

Less than 1km from the Atlantic, they're some of the most maritime vineyards anywhere in the world, and the combination of cool (and constant) breezes and regular sunshine is fantastic for Sauvignon Blanc, in particular. The average temperature here is only 17°C and, with the sandy, shell-filled soil, the wines have a crunchy minerality that's brilliant with the local seafood.

Fittingly, the winery itself is in an old crayfish-packing factory right down on the seafront, making it one of the most unusual you'll ever visit.

MULLINEUX & LEEU FAMILY WINES, SWARTLAND

Chris and Andrea Mullineux's story is fairly representative of the revolution in the Swartland in the last ten years. They were attracted to the region because of the pockets of amazing old vineyards hidden away on the vast estates. And though they couldn't – at first – afford to buy land, they could select their favourite parcels of fruit, buy grapes and make the wine.

Chris takes care of the vineyards while Andrea makes the wines. They're a hugely impressive team. The wines are sensitively made, elegant – almost understated – and have won over critics everywhere. They've twice been named winery of the year by the esteemed *Platter's Guide*.

They run weekly tastings at their farm in Riebeek Kasteel (you'll need to book ahead), which give you a flavour of the Swartland in general and their estate in particular. But if you're staying round Stellenbosch and can't arrange a visit here, it might be easier to pop into their Leeu Estates Wine Studio. In the lush loveliness of Franschhoek, it's open for tastings every day.

Independence drive

The Swartland has become one of the trendiest wine-producing regions in the world – a magnet for young, talented winemakers with a bohemian vibe. The Swartland Independent is a group of 22 small wine producers obsessed with making wines of real character. Their shop, the Wine Kollektive in Riebeek Kasteel sells the lot, and once a year (usually in November) they host a joyous celebration of food and wine.

AUSTRALIA & NEW ZEALAND

AUSTRALIA

Since the 1980s, Australia has had probably more influence on global wine trends than any other country. It's the fifth-biggest producer in the world (after France, Italy, Spain and the US), but whereas those countries have large wine-drinking populations, Australia is home to just 24 million people. And because they've had to export to survive, their ideas have gone global, influencing wine drinkers and producers everywhere.

The country made its name with the classic 'sunshine in a bottle' wines of the '80s and '90s – great dollops of exuberant fruit that burst into the uptight world of European wine like a stag party gatecrashing a whist drive. Big, blowsy, joyful and, crucially, accessible, they made wine fun.

The problem, in a sense, has been getting wine drinkers to move on from that image. The country does still make plenty of ripe, round, technically correct wines, but the industry's focus has shifted to the search for regional expression, for the right vines in the right sites to compete with the finest in Europe. It's moved, if you like, from being about shiny tanks and winemaking techniques to vineyards, terroir and dirt.

For the wine visitor, Australia is both daunting and magnificent. Daunting because of the sheer distances involved (it's a 4,000km journey from Margaret River in Western Australia to the Hunter Valley in New South Wales); magnificent because wine visits here are wonderful things. Actual tours of the winery or vineyards aren't that common Down Under – here it's more about visiting the cellar doors. These tasting and retail areas aren't even always at the same location as the winery itself, and are often more like bars that just happen to have a great wine selection and knowledgeable staff. Fun, relaxed and informative – sometimes with fantastic coffee thrown in, too – they're a wonderfully unpressured and unstuffy way of enhancing your wine education.

If wine is at the top of your list of priorities, you need to be in South Australia. It's still the epicentre of the country's wine industry – the irrigated Riverland region along the Murray River pumps out millions of litres of supermarket wines every year. But it's also home to many of the country's most famous quality regions: McLaren Vale, the Adelaide Hills – both within day-trip distance of Adelaide – and Coonawarra to the south and the Barossa and Eden Valleys to the north. You could spend weeks here and barely scratch the surface, so pick your visits with care.

Victoria has myriad wine regions and they're probably too spread out for you to feasibly visit them all in a fortnight – unless you like spending a lot of time in the car. But two of the best areas, the Yarra Valley and Mornington Peninsula (both big on Pinot Noir and Chardonnay), are handily close to the magnificence of Melbourne, and there's no shortage of decent wineries set up for thirsty tourists.

You need more commitment to see the most famous wineries of Western Australia. Margaret River is a few hours' drive south of Perth, but for the serious wine lover it's well worth the effort. Wine may have come late to this part of Australia (the first vines went in in the late 1960s), but the planting was done with knowledge by savvy doctors who'd worked out that the climate wasn't unlike that of Bordeaux. Today, although it's a small region, 'Margie' produces 20 per cent of all of Australia's premium wine.

If you're in New South Wales, the closest wine region to Sydney is the Hunter Valley – 150km to the north – and it's understandably popular for weekend visitors. More humid than the other wine-growing regions, its wines are distinctly different, described by Hunter legend Bruce Tyrrell as about 'fruit and acid, not tannin and alcohol'. Certainly, it's one of those New World regions that has created a style all of its own. Aged Hunter Valley Sémillon – all lime, toast, nuts and honey with stiletto acidity – is one of the world's great whites.

If you're out this way, consider heading up into the mountains. The higher altitude regions of Orange, Cowra and Mudgee – even Canberra – are making increasingly interesting wines.

Finally, there's Tasmania. Thirty years ago, when Aussie wine was all about fruit ripeness, it was seen as a weird, somewhat masochistic addition to the country's wine scene. But as the pendulum has swung towards lightness and elegance, so its cool-climate credentials have come to be seen as a real boon. It's the place to come if you want slimline whites (including Riesling), Pinot Noir and sparkling wine, plus amazing scenery.

NEW SOUTH WALES

KOOMOOLOO, ORANGE

When a producer with over four decades of experience and several 'winemaker of the year' accolades settles in a region, it's worth paying attention. Philip Shaw stumbled across this site by accident in the late 1980s from a height of several thousand feet – when he noticed its high, undulating terrain from a plane.

After further investigation, he bought some of it and planted getting on for 50 hectares. But it was only many years later that he attempted to make wine with the fruit – he wanted the vines to be mature enough to do the land justice.

It's easy to see what attracted him. Located 900m up on the slopes of an extinct volcano, these are some of the highest vineyards in Australia – cold enough for snow in the winter, and, more importantly, with significantly lower temperatures throughout the growing season, too. They're perfect for creating elegant, bright-fruited wines.

Visit Koomooloo's bluestone barn and you won't find big, syrupy Chardonnays or glutinous Shiraz, but rather wines of poise, elegance and finesse, made by a real expert. The Shirazes, in particular, are fantastic. If you like the northern Rhône style – all pepper and spice, rather than rich fruit – you'll love these.

At 260km west of Sydney, it's clearly a commitment to get here, but there's no shortage of seasoned observers who think Orange is really going places.

MOUNT PLEASANT, HUNTER VALLEY

In 1880 Charles King, an English immigrant, planted his vineyards near Pokolbin at the southern end of the Hunter Valley. Forty years later, a 24-year-old called Maurice O'Shea, who had studied winemaking in France, persuaded his French mother to buy the property and a couple of parcels of land next to it.

By the 1940s, after the Mount Pleasant estate had been bought by a big Australian wine family, O'Shea was firmly established as one of the country's most respected winemakers, an early advocate of the use of oak-ageing and of blending different regions and varieties together. One of the founders of the modern Australian wine industry, he did as much as anyone to encourage the shift from fortified to table wines.

The cellar door has a wide range of styles to go at. Unsurprisingly, there are plenty of Sémillons, Chardonnays and Shirazes, so you'll get a good idea of the Hunter Valley style. But try some of the b-side wines as well. Comprising more experimental varieties and blends, they're an interesting range – the kind of thing of which Maurice would have doubtless approved.

TYRRELL'S WINES, HUNTER VALLEY

The Tyrrell family arrived in Sydney in the 1850s, buying a large Hunter Valley estate within ten years. The first slab hut was built in 1858 and six years later they harvested their first wine crop.

Things trundled along for the best part of a century before Murray Tyrrell took over. One of the great characters of Australian wine, he was the first to plant Chardonnay in the country, and started the Vat 1 Hunter Sémillon – one of, if not *the* best expressions of the grape variety anywhere in the world, ageing with the grace of a fine German Riesling.

Both Murray and his son Bruce (still involved with the winery) have received Members of the Order of Australia awards for their services to the country's wine industry, though they could equally have been for raconteurship. There's no shortage of stories here – and the fact you can see the original 160-year-old hut as well as the old winery buildings and the Short Flat vineyard (home to Vat 1 Sémillon) is just the icing on the cake. The tour is super-cheap, but there's only one a day so don't be late.

Unusually for an Australian winery, there's no restaurant, but there is a barbecue area, which you can use for free. Take some yabbies and a lemon to enjoy with the Sémillon.

VICTORIA

DE BORTOLI, YARRA VALLEY

One of the larger producers in the Yarra, De Bortoli does everything from its famous Noble One dessert wine to port, sparkling wines, cheery rosés, succulent whites and ambitious reds – the full cornucopia of what can be made in the Yarra.

The story's a good one, featuring Italian immigrants fleeing their war-torn homeland, sleeping under a water tank, and hitting upon becoming wine producers almost by accident. It was a glut year, prices plummeted, and so farmers opted to leave their grapes on the vine. Vittorio de Bortoli picked them for free, crushed them and sold the wine back to them!

Tastings at their cellar door are well-priced, and the fee is redeemable if you buy anything. Winemaker Steve Webber is particularly excited by the potential of Shiraz in the Yarra, especially in cooler vintages, so see if there are any to try. If not, the Riorret Pinot Noirs ('terroir' backwards) are structured, textural and elegant. The stickie, meanwhile, is like dried fruit dipped in honeycomb. And if you're not keen on dessert wines, you can always wash it down with one of De Bortoli's beers afterwards...

FOWLES WINE, STRATHBOGIE RANGES

You don't make it into the Victorian Tourism Awards hall of fame without having something special, and for the sybaritic wine lover, this is a great visit.

Matt Fowles, the former lawyer who set up this winery 130km north of Melbourne, is keen on striding through the nearby Strathbogie Ranges with a gun, looking for grub. An all-round fan of food and wine pairing, he's created two wines specifically to match the local game, titled Ladies Who Shoot Their Lunch and Are You Game?

His celebrated Cellar Door Café is open seven days a week, and has its own Are You Game? experience, involving a tutored tasting and four dishes paired with various wines. But if you fancy something more wine-driven, its Stone Dwellers Experience incorporates a bus ride to the vineyards and winery for tastings direct from tank and barrel and an in-depth look at why the wines from this particular range taste like they do. Hint: the granitic soil might be a factor.

Afterwards, it's back to the winery for a two-course meal matched with wines from the Stone Dwellers range, making for a truly holistic appreciation of the whys, hows and what-to-do-withs of wine production.

INNOCENT BYSTANDER, YARRA VALLEY

Just over an hour out of Melbourne, in Healesville, Innocent Bystander is as much a social event as a winery visit. An airy wood-floored restaurant (serving excellent wood-fired pizzas) with a huge square central bar, it's a fun, relaxing place to spend a few hours tasting, chatting and eating – and great for anyone making their first steps into the world of wine.

There are neophyte-friendly styles such as Moscato and prosecco as well as more 'grown-up' Chardonnay, Pinot and Syrah. And if you're looking for something less ordinary, it also has Tempranillo, Arneis and a succulent Pinot Gris.

It's open late, too, so if you're using Healesville as a base to tour the Yarra, head here for a relaxed evening meal. You might also like to cleanse your palate with some of its home-made cider.

MONTALTO, MORNINGTON PENINSULA

Montalto, towards the southern end of the Mornington Peninsula, is the place to come if you want 'experiences' rather than just to try a few bottles.

There's an excellent restaurant, rentable picnic tables (and no, you can't bring your own food – this is Mornington) and, finally, there's the outdoor art. Thirty permanent sculptures are scattered throughout the property on a 1km-long sculpture trail, some obvious, others more hidden away among the vines and wetlands.

Of the wine options, none is especially cheap, though the Ultimate Pinot Lovers Road Trip looks the most interesting. You begin with a tasting from the barrels in the winery, before visiting the Peninsula sites that provide the fruit for Montalto's single-vineyard range.

It's a great way of appreciating the factors that affect how the wine tastes. You get to try the range afterwards at the cellar door and during a six-course lunch.

PORT PHILLIP ESTATE, MORNINGTON PENINSULA

More or less in the middle of the Mornington Peninsula, this place has the advantage that it allows you to try (and buy) the wines of not one, but two really good estates. Port Phillip and Kooyong are both owned by the Gjergja family: the former, where the tasting room is located, was planted in 1987, on a north-facing amphitheatre; Kooyong, set up eight years later, is at the northern end of the Peninsula. Both are particularly rated for their Chardonnays and Pinot Noirs.

Just as striking as the wines is the winery itself. Sitting on a ridge, looking over the vineyards, it has glorious views out towards the sea, while the dining room's floor-to-ceiling windows make for a light, airy cellar door that backs out on to expansive timber decking. It's impressive but low-impact, and has deservedly picked up a string of architectural awards.

The winery is not open to the public, but the wines make it worth a stop-off. Its Mornington Peninsula Master Class looks at three different Mornington terroirs, while straight tastings are super-cheap and any costs are refunded should you buy a bottle. Which, unless you have the palate of a barbarian, you will.

TAHBILK, NAGAMBIE LAKES

Established in 1860, Tahbilk is one of the grand old names of Australian wine. It's the oldest winery in Victoria, and the fifth oldest in the country. Even its 'new cellar' was built in 1875.

You can also see one of its original 1860 vineyards. The vines continue to produce – in tiny quantities – and it still makes a wine from them: the 1860 Vines Shiraz. (Don't expect to get a glass of it at the cellar door, though.) It also has some 90-year-old-plus Marsanne vines that it claims are the oldest in the world and, at 40 hectares, are also probably one of the largest single plantings of the variety.

A tasting here is a stimulating experience, with history dripping out of every pore. The whites might use modern methods, but the reds are still fermented in big old wooden vats – a technique that's barely changed in the last 150 years.

'Tabilk' (the 'h' was added later) means 'place of many watering holes' in the language of the local aboriginal Daung-wurrung clans and the 1,200-hectare estate certainly has no shortage of the wet stuff. Here you'll find 400 hectares of wetlands and wildlife reserve backing on to the Goulburn River and any number of creeks and backwaters. The place is big on eco-tourism: it has 4km of trails and boardwalks to explore and offers 30-minute cruises in its eco-friendly electric boat.

If you're feeling flush, the five-hour Ultimate Tour takes in everything from wetlands to winery to blending with a three-course lunch thrown in. For what you get, it's good value.

Tahbilk is a charming, multi-faceted visit. Just over an hour and a half from Melbourne, it's doable as a day trip. Or, as it's situated off the Hume Highway, it also makes a handy stop-off if you're heading north-east.

YERING STATION, YARRA VALLEY

This is the site of Victoria's first vineyard, planted in 1838, and while it's had its ups and downs in the intervening couple of centuries – not least an unpleasant brush with phylloxera that trashed vineyards across the state in the early 20th century – it's still one of the most influential.

The cellar door is housed in the original 1859 winery building and walk-in tastings are free. There's a large range to go at (including sparklers), though you might want to consider upgrading to a private tasting. They're not expensive, and will get you access to the Estate, Village and Reserve wines, which are a step or two up from the standard range.

Since the family who own Yering Station also own Mount Langi Ghiran and Xanadu wineries from the Grampians (Western Victoria) and Margaret River, respectively, you can also try wines from different regions in the one visit – a big bonus if you're not touring the country.

Yering Station isn't just about the wine, though. There's a nice restaurant and an art gallery, with an impressive track record of showcasing established and emerging Australian artists. Add it all together and it makes for a bucolic day trip just an hour from Melbourne.

TEN MINUTES BY TRACTOR, MORNINGTON PENINSULA

An odd name for a winery? Perhaps. But it makes sense. These guys started out with three vineyards that are – you guessed it – ten minutes apart as the tractor trundles. It sums up what they're about – differences in terroir.

While more expert tasters will enjoy sifting out the differences between the various single-vineyard wines, this is also a good place for less-experienced visitors to get to grips with the four grape varieties grown here. Understanding what Chardonnay, Pinot Noir, Pinot Gris and Sauvignon Blanc taste like in Mornington in the hands of an expert team is reward in itself.

It's a nice place to hang out for a bit, too. The restaurant is headed up by a chef and sommelier who both have lots of experience at top European venues.

SOUTH AUSTRALIA

ALPHA BOX & DICE, MCLAREN VALE

If you're getting a bit tired of the same-old, same-old, head here. Alpha Box & Dice was set up as a 'laboratory for viticultural exploration' in 2008 and has been shaking things up ever since.

The idea when it started was to create a different wine for every letter of the alphabet. Today the names run from Shiraz-Durif blend Apostle to its Zaptung prosecco, and the plan is to fill up all 26 spaces. The concepts behind the wines are fun, interesting and make you think – a long way from the usual 'we wanted to express the terroir' spiel that most places trot out.

Its big things are 'minimum intervention' and using less typical European grape varieties grown across South Australia. There are all sorts of weird and wonderful creations here – from (southern Italian) Aglianico or (Piedmontese) Nebbiolo and Barbera to Mediterranean/Australian blends (Tempranillo or Sangiovese with Cabernet) – all delivered with wit and joy. The world of wine needs more places like this.

D'ARENBERG, MCLAREN VALE

Chester Osborn – long of hair, loud of shirt, flamboyantly opinionated – is an unmissable character in the Australian wine world. He's not someone to do things by halves, which explains why the company uses old-fashioned basket presses (slow, labour-intensive, but gentle) to make its wines. As if that weren't sufficiently old-school, the reds are still foot-trodden during fermentation as well.

The results, though, speak for themselves. Chester's wines might be big on fruit flavour, but they're balanced, and low on oak influence.

This is not a visit where you stand around in cellars poking at barrels. This is a visit where you enter 'the Cube'. Looking rather like a half-twisted Rubik's Cube rising out of the vineyards, the glass, five-storey visitor centre was inspired by an idea Chester had in 2003. Winemaking, he reasoned, was a puzzle, so why not create a visitor experience that encapsulates that?

It's brilliantly done. There are any number of stimulating elements to a visit here, from art, food and themed wine tastings to a wine inhalation room and a virtual fermenter. Already an icon in the Vale, it's unmissable in every sense.

FIRST DROP, BAROSSA VALLEY

Ever think there's too much reverence attached to wine? Too much nodding politely and bowing and scraping before the centuries of heritage, and that sometimes all you want is something good to actually drink? If so, you're on the same page as Matt Gant and John Retsas.

Their range of wines is modern and quirky – with plenty of Spanish and Italian varieties in there both as single varietals and blends – but even their classic

Australian styles have a deftness of touch that is 21st century in feel rather than a homage to the 1990s. Their Barossa Shiraz, Mother's Milk, for instance, is a juicy drinker rather than a heavy sipper – what Aussie winemakers call 'smashable', meaning it's moreish enough to keep you pouring glass after glass until the bottle has mysteriously emptied.

Their Home of the Brave tasting room in Nuriootpa is a relaxed, fun place to pop in for a taste of the deft new direction in which Australian food and wine are heading. You might want to leave the car at home, though.

GROSSET, CLARE VALLEY

There's nothing showy about Grosset. It isn't a winery that has fancy visitor centres, themed tastings or guided tours. What it has is great wines, particularly Riesling, of which it is Australia's acknowledged master.

At the southern end of the Clare Valley, it's a small winery – it makes only nine wines each year, production is never more than 11,000 cases, and it owns just 22 hectares of vineyard – but it punches well above its weight.

Get one of its experts to explain to you how the same valley can produce elegant dry whites and full-bodied reds. Tasting the mountain-stream purity of its Polish Hill Riesling in situ is worth the visit alone, but make sure you compare it to its sister wine from Springvale.

JACOB'S CREEK, BAROSSA VALLEY

When Johann Gramp first stuck his vines in the ground alongside the less-than-mighty channel of Jacob's Creek in the 1840s he probably wasn't thinking much beyond making wine for himself and his family; maybe selling a few spare bottles to the neighbours. Yet from these humble beginnings, JC has gone on to be the wine that launches a thousand dinner parties all over the world every week.

It's tempting to define Jacob's Creek entirely by the affordable varietal wines that form the bedrock of its range, but if you come to the visitor centre, you ought to try some of its Heritage bottles if you can. Its Steingarten Riesling is one of the country's best, while the Centenary Hill Shiraz and Johann Shiraz/Cabernet are extraordinarily good for the money.

This a place where you could spend several hours, enjoying the walking and cycling trails, picnicking in the vineyards, themed tastings and one of the country's best-value 'blend your own wine' experiences. But it's also possible just to roll up for a taste at the bar. The staff can fill you in on the history of the brand, and you can visit the vineyard right outside to learn about the grape varieties.

If you want, you can even make the five-minute drive to the site of Johann Gramp's original homestead, winery and vineyard from 1847.

THE LANE VINEYARD, ADELAIDE HILLS

Adelaide's food scene rather ran out of ideas in the early years of the millennium, and while it's very much on the up again now, one place has continued to pack in food and wine lovers since it opened. Only half an hour south-east of the centre of Adelaide, The Lane is recognised as the winery restaurant that put the Adelaide Hills on the map food-wise, and a flagship destination for anyone in search of an epicurean afternoon.

In summer it usually has a couple of levels of walk-in tasting available. If it's on offer, go for the Estate Tasting. It's a bit pricier than the standard Block Series Tasting, but will get you really good wines. For a further marginal upgrade, you can get the wines matched with small but tasty bites from the kitchen. It's not necessarily a lunch substitute, but it's nice to experience a flight put together by both the winery and a properly decent restaurant.

If you fancy something more active, you can have a go at blending your own wine or even making your own cheese. Why not do both and take home your own hand-made food and wine combination?

PENFOLDS, ADELAIDE HILLS

Set up by Dr Christopher Penfold and his wife Mary with cuttings they had brought with them from Blighty, the Magill Estate could be described as the birthplace of Australian wine. The first vines went into the ground here in 1844, and though the good doctor himself saw wine as a useful tonic for his patients, rather than a civilised accompaniment to his Sunday roast, the Penfolds' influence on the country's wine scene grew and grew. By the 1920s it was making a third of all Australian wine.

And yet this is not a story about size, but about new thinking, ushered in by winemaker Max Schubert. After visits to Europe, Schubert wanted Australia to move away from the traditional fortified style and produce table wines that were serious and age-worthy.

He began experimenting and the result was the iconic Penfolds Grange – a wine that re-set the bar for New World wines in general and Australian wines in particular. It remains at the top of the wine pyramid today.

Only 8km from the centre of Adelaide, the Magill Estate is a must-visit, taking in the atmospheric old winery and original vineyards along with a tasting.

But if you're only going to do a handful of wineries, this is one where you should consider the (not inexpensive) upgrade to the Ultimate Penfolds Experience. Not only do you get to see the original Grange Cottage (Christopher and Mary's 1844 home), but you also get to try some Grange as well.

PETER LEHMANN, BAROSSA VALLEY

The Barossa might be one of the star Australian regions, but it's known tough times – and that it got through them was in no small part down to Peter Lehmann. In the late 1970s, grape prices bombed in the valley, and large companies abandoned the place. Small growers were facing destitution.

Lehmann – a fifth generation Barossan – was horrified. Refusing to sit back and watch friends and neighbours go to the wall, he borrowed money to buy their fruit and make wine. Later, to keep the business going, he took wine orders and payment in advance from customers, promising to deliver them the wine in two years when it was ready. Nothing was written down. He was an honourable man and people trusted him to keep his word.

It's a great legacy to leave behind and the heart-warming story adds an extra level of interest to any visit here. As well as custom-made tastings (plus some absolutely top-notch Shiraz), the cellar door team are also able to arrange vineyard walks and winery tours. The Taste of the Vineyards option, where you get to sample wines from the 14 different sub-regions of the Barossa, is a great way to understand the area.

SHAW + SMITH, ADELAIDE HILLS

There's no shortage of lovely producers to visit in the well-heeled gentility of the Adelaide Hills. Even so, Shaw + Smith's millennial winery stands out. It was set up by two winemaking cousins, who describe their wines as 'modern Australia' and 'nothing to do with the wines of the past'.

Airy and elegant, the tasting room has a modern feel, too, and with views straight out on to the slopes of the Balhannah vineyard it's a relaxed place to spend an afternoon. If it's hot, you should also see a marked difference in temperature from down in the city – one of the reasons that Chardonnay, in particular, works so well up here.

There are two wine flights available, a standard option and a limited release of rare, older and single-vineyard wines. The best varieties are Shiraz (which took them a bit by surprise) and Chardonnay, which is well-established as the Hills' standout white. All the wines are great, but the Balhannah Shiraz (grown round the winery) and Lenswood Chardonnay (10km to the north-west) are particularly high class.

Both wine tastings are served with side dishes, but if you want to up the ante, there's also a Friday Table. It's pricey, but you get to go behind the scenes with a hosted tour, tasting and lunch.

WYNNS, COONAWARRA

Coonawarra is one of the few regions in Australia where you can easily walk from one wine estate to the next. So if you come here, it's worth parking the car, popping on your walking boots and making a day of it. Brand's Laira, Di Giorgio, Redman and Zema Estate make up a nice 5km circuit in the heart of Coonawarra and its famous terra rossa soil.

The organisers rather optimistically suggest that the Wineries Walking Trail can be completed in three hours, but this assumes a 20-minute stop at each producer and, presumably, eating on the go. Most of the places offer not just tastings, but also cheese, food platters and coffee – so there's plenty to make you linger.

Of the five wineries on offer, Wynns is a great place to start and finish. It's the oldest in the region, and if you've ever savoured one of its bottles at home, seeing the famous three gables that appear on its labels is an exciting moment. There's also the chance to make up your own Coonawarra blend.

YALUMBA, EDEN VALLEY

The Eden Valley is home to several seriously good wineries. A couple of hundred metres higher than the floor of the Barossa, it makes excellent Riesling as well as top-notch Shiraz. These guys are also famous for their work with Viognier: their top-end Virgilius is recognised as one of the best examples in the world.

Yalumba has a great story behind it – immigrant arrives, works hard, buys land, makes money from Gold Rush, reinvests it, creates successful wine estate. Perhaps the best bit, though, is that it's still in the hands of the original family, which isn't, sadly, all that common in the Barossa.

The cellar door will give you a look at the basics of the region, plus a range of decent wines, but I'd suggest booking a visit. Over the course of two hours, the Yalumba Unlocked gives you the full winery story, a private tour of the grounds and old buildings, a visit to the cooperage (highly unusually, Yalumba makes all its own barrels), a look at the cellar full of the family's old bottles, and a private tasting of the top wines. It's exceptional value.

You need to book 48 hours in advance, but as numbers are limited to just four, try to do so a couple of weeks ahead.

There's any number of great wines here, but if you can try the Octavius (Shiraz brother of the Virgilius, from properly old vines), you're in for a treat.

WESTERN AUSTRALIA

CAPE MENTELLE

One of the 'founding five' wineries of Margaret River, Cape Mentelle was set up in 1970 by David Hohnen and his two brothers. The initial 16 hectares of their Wallcliffe vineyard are still in production today, home to the Cabernet Sauvignon vines that make their most famous wine.

Cape Mentelle's Cabernet made a huge impression in the early 1980s when it won the coveted Jimmy Watson Trophy (given to Australia's best one-year-old red wine) two years on the trot. It remains an icon today, though their work with the 'other' classic Margaret River style, the white Sauvignon Blanc/Sémillon blend, has been almost as ground-breaking.

Australian wineries aren't big on cellar tours, so jump at the chance to do this one. It's not expensive and the hour includes a tour of the Wallcliffe vineyard and the winery. There's also a pricier 'tour plus food match in the cellar' option.

To their immense credit, this is no dry intellectual visit. Tastings at the cellar door are free, and they have activities to keep small kids engaged long enough for the adults to taste at least a couple of wines in peace. For older children, there are *pétanque* pits as well. A great winery, with a lively offering, perfectly positioned for a visit on the way back from the beach... what's not to like?

CULLEN

The Cullen story is, in a sense, Margaret River's wine history in microcosm. Like so many wineries, it was started by a doctor, Kevin Cullen, and his wife Diana in the late 1960s, with small experimental plantings. The results were so successful that by the early 1970s their whole cattle farm had been turned over to viticulture, and the winery quickly acquired a reputation as one of the best in Australia.

By 1998 the estate was already being farmed organically, but since 2004 Kevin and Diana's daughter, Vanya, has taken the vineyards and winery fully biodynamic, working in tune with the lunar rhythms and using homeopathic preparations for the vines.

There's no question that it's working. Vanya Cullen is one of the most respected winemakers working today, her wines consistently standing comparison with the best in the world.

Brilliantly, if you visit, it has a self-guided 'spiral garden' where you can see, touch and read about the various elements of biodynamism. This is free, as are basic tastings at the cellar door, though you might want to consider paying to sample a few back vintages from the Enomatic machine. With paid-for private vineyard tours and tastings, as well as a restaurant, this is a fabulous chance to understand what makes one of Australia's best wineries tick.

HOWARD PARK

As with many Australian wine labels, when John Wade set up Howard Park (named after his father) in the mid-1980s he didn't own any vineyards. Instead he bought in fruit from growers across this corner of Australia, from both Margaret River (facing west on to the Indian Ocean) and the Great Southern region down near Albany, which looks on to the Southern Ocean.

The company has grown over the intervening decades, but still makes wines across the two regions. And it means the chance to do comparative tastings is one of the joys of a visit to its Margaret River cellar door near Wilyabrup. It's particularly useful if you want to get an idea of what the remote Great Southern region is like without schlepping the extra 300km from 'Margie'. Since the winery also imports Pinots from Burgundy, you might get to do a northern/southern hemisphere Pinot/Chardonnay comparison, too.

And if your trek round Australia has left you craving bubbles, Howard Park makes a decent range of 'méthode traditionelle' sparkling wines using the champagne grapes, Chardonnay, Pinot Noir and Pinot Meunier.

LEEUWIN ESTATE

With its art gallery, restaurant, summer concerts and imaginative range of 'experiences', Leeuwin Estate wouldn't look out of place in the heart of Napa Valley. For wine tourists in search of a slick, glossy, entertainment-filled few hours, there's no higher praise.

Fortunately, it's not all front. The wines are terrific – its Art Series in particular has serious chops – and as one of the 'founding five' wineries it deserves credit for creating the Margie bandwagon rather than jumping on it. As founder Denis Horgan puts it, 'we had to do something to get people to come down here'.

There's a stimulating range of tastings, visits and food-matchings depending on the depth of your wallet. A tasting at the cellar door, combined with one of the big-name late-summer concerts (book way in advance), could be a great way to finish off a visit to the region.

PIERRO

Have you heard of the ABC movement – Anything But Chardonnay? It was a reaction to the big, blowsy Chardonnays of the 1990s: people decided they were vulgar and unbalanced and that they would rather drink anything else instead. While the ABC founders may have had a point about some of the more pneumatic bottles tottering along at the time, it was a ludicrous, showy response that took no account of the thousands of great Chardonnays out there.

If you've ever been tempted to write the grape variety off, you need to come to this cellar door. Set up by Dr Mike Peterkin, Pierro makes one of the best Chardonnays in the New World. Rich and powerful, but balanced and poised, it is a Beyoncé of a wine – full-figured, sassy and dignified.

STELLA BELLA

What happens when you merge cool-climate Australia with French influences? Head here to find out. Stuart Pym had worked at Domaine de Chevalier in Bordeaux before he bought the Suckfizzle vineyard in 1996, and the European influence is evident in the elegance of his wines – particularly the superb Suckfizzle white, a Sauvignon Blanc/Sémillon blend that's one of the region's best. The taut, grainy Cabernet also shows off this cooler southern end of Margaret River really well.

Just a short trundle south-east of Margaret River town, this is an intimate, unpretentious cellar door visit with a human face and great wines.

VOYAGER ESTATE

Yes, that really is a Cape Dutch building. And no you're not in South Africa, as the giant (15m!) Australian flag unfurling in the Fremantle Doctor breezes makes obvious.

Voyager Estate is something of a one-stop shop for curious wine tourists. From vineyard visits to food matches, winery tours to customised tastings, there's something for every level of knowledge and interest.

The seven-hour Wine Essentials Day is probably the best crash course in grape growing, tasting technique, food matching and winemaking you'll find anywhere in the world. It comes at a price, but there are few quicker ways to get from 'uncertain amateur' to 'confident neophyte'. Otherwise, the Cabernet and Chardonnay By the Fire experiences will help you get under the skin of how these key Margaret River varieties are grown, made and aged.

With an excellent restaurant on site as well, this is somewhere to come for a lengthy visit.

TASMANIA

JOSEF CHROMY

Cool, wet and wild, Tasmania is a tough place to make wine. But when you've fled war-torn Czechoslovakia (as Josef Chromy did at the age of 19), dicing with guard dogs, minefields and trigger-happy soldiers on the way, it probably seems pretty benign.

Certainly, Chromy's had big success in the region in which he arrived in the 1950s and has stayed commendably loyal to ever since. Before deciding to set up his own venture at the ripe old age of 76, he was behind the growth of many of Tasmania's best-known wineries.

The cellar door, ten minutes from Launceston Airport, does super-cheap tastings, as well as daily vineyard/winery tours a few days a week for those who book in advance.

But it also has some interesting themed offerings, too, including a chance to get into how sparkling wine is made (and to blend your own); a two-hour drive far into the vineyards; and even a fly-fishing course on the lake, which can be incorporated into a winery tour, tasting and lunch.

PIPERS BROOK

On the go since the early 1970s, Pipers Brook is a 'Tasmania in a nutshell' kind of visit. You can do self-guided tours through the vineyards to get a flavour of the terroir and drink in the views of the Tamar Valley, before settling down to a tasting of an impressive range of classic cool-climate wines. There's a small charge for the tasting, but it comes off anything you subsequently buy.

Food-wise, the offering is limited to plates of local cheeses, but on the plus side it does have an area 200m from the cellar door where you can pitch camper vans for free – not something on offer at too many wineries. So if you're touring Tazzie in a motorhome, this could be a unique chance to wake up in a winery.

MOORILLA

Tasmania has always attracted mavericks and gamblers, and two of them are behind Moorilla. First came Harvard-educated Italian Claudio Alcorso, the man behind Australia's Sheridan fashion label. When he bought the estate in 1948 and told the regional government that he planned to plant vines, it wasn't impressed, telling him in no uncertain terms to plant apples and pears instead. He went ahead anyway.

Fifty years later, Tasmanian local and professional gambler David Walsh bought the estate and decided that what the island also needed was a Museum of Antiquities (of course), which he duly opened in Alcorso's modernist villa. The place has since gone on to become one of Australia's top modern art museums, and makes for an unrivalled opportunity to – as it puts it – 'talk crap about stuff you don't know much about'.

The cellar door does tastings of its wines and its Moo Brew beer, and you can arrange tours of both winery and, up the road, the microbrewery. Or you can just sit in the café and wine bar and drink in the dreamy view along with your Riesling.

And since you can get a ferry here from Hobart (25 minutes down the River Derwent), you might not need to spit so assiduously at the tastings...

WINTER BROOK VINEYARD

Also up in the Tamar Valley is Winter Brook Vineyard. It's a boutique operation (just three hectares), low on frills and big on heart. The tasting room is open all year round, but only on Fridays, Saturdays and Sundays. That's because owners, Frank and Nicole Huisman, do pretty much everything.

Their wine shtick is 'naturalness' with minimal intervention at all stages. It's a brave decision in the Tasmanian climate, so be sure to ask about how they do it if you visit. Having emigrated here from Amsterdam in 2010, they're not afraid of bold moves, and as well as the usual Taz grapes of Chardonnay, Riesling and Pinot Noir, they also have German/Austrian grapes Dornfelder and Blaufränkisch.

If the sun is shining, they're happy for you to bring a picnic and rug and flake out in their vineyards with one of their bottles.

NEW ZEALAND

No wine country has gone from zero to hero as fast as New Zealand. As recently as the early 1970s its wine production was largely limited to bad imitations of forgettable off-dry German wine styles. Nowadays, the country's bottles are a must on retailers' shelves and wine lists from Beijing to Berlin.

So what happened? The dramatic upturn can be traced back to one moment: when the country's biggest wine firm, Montana (now Brancott Estate), decided to plant Sauvignon Blanc in the top corner of the South Island. The first vintage from Marlborough was in 1979, and by the mid-'80s it was clear something special was going on. This was Sauvignon Blanc, Jim, but not as we knew it. By the time the now renowned Cloudy Bay appeared in the mid-1980s, critics were already hailing it as potentially the best expression of the grape anywhere in the world.

Whether you agree with the hyperbole or not (and the growers of Sancerre surely have a thing or two to say about it), it's unquestionably true that 'Kiwi Sauvignon' is a unique and colossally popular style that has been driving New Zealand's renaissance for the last 40-plus years. A trip to the alluvial plains of the Wairau Valley could be seen as a pilgrimage as much as a wine tasting.

But if you head to Marlborough, don't limit yourself to Sav; there's good sparkling wine and very good Pinot Noir, too. And don't think New Zealand's wine offering begins and ends round Blenheim, either – it's scattered liberally throughout the country. On the downside, this means it's hard to get a strong idea of what's going on without putting in some serious miles. But on the upside, since New Zealand is a country that lends itself to touring, you'll find interesting producers happy to tell you about their regions and wines wherever you go.

There are vineyards close to Auckland, as well as over 100 producers around an hour from the adventure playground of Queenstown, Central Otago. Head north from Christchurch towards the whale-watching/dolphin swimming at Kaikoura and you'll go past dozens of Waipara wineries, while Martinborough is just an hour or so over the beautiful Tararua Ranges from Wellington.

NORTH ISLAND

ATA RANGI, MARTINBOROUGH

For most people, skinning Welsh rugby legend JPR Williams in a Lions match would be the highlight of their life. But for Clive Paton (who did just that), his legacy will be his work with Ata Rangi.

He put in his first vines on the edge of Martinborough in 1980 when he realised that it had a similar climate to Burgundy. It was a gamble, for sure. Temperatures in this south-eastern corner of the North Island might be low (which Pinot generally likes), but the winds are fierce and the vines struggled mightily in the early years. But his faith was vindicated. Ata Rangi (which means 'new dawn') has long been recognised as one of the best Pinot Noirs in the country, and in the top tier anywhere in the world.

Visit the cellar door and you might get lucky and run into Clive or his wife Phyll – they're wonderfully informed, unassuming commentators on the geography of the region and New Zealand wine in general. They run two sessions a day – there's no charge, but you need to book. They only make a handful of wines, and though the Pinots are the stars, the Craighall Chardonnay and (Alsace-like) Pinot Gris are also excellent.

If you're visiting New Zealand in the run-up to Christmas, keep an eye open for the Toast Martinborough festival (usually late November) – a fun celebration of food, wine and music.

CRAGGY RANGE, HAWKE'S BAY

It's astonishing to think Craggy Range was only set up in the mid-1990s. In little more than 20 years it's become one of New Zealand's most respected wineries.

It's the project of businessman Terry Peabody, who took years to find the right site, having first looked in Europe, Australia and the US before settling on this sun-filled corner of the North Island. He's skimped on nothing – not for show-off purposes, but to create great wines.

A trip to his winery in Havelock North, just outside Hastings, is one of the best visitor experiences in the country, with a variety of fairly priced themed tastings, the chance to tour the facility and grounds, a decent restaurant and a variety of lodges and cottages to stay in. Maybe pop in here after spending the day exploring the famous Art Deco magnificence of Napier 25km away.

MILLTON VINEYARD, GISBORNE

Further up the coast, above Hawke's Bay, Gisborne is the place where Captain Cook first made landfall in 1769. These days, though, it's the region's wines that really merit exploring.

James and Annie Millton set their winery up here in 1984 after spells working at estates in France and Germany, and over the last 35 years have built an impressive reputation. Today Millton Vineyard is acknowledged as one of the top family-run wineries in the country.

If you're concerned New Zealand is just going to be about Sauvignon Blanc and Pinot Noir, you need to pay this place a visit. It has a wide range of brilliant wines, including Chardonnay, Riesling, Viognier, Chenin Blanc and Syrah.

Visit the cellar door and you can discover all about what makes the Gisborne region different. You should also ask about James and Annie's commitment to biodynamic viticulture. They very much believe that wine is grown not made, and use only natural preparations to treat their vines.

OBSIDIAN, WAIHEKE

Waiheke Island is about 20km east of Auckland, in the Hauraki Gulf. It's a beautiful place to visit, with dozens of amazing beaches – the reason so many Aucklanders have holiday homes here.

The island is a relative newcomer wine-wise, but it already has an impressive reputation, particularly for its Syrahs. And Obsidian, in Onetangi, is something of a hidden gem. Tucked down in a little valley, it hosts its tastings on a vine-covered patio behind a rustic shed. Blingy it ain't, but it has heart and charm.

The wines are very different from what you get in the rest of New Zealand: Syrah and Pinot Gris have some currency in the Land of the Long White Cloud – but Viognier, Montepulciano and Tempranillo are far less common.

There's nothing to stop you taking a bottle to the nearby beach, 15 minutes' walk away, to while away a balmy summer afternoon. But you could also make Obsidian part of a wider visit. There's a 'secret' walking track through vineyards and bush that connects it to nearby Tantalus Estate. Recently refurbished, this is a less rustic operation, with an excellent restaurant, craft brewery and a handsome cellar door.

TE MATA, HAWKE'S BAY

Site of one of New Zealand's oldest wineries, Te Mata is proof that the clock was running in the country's wine world in the 19th century. Hearteningly, what's made here now is a lot better than it was back then. Te Mata produces some very good – and long-lived – red wines, making the most of the Hawke's Bay sunshine.

Even a tasting at the cellar door needs to be booked 24 hours in advance, so you're probably best off arranging one of the tours as well. You'll get to see the country's oldest barrel room, the Stained Glass Cellar, and some of the sun-soaked Havelock Hills vineyards. Make sure you ask about the legend of Te Mata o Rongokako (the face of Rongokako) as well.

VILLA MARIA, AUCKLAND

There's no excuse not to stop off at the Villa Maria cellar door in Auckland. It's a few minutes from the airport, heading towards the city – perfect for a quick sharpener after a long flight, or as a last dose of civilisation before 12 hours of airplane hospitality.

Villa is New Zealand's second-biggest wine company, after Brancott Estate, but it has a very human story, built up largely by one man. George Fistonich began making wine in 1962, aged just 21, with grapes grown on land he leased from his Croatian immigrant father. He gradually expanded to take in wines from across the greater Auckland area before moving into the rest of the country.

It makes a wide range of wines, so a visit lets you try everything from Hawke's Bay Syrah and half-a-dozen types of Marlborough Sauvignon Blanc to Gisborne Viognier and sweet wines.

A small fee will get you a tour of the winery and bottling hall, plus a video explaining the whole story. And if you do somehow miss the cellar door here, there's also one in Marlborough with a similarly large range of wines.

SOUTH ISLAND

BLACK ESTATE, WAIPARA

If you need a place to break up the drive from Christchurch up the coast, Black Estate, 60km north of the city, could fit the bill. Not only does it have one of the country's best winery restaurants, but also a great range of biodynamic and organic wines.

Riesling you expect from a Waipara winery, but there's also Chenin Blanc, Chardonnay, some good Pinot Noir, Cabernet Franc (rare in New Zealand) and a super-trendy 'pét-nat' – a 'pétillant naturel' wine that's lightly fizzy and made in a style that pre-dates champagne techniques by centuries. An interesting and modern cellar door, in other words.

Since there's also a bed and breakfast (and bikes you can borrow for free), it could serve as a useful base if you want to explore the wider area and its wineries.

BRANCOTT ESTATE, MARLBOROUGH

This is where it all began. The first Sauvignon Blanc vines were planted on this site in Marlborough in 1975 and the rest, as they say, is history: a 'Savalanche' of wines – ranging from fresh and grassy to pungent and tropical, and now even taking in a bit of oak-ageing – has been spreading across the globe for over 30 years since.

You can acquaint yourself with all the styles (and sub-regional differences) at Brancott's cellar door with a themed exploration of Marlborough's most famous grape, but if you want more variety, there are also well-priced range tastings. Either way, make sure you try the Sauvignon Gris – it's rare and it's good.

The helicopter tour of the vineyards looks both pricey and slightly missing the point – the cycling tour, with guide, gives a better take on the Wairau Valley. For something completely different, you can also meet its resident falcon, which keeps birds away from the vines in a way that is both eco- and camera-friendly. Meanwhile, its glass-box restaurant has quality food and cracking views over the rustling hectares of Sav.

CLOUDY BAY, MARLBOROUGH

It's not always possible to visit a country's most famous winery. But you can in New Zealand. Cloudy Bay was set up by David Hohnen (see Cape Mentelle, p263), who took the name from Captain Cook's description of the muddy water where the Wairau River washes into the Cook Strait.

Fortunately, the place isn't just trading on its reputation. There are a host of activities to satisfy the most demanding visitor. For those who just want to taste, there's an attractive cellar door (including a large terrace with views out on to the vineyards and lots of lawn space for general flopping) and, in summer, there's also a raw bar where you should try its fizz, Pelorus, with oysters.

But it has a raft of tailor-made experiences too, from straight tutored tastings and food matchings to vineyard tours, helicopter trips and a half-day excursion to Marlborough Sounds on a 50-foot yacht. The chance to drink Cloudy Bay while bobbing up and down in the body of water it's named after puts a whole new spin on drinking wines in the place they are from.

FELTON ROAD, CENTRAL OTAGO

Nigel Greening, the always-entertaining owner of Felton Road, says its Bannockburn base is both the hottest and coldest place in New Zealand 'often on the same day'. It gives you some idea of how it's possible to make wine here. The growing season is short, but it's intense, with lots of sunlight and day/night differences of 20°C.

In less skilful hands – or on less good sites – this can result in rather blowsy wines, but Felton Road is one of Central Otago's A-list producers. Biodynamic in the vineyards and hands-off in the winery (Greening describes his winemaking as 'medieval'), it turns out wines that are elegant, textured and serious. Compare its Pinot with that of Rippon (p275, just to the north) and Ata Rangi from Martinborough (p269), to tick off three of the country's best. Don't miss its superb Chardonnays, either. Tastings are available during the week only and need to be booked in advance.

GIBBSTON VALLEY, CENTRAL OTAGO

It takes real guts to be the first to plant vines in a region. Particularly when everyone thinks you're crazy for doing so. There's not a lot between Central Otago and the South Pole – it's the most southerly wine region in the world – and most felt it was too cold for grapes. But Alan Brady thought differently, and after 35 years and dozens of wineries following his lead, he's been proved right.

Gibbston Valley has a wide range of wines to try – from fizz and Riesling to Chardonnay, dessert wines and Pinot Noir. Its cellar, blasted out of the rock, is the largest in the country, and understandably popular with the thousands of tourists who flood into nearby Queenstown every year.

There is a range of tasting and visit options, including the addition of a meal in the restaurant and pick-up and drop-off from Queenstown if you don't have a car – or feel a disinclination to use the spit bucket. Rather brilliantly, you can hire regular or e-bikes to go zipping along the trails round the winery and it also puts on a summer concert (January) that attracts impressive acts year after year. And if all that isn't enough, there's a cheesery, too.

Gibbston Valley is a great visit in itself, but it can be handily worked into a range of day trips from Queenstown. The atmospheric Gold Rush centre of Arrowtown is just a few kilometres away, or if you want a shot of adrenaline before your Pinot, you could try a bungy jump at Kawarau Gorge, the world's first bungy site.

MAHANA, NELSON

Say what you like about the British royal family, but they tend to get some choice visits lined up for them. So the fact Prince Charles stopped off here in 2015 ought to be a decent starter recommendation for you.

Once known as Wollaston estate, Mahana has upped the ante over the last decade or so. The super-modern winery, on four levels, uses gravity to get grapes from crusher to bottle, the vineyards are both organic and dry farmed (ie no irrigation) and the wines are exciting. It makes textural Sauvignon Blancs that are more ambitious than most from New Zealand, as well as one of the country's best Rieslings (Dr Schaeffer), and a skin-contact 'orange' Pinot Gris that's a real experience.

Mahana Villa is a great place to stay if you're looking for a bit of luxury: wooden floors, art on the walls and floor-to-ceiling windows with fabulous views out over the vines. A royal experience indeed.

Note: check there are no events on before visiting as it's popular for weddings.

NEUDORF, NELSON

Nelson is a fantastic place for tourists – all sea and protected parkland – yet few people come here for the wine, preferring to head off to the admittedly stunning Abel Tasman National Park for seals and sea kayaking instead.

It's a shame, because there are some interesting smaller producers here, and Neudorf, in the Moutere Hills, is one. Moutere means 'floating land' in Maori – so called because the regular mists make the hilltops look like they're hovering on the clouds. The climate is warm, rather than hot, which explains why (barring a bit of Pinot Noir) all the wines are white: Chardonnay and Sauvignon, as you'd expect, but also Riesling, Pinot Gris and the star Spanish white variety, Albariño.

They're of uniformly high quality, and the team who makes them are friendly, passionate and approachable. They'll talk to you for hours if you want to learn, and are super-happy for you to stretch out with a picnic in their grounds. If you've forgotten to bring food, there's even a small deli on site.

PEGASUS BAY, WAIPARA

Like many wine estates, 'Peg Bay' began life as a sheep farm, with Ivan Donaldson – head of neurology at the hospital in Christchurch – making wine in his spare time. Shades, perhaps, of the doctor-driven wine scene in Margaret River. And just like in Western Australia, what began as a hobby has blossomed into something special. Still family-run, this place is recognised as one of the best producers not just in Waipara, but in the whole of New Zealand.

It has a good range of wines, but any visit here should be mostly about Riesling. Pinot Noir, too. But definitely Riesling. Seeing the differences between its Bel Canto and Pegasus Bay expressions is like hopping from Austria to Germany.

The restaurant is seriously good and, interestingly, the food is geared around the wine list to create an experience where both components add up to greater than the sum of their parts.

RIPPON, CENTRAL OTAGO

There are wineries with a view, and then there's Rippon. If you've ever read an article about Central Otago, chances are it'll have been accompanied by a photo of this place. The vista from the estate towards Lake Wanaka, with its rows of vines marching down towards the water's edge, against a backdrop of the jagged peaks of the Southern Alps, is breathtaking – as famous as the views down the Douro or in the medieval villages of Alsace.

There are no bells and whistles here – just half-a-dozen really good wines available to taste for free. The Pinots are the stars, but the Rieslings, the (highly unusual) Gamay and (even more unusual) Riesling/Sylvaner cross Osteiner are also worth a look. If you can tear your eyes away from the landscape, that is.

YEALANDS, MARLBOROUGH

Peter Yealands set out in 2008 with the goal of creating the world's most sustainable winery – back when the approach was much less common. It wasn't his only brave decision. To get to the estate, you have to head south over the Wither Hills from Blenheim, into the Awatere Valley – a place most in the Marlborough heartland considered too cool and difficult to grow grapes.

Plastered with solar panels, the Yealands winery looks like some kind of *Star Wars* spacecraft. It runs complimentary wine tastings seven days a week, as well as a self-guided vineyard visit (download a free app, or pick up a map from the cellar door). This 40-minute walking tour outlines its vineyard philosophy, and leads you to wonderful views of the Cook Strait – on a clear day, you can see across to Wellington at the foot of the North Island. On a hazy day, you'll have to content yourself with the chickens and Babydoll sheep, which can make this a good visit for those with smaller children in tow.

Vine routes

There are a number of decent trails and themed tours in New Zealand, but the 4 Barrels Walking Wine Trail in Central Otago is particularly recommended. A newly developed 8km walk, it takes in four Cromwell wineries: Misha's Vineyard, Aurum Wines, Scott Base, and Wooing Tree Vineyard. Less than an hour from Queenstown or Wanaka, it takes you through vineyards, along Lake Dunstan, and to cellar doors where you can enjoy wine tastings and meals. It's scheduled to take three-and-a-half hours, but you'll probably want to make a day of it.

ASIA

Nowhere else in this book are the distances between the wine regions so vast, the number of vineyards so scarce. It's nearly 7,000km from the wine-growing western edges of Asia to China, and much of what lies in between is a viticultural (and sometimes literal) desert.

Historically speaking, the differences are vast, too. On the one hand, in Ningxia, you have one of the fastest-growing and most interesting new wine regions on the planet. Georgia, meanwhile, genuinely is the birthplace of winemaking. There is evidence of wine production here dating back to Neolithic times.

Asia might not be the first continent that springs to mind when it comes to wine, but it holds the key to its earliest days and, if some observers are to be believed, its future, too.

CHINA

Wine is exploding in China. It's now one of the biggest markets in the world and continues to expand every year. It runs at two speeds, though: imported wines are doing well (and growing), whereas most of what's produced domestically is pretty poor. But there is burgeoning fine wine production, too, as Chinese winemakers try to create their own versions of Bordeaux – often complete with big blingy châteaux.

Most of this fine winemaking is centred on Ningxia. On the southern edges of the Gobi desert, it's high and dry enough to have echoes of Mendoza in Argentina – particularly with the Helan Mountains as a picturesque backdrop. Unlike Argentina, however, it has a wildly extreme climate, with temperatures of 35°C in the summer, and almost as far the other side of zero in winter. Vines need to be covered in earth to survive the coldest months.

CHATEAU CHANGYU MOSER XV, NINGXIA

There's no shortage of ambition at this winery. A collaboration between huge Chinese wine producer Changyu and globe-trotting Austrian winemaker Lenz Moser (whose relatives are still making wine in the homeland – p156), it's had money and expertise thrown at it from the start. Changyu – which was started back in the 19th century – sees this as the boutique jewel in its crown, and the result is a spectacular 16th-century-French-style château and wines of serious intent.

Its vineyards are still relatively young, but Lenz is already excited. He likens the buzz and energy in Ningxia to that of Napa Valley in the late-1970s, which gives you some idea of how we might be talking about the place by 2050.

It's well set up for tourists. Not only is it open 365 days a year, but it also has 3D videos on the company and the winemaking process, tours of the winery, a museum about the history of wine in China, and – of course – the chance to taste and buy. You can even get your own labels made up for your favourite wine, which it will post out to you. And if you're there around harvest time (September/October), you can go out and taste the grapes, too.

SILVER HEIGHTS, NINGXIA

If you were going to make a film about a winery, you could do worse than use the story behind Silver Heights as your starting point. It starts with a Mr Gao Lin planting vines in the desert in Ningxia. He then packs his daughter Gao Yuan off to France to learn how to make wine. She works at Calon Ségur in Bordeaux, falls in love with the French winemaker, and returns with both a winemaking qualification and a husband.

A few years later, they are running a small winery, making (five) thoroughly decent wines from Cabernet Sauvignon, Merlot and Chardonnay. They have two locations to visit – the original 'Farm' in Yinchuan, the capital of Ningxia, and a newer place an hour or so to the north, up near the Helan Mountains.

Currently, visits are only to the Mountain facility – and by appointment, though it does include a look round the winery, cellar and vineyards. The Farm, when converted, will make a more tourist-centred facility.

It's a small operation – more like visiting a boutique French producer than a Napa tourist trap – and since visitor numbers are relatively low, it tends not to have lots of bottles open. All of which means that you'll need to buy anything you want to taste. It doesn't make it especially cheap, but the wines – and story – are definitely worth it.

GEORGIA

Georgia, you say? Georgia? Yes. Absolutely. Not only is it a fascinating place to visit in itself, it's also home to the oldest ever archaeological evidence of winemaking – dating back to 6,000BC. The Georgians aren't exaggerating when they describe their country as the birthplace of wine.

As well as the heavyweight history behind it, it's also having a bit of a moment. There's a growing interest in its unusual indigenous grape varieties, but even more interest in its traditional way of vinifying and ageing wines in giant clay amphorae – *qvevri*. The growth of 'concrete eggs' for fermenting wines (which you'll see everywhere from Marlborough to Mendoza) all comes back to this traditional Georgian winemaking technique.

If a self-guided trip to the Caucasus sounds daunting, there are some good companies that will put a bespoke itinerary together for you: Taste Georgia, which specialises in food and wine tours, is one of the best.

BABANEURIS MARANI, KAKHETI

If you want a one-stop visit with a difference, put this place on your list. 'Chateau Baba' is a relatively small estate (just 11 hectares) with a boutique hotel attached, in the foothills of the Greater Caucasus mountains.

Its wines are all made from local grapes – the two stalwarts Rkatsiteli and Saperavi, plus Mtsvane and the marvellously named Kisi (pronounced 'kissy'). A floral, perfumed variety, it's well worth a look. All of them are fermented and aged in *qvevri*.

Alongside winery tours and tastings, it offers everything from hiking to horse riding and mountain biking, as well as providing access to exclusive trails through the woods of the Babaneuri nature park. If you come during the vintage, you can even help it with some picking.

With nine rooms, a heated outdoor 18m swimming pool and a restaurant, this could make a great base for exploring the historical sites, natural beauty and wineries of Georgia's main wine region.

MOSMIERI, KAKHETI

On a slope looking out over the Alazani Valley, Mosmieri (which means 'wine lover' in old Georgian dialect) sees itself as very much at the forefront of the country's wine renaissance. It uses only local grape varieties, and positions them firmly upmarket.

Because it makes wines in both a traditional and modern style, you can compare its (80 per cent Rkatsiteli) steel-fermented Tsinandali white with the (100 per cent Rkatsiteli) *qvevri*-fermented Kakhuri. The differences in colour, flavour and texture are marked – and it's all down to the use of amphorae.

It's always open for tastings and is happy for you to wander round the vineyards that surround the winery. You can even have a go at crushing some grapes with your feet in a traditional *satsnahkeli* at harvest time. If you're confident of your foot hygiene, you can drink the juice, too.

There are up to ten wines to taste, including samples from both the fermenting tanks and barrels. After which there's a large bar and restaurant, complete with courtyard, fountain and big terrace, ideal for sitting and soaking up the Georgian sun in the summer or early autumn. You can also see into the winery through its floor-to-ceiling windows.

CHÂTEAU MUKHRANI, MTSKHETA

A royal estate that planted its first vines in 1875, Mukhrani is a decidedly aristocratic producer. In the 19th century it even used to supply the Russian royal family. Billed as the 'first Georgian wine château', its castle and cellars took 12 years to build and, now fully restored, the latter are home to 60,000 bottles, ageing peacefully.

It has an interesting mix of international and local grape varieties (Cabernet Sauvignon and Sauvignon Blanc among the Mtsvane, Rkatsiteli and Saperavi), so if you've ever wanted to know what Chardonnay tastes like in the Caucasus, this is your chance. Ask nicely and it might also let you try the traditional off-dry reds – they're quietly crowd-pleasing.

In a sense, the place itself is the star. You can do a tour of the castle, grounds, winery and cellars (complete with full history of the Georgian royal family) for not very much at all. But it seems crazy not to throw in a three-wine tasting (red, white, and rosé) as well. More expensive options simply add in a sweet, fortified wine or *chacha* – Georgian grappa – so probably aren't worth the upgrade.

Just an hour from the capital Tbilisi, this is somewhere you can easily come if you're passing through and have half a day to spare.

LEBANON

They've been growing grapes in Lebanon for a long time – over 6,000 years. And no wonder – the climate makes it easy! The vineyards are mostly in the Bekaa Valley. Running roughly north/south, parallel to the coast, this broad strip of land has been the heart of the region's agriculture for thousands of years. Sitting between two mountain ranges, it gets plenty of rain in the winter and autumn, while summers are so dry that few winemakers need to use treatments for their vines. And while it's hot, the Bekaa sits 800–1,000m above sea level, which provides mitigating sea breezes and a quick cool-off once the sun goes down, allowing the vines to rest.

There is ancient history absolutely everywhere you look in Lebanon. The ancient port of Byblos 40km north of Beirut is one of the world's oldest towns and gave the Greeks their word for book. Baalbeck, in the Bekaa, has some of the most awe-inspiring Roman ruins outside of the Italian capital.

CHÂTEAU KSARA, BEKAA VALLEY

The Jesuits certainly got about, and wherever they went they tended to take winemaking with them. It was they who first started farming a 25-hectare strip here back in 1857, with the intention of making Lebanon's first dry wine. Happily, in 1898, they also discovered some Roman cellars – 2km of them – which made ageing the wines somewhat easier. The latter are included as part of any visit to the country's oldest winery and are as atmospheric as any in the world. You don't need to book for the basic tours or tastings, but you will need to contact them in advance if you want more, such as food matching or a vineyard trip.

The winery was replanted with noble (as opposed to local) grape varieties in 1991, so this is mostly about Cabernet Sauvignon, Chardonnay and the like. But the blanc de blancs – a blend of Chardonnay, Sauvignon Blanc and Sémillon is both good and unusual.

CHATEAU MUSAR, GHAZIR

The Hochar family arrived in Lebanon from France with the Crusades, and have stayed there ever since – though it wasn't until the 1930s that Gaston Hochar planted a vineyard in the Bekaa Valley. Without a question, Lebanon's most famous winery, Musar is known for its deep, rich red wines, in particular. A blend of Cabernet Sauvignon and the southern French varieties Carignan and Cinsaut, the Grand Vin, from old, unirrigated bush vines, is a heady beast that lasts for decades. In its longevity it perhaps echoes some of the French influence in the winery's creation (Hochar was friends with Ronald Barton of Bordeaux's Château Léoville Barton – see p32). But the exotic, swirling flavours are pure Lebanon.

The winery is not near the vineyards – it's in Ghazir, 30km up the coast from Beirut, and on the way to Byblos if you fancy some ancient culture after your Cabernet. It's not open for drop-ins, but you can arrange a visit in advance. You'll see the fermentation area, barrel and bottle cellars, and the bottling line – and it also throws in a tasting of half-a-dozen of its wines. Not bad at all, for free!

DOMAINE DES TOURELLES, BEKAA VALLEY

Founded by Frenchman François-Eugène Brun back in 1868, Domaine des Tourelles seems almost frozen in time: there are old Bakelite phones in the offices, and it still uses concrete tanks to ferment the grapes. While these are becoming trendy again in some parts of the world, here they never went out of fashion.

Some of its vineyards are seriously old, too – up to 70 years – and, this being the dry, breezy Bekaa, they're farmed organically. Shop-bought yeasts? Forget it. This is wild-ferment territory, with whatever yeasts that happen to be on the grapes when they're picked kick-starting the fermentation naturally.

Unusually for Lebanon, its main red grape is Syrah, rather than Cabernet Sauvignon, which it makes into a single varietal and also blends with Carignan, Cinsaut and, yes, Cabernet. They're polished wines with interest and class.

It has a small shop of its own on Rue Monot in Beirut where you can buy and taste. The winery itself is in Chtaura, east of the capital. Not far from Château Ksara, you could easily do the two wineries one after the other.

Visits here are pretty fluid. Turn up unannounced and you'll get a quick look round and a tasting. Phone ahead to book a time and you'll get the full two-hour vineyard/winery/cellar tour, and a range of wines to sample. The big sacks of aniseed gently perfuming the air are explained by the fact that it's also Lebanon's largest producer of the spirit arak, so you should probably try that, too.

IXSIR, BATROUN

You need to make a bit more of an effort to come to Ixsir. It's not based in the Bekaa Valley, like most of Lebanon's wineries, but in the northern hills, closer to Tripoli than Beirut. But is it worth the effort? You'd better believe it.

The winery is super-modern, sustainable and beautiful, and the wines are very good. Grown on hill-side terraces at 1,800m above sea level, these are the highest vineyards in the northern hemisphere. Unsurprisingly, the views over the limestone crags towards the Mediterranean are spectacular, so it makes sense to stay for lunch so you can drink them in along with your wine. You need to book 48 hours in advance, but it does offer tours and tastings every day.

FRANCE

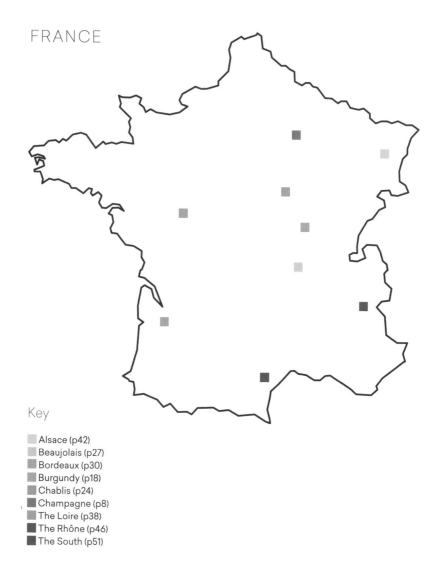

Key

Alsace (p42)
Beaujolais (p27)
Bordeaux (p30)
Burgundy (p18)
Chablis (p24)
Champagne (p8)
The Loire (p38)
The Rhône (p46)
The South (p51)

MAPS

ITALY

Key

North East (p60)
North West (p68)
Chianti/Tuscany (p73/p79)
South (p83)
Sardinia (p87)
Sicily (p87)

SPAIN

Key

Andalucía (p120)
Catalonia (p100)
Duero Valley (p113)
Galicia (p106)
Rioja (p92)

ACKNOWLEDGEMENTS

I could never have written this book without a lot of help from a lot of people: wineries who have hosted me, poured me wine and answered my questions; generic bodies who have organised trips for me down the years and helped me out with Facts and Information; experts in various fields who have pointed me in the right direction when I got stuck at various writerly crossroads, and the myriad winemakers I've met who have filled in the gaps in my knowledge and talked so eloquently and passionately about what they do.

I'll probably miss a tonne of you out, so apologies in advance to anyone who feels neglected. Blame it on the Riesling... A big shout out (in no particular order) to Tom Perry, Matt Walls, Anne Krebiehl, Francoise Perretti, Steve Burns, Maria João de Almeida, Rosamund Barton, Gina Millani and Mark Chandler, Jim Budd, Dante Cecchini, Jo Black, Chris Appleby, Angeline Bayly, Kate Sweet, Rod Smith, Rosemary George, Chris Stroud and the team in Auckland, Emma Baumann and everyone at Wine Australia, Susan Spence, Gustavo Crespo, Jo Wehring, Anita Jackson, Sarah Abbot MW, Javier Zaccagnini, Juan Pablo Quijada, Emma Wright, Keith Isaac, the team at Imbibe Magazine, and Damian Riley-Smith for giving me the job that got me into booze writing over 20 years ago.

Respect and gratitude in abundance, too, to the team at Quadrille, particularly designer Katherine Keeble, editor Nick Funnell – genially ruthless about fact-checking, illustrator Aurelia Lange for her wonderful artwork, and the marvellous Zena Alkayat, who has pulled the whole thing together while tolerantly preferring carrot to stick.

Finally, a heartfelt thank you, too, to my parents for making wine a part of everyday life when I was a boy and probably wanted Coke; to my always lovely wife Bola who did a great job of pretending not to care that she came second to 300 pages of wine research for so long and remained a staunch supporter even when I was tired and grumpy; and to my kids Becky and Eddie for pretending to be interested when I told them about 'great wineries for families to visit'. The wine bug's gonna get you one day...